Educating Children with Fragile X Syndrome

D1282038

Fragile X syndrome is the most common inherited cause of learning difficulties, affecting a child's ability to tackle key skill areas such as literacy and numeracy, and causing behaviour problems and social anxiety. This definitive text will provide essential support and information for teachers, for whom meeting the educational needs of children with Fragile X presents demanding challenges.

The book benefits from the expertise of an international field of researchers, whose variety of perspectives contribute to this unique, multi-professional approach. Some chapters of the book are descriptive of the condition, whilst other chapters suggest practical intervention strategies, based on sound educational principles, expressed in accessible non-specialist terms. A range of important topics are considered, including:

- the physical and behavioural characteristics of Fragile X;
- the effects of Fragile X syndrome on learning;
- adults and women with Fragile X syndrome;
- medication and therapy;
- related conditions such as autism and attention deficit disorders.

As it breaks down the barriers of professional practice, this book establishes the groundwork for successful and valuable multi-professional teamwork. By providing immediate access to a body of empirical knowledge and advice from other disciplines, it will also encourage teachers to incorporate this approach into their own practice. No one responsible for the education of a child with Fragile X syndrome should fail to read this book.

Denise Dew-Hughes has vast teaching and lecturing experience. She is Specialist Advisor in Education to the Fragile X Society, UK.

Educating Children with Fragile X Syndrome

A Multi-Professional View

Edited by
Denise Dew-Hughes

In association with the Fragile X Society

 RoutledgeFalmer
Taylor & Francis Group

LONDON AND NEW YORK

First published 2004 by RoutledgeFalmer
11 New Fetter Lane, London EC4P 4EE

Simultaneously published in the USA and Canada
by RoutledgeFalmer
29 West 35th Street, New York, NY 10001

RoutledgeFalmer is an imprint of the Taylor & Francis Group

© 2004 Denise Dew-Hughes

Typeset in by Times by Keystroke, Jacaranda Lodge, Wolverhampton
Printed and bound in Great Britain by TJ International Ltd, Padstow, Cornwall

British Library Cataloguing in Publication Data
A catalogue record for this book is available from the British Library

Library of Congress Cataloging in Publication Data
A catalog record for this book has been requested

ISBN 0-415-31488-7

Contents

Illustrations

Tables

Figures

Contributors

Angela Barnicoat M.D. FRCP Consultant Clinical Geneticist at Great Ormond Street Hospital NHS Trust. She has been involved in research of the genetics of fragile X syndrome and is a Specialist Advisor to the Fragile X Society.

Richard C. Belser Ph.D Research Scientist in Behavioral Physiology, New York State Institute for Basic Research in Developmental Disabilities. Has worked with children with fragile X syndrome for 18 years, studying their sensory perception, arousal and language.

Marcia Braden Ph.D Consultant Psychologist in Colorado, specialising in diagnosis and treatment of developmental difficulties. Has been working with children with fragile X syndrome for 20 years and published many standard texts on assessment and educational strategies.

Barbara Carmichael M.Sc. Clinical Nurse Specialist and Counsellor in Genetics for NE Thames Region, with responsibility for families in South Essex. A founder member of the Fragile X Society, has family members affected with fragile X syndrome.

Kim Cornish Ph.D Developmental Neuropsychologist, holds the Canada Research Chair in Neuropsychology at McGill University, Montreal, also Special Professor in Nottingham University's Faculty of Medicine. Has worked with the Fragile X Society for many years on research projects.

Denise Dew-Hughes Ed.D Teacher, researcher and author in special education for 20 years, specialising in pupils with pervasive developmental disorders, such as fragile X syndrome and autism. Specialist Advisor for Education to the UK Fragile X Society. Conducted national survey of the education of young people with fragile X. Government-funded post-doctoral research investigated pupils with challenging behaviour and professional development for teachers. Currently teaching and researching in Oxford.

Charles Gibb Chief Educational Psychologist, Fife Regional Council, Scotland. Specialist Advisor to the Fragile X Society and author of their education booklets.

Dido Green Specialist Head Paediatric Occupational Therapist at Guy's Hospital, London, managing OT services to in-patients, neuro-motor and neurodisability clinics. Current research investigates social and motor difficulties, with clinical input, for children with

Complex Developmental, Learning and Social Communication Disorders. Has worked with children with fragile X syndrome since 1990.

Randi Hagerman, M.D. Developmental and Behavioural Pediatrician, holder of the Tsakopoulos-Vismara Chair in Pediatrics, University of California. Medical Director of the Medical Investigation of Neurodevelopmental Disorders Institute. An internationally recognised clinician and researcher in developmental and behavioural paediatrics, she has spent over 20 years doing clinical work and research into fragile X syndrome. Author of many standard texts on diagnosis, treatment and research in fragile X syndrome, including medical, psychopharmacological and educational treatments. Co-founder of the U.S. National Fragile X Foundation, Board member of and scientific advisor to their Scientific and Clinical Advisory Committee.

Greg O'Brien is Professor of Developmental Psychiatry, University of Northumbria, but is primarily a clinician, active in research, teaching and service development. His research promotes the recognition, classification and understanding of severe behaviour problems – these are the most significant cause of exclusion among people with learning disability.

Lesley Powell Ph.D is an educational consultant and clinician in Perth, Western Australia. Has researched and published in fragile X for 10 years; now focuses on the education of girls. She is Special Advisor to the Fragile X Support Group of Western Australia.

Gaia Scerif Researching neurocognitive development with Professor Annette Karmiloff-Smith at the Institute of Child Health, University College, London. Joined Professor Kim Cornish on the UK's first project investigating early attentional development in young children with fragile X.

Kate Schnelling Ed.D. Deputy Head of a Special School. Formerly Education Officer for pupils with emotional and behavioural difficulties. Originator of the Family Nurturing Network in the UK, recommended by the DfEE Green Paper 'Excellence for all Children' (1997) as excellence in practice. Publication subjects include the Code of Practice and pupil exclusion.

Vicki Sudhalter Ph.D Research Scientist in Psycholinguistics with the New York State Institute for Basic Research in Developmental Disabilities. Developed the Clinical Psycholinguistics Laboratory, Jervis Clinic NY; Has researched and published extensively on the behavior and language of children with fragile X for 17 years.

Catherine Taylor Specialist Speech and Language Therapist for Child Mental Health Learning Disability Service, St Georges Hospital, London and South Thames College. Along with Dr Jeremy Turk, has responsibility for a substantial number of clients with fragile X.

Julie Taylor Head of a Specialist Unit for children with autistic spectrum disorders, AD/HD and fragile X.

Jeremy Turk M.D. Senior Lecturer in Child and Adolescent Psychiatry, St. George's Hospital Medical School, London University. Consultant Child and Adolescent Psychiatrist, Southwest London and St George's NHS Trust, and Consultant Psychiatrist,

National Autistic Society Centre for Social and Communication Disorders. Main clinical interests: emotional and behavioural problems in children with developmental disabilities. Researched, lectured and published extensively on developmental and behavioural consequences of genetic causes of learning disability, in particular fragile X syndrome. President Elect, Royal Society of Medicine Forum on Learning Disability and co-author of *Child Psychiatry: a Developmental Approach.*

Claire Wolstencroft Mother to two teenage boys, one with fragile X. She has worked as a special needs support teacher in her son's residential school.

Acknowledgements

I owe a great deal to the help and support of the British Fragile X Society and its sister organisations in the USA, Canada and Australia. I would also like to acknowledge the generosity of the many professionals who have donated their time and expertise to this book. Above all, my thanks go to the young people with fragile X syndrome who have always been a delight to teach, and to their parents.

Introduction

Fragile X syndrome and education

Denise Dew-Hughes

Educating a child with fragile X syndrome, or any child with complex learning difficulties, challenges the professional knowledge and practice of teachers. Each child is unique in its needs and skills and all good teachers differentiate their practice accordingly, but the child with exceptional needs requires something exceptional from the teacher.

Pupils with pervasive developmental disorders, such as fragile X syndrome, present with complex, diffuse and global educational needs. Their learning difficulties are compounded with behavioural, physical and medical problems, and influenced by complex personal and environmental factors. Teachers confident in meeting a wide range of learning needs might well consider their skills insufficient when these needs are combined within a single pupil.

This dilemma affects all teachers as the boundaries between mainstream and special education become less clear cut. More children with learning difficulties are educated alongside normally developing peers, and classroom teachers have statutory responsibility for identifying and meeting special needs. Mainstream schools have become more inclusive, delivering a broader education, while special schools have assumed additional roles as advisory and support centres. Conditions such as fragile X present a wide range of learning difficulties and cross boundaries of school placement, but still require special expertise and understanding from teachers.

The transition of pupils with special needs between specialist provision and mainstream schools has coincided with an increased perception of human rights within a non-segregated society. Pre-judgements, stereotyping and reduced expectations of ability of people with learning difficulties are rightly resisted from a human rights standpoint. At the same time, increased scientific diagnosis of learning difficulties, endorsing medical and genetic causation, has reawakened the spectre of the 'pupil deficit' model of special educational needs. Diagnosed disorders giving rise to complex learning difficulties retain strong links with pathology and genetic causation. This presents a risk of pre-judgement of ability or provision according to diagnosis, even though such pre-determination would rightly be rejected on grounds of human rights. Education requires a firm foundation of professional knowledge and ideology to incorporate these two seemingly oppositional concepts.

Teachers responsible for pupils with pervasive developmental disorders and complex learning difficulties face professional challenges as well as ideological issues. Although initially trained to meet special needs, teachers may consider themselves under-qualified to deliver the specialist education to which these exceptional pupils are legally entitled. Initially, teachers might do well to reacquaint themselves with the basic elements from which they construct their professional practice. Faced with the exceptional child, they might construct a 'best fit' from their usual practice and then increase and improve their professional knowledge with specialised understandings and approaches. In this way, general practice becomes specialised.

Children with fragile X syndrome fit well within this process. They are not physically vulnerable; in general they have no more medical problems than other children. However, the learning difficulties associated with fragile X – short attention span, behavioural outbursts, speech and language difficulties, numeracy confusion and social anxiety – fall predominantly within an educational domain and are recognisable and familiar to teachers. All teachers at some time have to deal with these features in other pupils. They are common to a wide range of special conditions as well as the everyday practice of teaching and learning.

The professional knowledge of teachers involves knowing what to do to help someone learn, and knowing how and why it works. All teachers construct an individualistic professional knowledge from information, training, and experience, personalised with intuition, values and interests. These elements form a continuum ranging from objective, research-supported empirical evidence, to subjective personal value systems, intuitive knowledge and life-experiences (see figure 1). Training has a central location because students and tutors share an amalgam of subjective and objective knowledge.

Teachers locate themselves on the continuum by building their practice predominantly from one or more of the three basic elements. To become better informed and develop new skills and understandings, some teachers read or research, some prefer in-service training, and others draw on their own or shared experience. Some practitioners are most effective and flexible in their practice when combining these elements in equilibrium.

This book provides the basic elements of teachers' professional knowledge. To construct a suitably specialist practice, teachers must access information and clinical experience from other practitioners. However, information from other fields is not always tailored to the needs of education, nor expressed in terms intelligible to teachers. Information, experience and training from other professionals, therapists and advisors can be irregular and insufficient to meet the daily requirements of classroom practice. The purpose of the book is to gather together professionals whose disciplines impinge on education and direct their specialist expertise towards the practical needs of teacher and pupil. Assumed into teacher understandings and blended with normal classroom practice, this multi-professional expertise can help teachers construct the specialist practice required by exceptional children.

This process would make little improvement to education if it were limited to producing better teachers for children with exceptional or complex needs. If multi-professional expertise

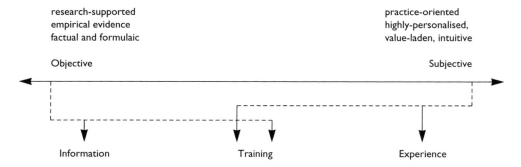

Figure 0.1 A continuum of professional knowledge

were condition-specific, teachers would need to learn new skills for every different pupil condition they encountered. But teachers developing their professional knowledge to meet specific pupil needs commonly find that new skills can be applied to improve more general practice. Insight into multi-professional practice thus improves teaching by developing new understandings and skills, which are applicable to a wider range of pupil difficulties and strengths.

Maintaining distinctions between academic theoreticians and the practising teacher or clinician imposes a further limit to improved practice. Where these distinctions prevail, true reciprocity of information and reflection are impossible. Academic findings can inform and improve practice only when accessed and used by the practitioner. At the same time, the experience of classroom practitioners provides a rich vein of material for the academic researcher.

The advantages of these reciprocal processes, between general and special needs, as between theory and practice, is demonstrated by the contributors to this book. What they identify as good practice for pupils with fragile X is recognisable as good, general classroom practice, enhanced with new understandings. The recommended skills and knowledge can serve not only the purposes of special practice, but also those of mainstream education by increased teacher competencies and flexibility of practice.

It is a common concern among teachers that constraints of time and funding limit input from other disciplines. Even if such expertise were provided specifically for their requirements, they cannot always have access to it or understand its specific purposes and terminologies. This book purports to meet teachers' requirements for the expertise of allied professional fields, expertise selected for its relevance to education, and written specifically for teachers' use.

In this way, a true multi-professional approach to education can be established, bridging the gap between theory and practice, and between special and general needs. Contributors to this book have backgrounds in all of these disciplines. The theory–practice dialectic is shared as a common goal, and the narrow applications of detached, scientific inquiry are avoided in favour of more general understandings. Because many contributors combine the roles of theoretician and practitioner, reciprocity is established and the ground laid for a philosophy of promoting improved practice through information and professional experience.

Adopting a multi-professional view of educational practice can thus enhance professional knowledge in teachers by increasing their deeper understanding of its nature and promoting its more effective application.

Structure of the book and individual contributions

Each chapter in this book has been designed to stand alone. Contributors record information and experience from their own specialist field and bring their personal perspective to the education of children with fragile X.

Part I concerns the person with fragile X syndrome. Professor Randi Hagerman describes the basic physical and behavioural characteristics of people with fragile X, and Dr Jeremy Turk outlines the importance of diagnosis. Professor Kim Cornish details the cognitive strengths and difficulties associated with fragile X. Dr Vicki Sudhalter and Dr Richard Belser focus on the importance of language and communication as social and educational tools. They describe the difficulties fragile X causes for language acquisition, and discuss the effects of arousal on the behaviour of people with fragile X, with an emphasis on the damage this causes to language. Dr Lesley Powell presents findings from her extensive studies on the particular difficulties and concerns of girls with fragile X.

Part II looks at educational issues in general. Dr Marcia Braden gives basic information about the effects of fragile X on education and learning. She expands the earlier discussion of cognitive strengths and weaknesses (Chapter 3). Dr Denise Dew-Hughes sets the findings of a national survey on school placement and provision for young people with fragile X within the ongoing debate over special and mainstream schools, and inclusive education. This chapter presents parents' views of their children's education. Charles Gibb identifies key issues in educational assessment and intervention, which underlie attitudes to special needs and provision. Dr Braden considers the methodologies of formal assessment and constructing a profile for individual children. These two chapters (8 and 9) focus on children with fragile X as individuals with learning needs. Many of the issues raised here are relevant to children with a wide range of special needs; rather than being confined to those with fragile X syndrome. Dr Kate Schnelling draws on expertise as Education Officer and Deputy Head Teacher to present a structured approach to gaining educational support, illustrated by examples from a recent national survey on children with fragile X, conducted by Dr Dew-Hughes.

Part III describes and evaluates educational strategies that have been successful in meeting the specific needs of children with fragile X. The practical application of such strategies is one of the main purposes of this book. Dr Braden lists classroom adaptations and recommendations for good practice and work habits. Julie Taylor, head of a school for children with autistic spectrum disorders, including fragile X gives details of her successful classroom practice. Claire Wolstencroft, herself a teacher and parent of a child with fragile X, discusses the importance of parents and teachers working together, and suggests ways to achieve a successful partnership. Auxiliary therapies are presented in detail by Catherine Taylor (Speech and Language) and Dido Green (Occupational Therapy and Sensory Integration Therapy). The importance of the role of structured therapeutic support and advice in successfully educating children with fragile X is emphasised by these two contributions.

Part IV considers the development, behaviour and psychology of children with fragile X syndrome. Professor Kim Cornish and Gaia Scerif describe development in the vital early years, comparing the child with fragile X against the normal developmental patterns with which teachers are familiar. Dr Jeremy Turk discusses the behaviour of children with fragile X, a primary concern for teachers. He identifies the causes of confusing and challenging behaviour patterns and suggests management strategies for meeting these challenges in the classroom. Professor Cornish and Julie Taylor look at the theoretical and academic relationship between fragile X and related conditions, such as attention deficit disorder with or without hyperactivity (AD/HD) and autistic spectrum disorders. They consider clinical versus aetiological diagnosis, the ways related conditions may overlap, and the need for differentiation in approaches. Dr Turk examines the issues surrounding the use of medication to address the behaviour of children with fragile X. He describes the practical use and effects of pharmaceutical interventions which may control hyperactivity, short attention span and impulsivity and promote learning for some children.

Part V considers the wider issues of family and social matters for people with fragile X syndrome. Dr Angela Barnicoat and Barbara Carmichael describe the basic facts of the genetics of fragile X, and the ways in which families may be affected. As an educational outcome, the position of adults with fragile X is then considered. Professor Greg O'Brien presents the findings of his longitudinal studies of adults and their continuing learning needs, which constitute a prime educational outcome. Professor Cornish describes the behaviour and cognitive profile of adults, and considers whether abilities decline or increase with age. Dr Powell discusses the needs of older girls and women, who have lived with educational difficulties, and are coping with bringing up children with fragile X while dealing with their own emotional and social problems. Dr Turk ends by focussing on the more personal aspects of support for people with fragile X and their families.

Part I

The child with fragile X syndrome

Chapter 1

Physical and behavioural characteristics of fragile **X** syndrome

Randi Hagerman

It is essential for educators to know about fragile X syndrome because this common disorder presents a variety of behavioural and cognitive problems, which continue from infancy throughout life. Fragile X has many consistent features, but each child has a different set of background genes that may be influenced in different ways. Some children may have mild learning difficulties, whereas others may have severe learning disabilities and autism. Some may have severe outbursts and aggression whereas others are easygoing.

A detailed description of the genetic implications of fragile X syndrome can be found elsewhere in this book. This chapter describes the physical and behavioural characteristics of fragile X which, put simply, result from the absence or deficiency of a protein responsible for early brain development.

High functioning individuals

Approximately 15 per cent of males with fragile X are considered high functioning; their intelligence is average or even above. These boys often have fewer of the physical and behavioural features of fragile X (see tables 1.1 and 1.2). The intelligence level of most boys with fragile X will decrease over time, although some who are less severely affected can maintain a normal to borderline range of intelligence level into adulthood. Most children with fragile X have a mild to moderate range of learning disabilities. Sometimes the diagnosis of fragile X is delayed until middle childhood, particularly in the child who is higher functioning and has fewer features of fragile X.

Early features

At birth, infants with fragile X commonly have a large head circumference, poor muscle tone (hypotonia) and mild difficulties in coordination. Parents may not know in the first year that there is a developmental problem with their child unless the hypotonia is severe and early motor milestones such as sitting, crawling, and walking are delayed. More typically, the parents become aware of significant problems with delays in speech and language development. By the age of two, children with fragile X are usually not speaking and this precipitates paediatric evaluation and a subsequent diagnosis. Educators will usually see children with fragile X in an early childhood intervention programme.

Table 1.1 Percentage of prepubertal boys and girls with features

Behavioural feature	Males with full mutation		Male mosaic (n = 30)	Females with full mutation (n = 40)
	Fully methylated (n = 103)	<50 per cent methylated (n = 10)		
Hand-flapping	83	70	93	40
Hand-biting	56	10	37	20
Hyperactivity	70	30	70	55
Perseveration	85	90	90	70
Aggression	42	10	33	28
Shyness	73	80	60	83
Anxiety	68	90	63	58
Panic attacks	25	30	27	25
Poor eye contact	86	70	80	73
Tactile defensiveness	81	60	80	68

Adapted from Hagerman RJ (2002) The Physical and Behavioural Phenotype. In Hagerman RJ and Hagerman PJ (eds) *Fragile X Syndrome: Diagnosis, Treatment and Research*, Third Edition. The Johns Hopkins University Press, Baltimore, Maryland, pp. 3–109.

Table 1.2 Percentage of prepubertal boys and girls with features

Physical feature	Males with full mutation		Male mosaic (n = 30)	Females with full mutation (n = 40)
	Fully methylated (n = 103)	<50 per cent methylated (n = 10)		
Long face	50	20	47	48
Prominent ears	69	50	70	68
High-arched palate	62	40	57	53
Hyperextensible finger joints	72	70	77	60
Double-jointed thumbs	55	50	30	38
Single palmar crease	22	10	17	15
Hand callouses	13	0	13	0
Flat feet	72	80	83	60
Heart murmur or click	1	0	0	0

Adapted from Hagerman RJ (2002) The Physical and Behavioural Phenotype. In Hagerman RJ and Hagerman PJ (eds) *Fragile X Syndrome: Diagnosis, Treatment and Research*, Third Edition. The Johns Hopkins University Press, Baltimore, Maryland, pp. 3–109.

Autism and fragile X

Approximately 25–35 per cent of young children with fragile X have a diagnosis of autism because of their social withdrawal, poor eye contact, severe deficits in social interaction, perseverations in behaviour and speech, and stereotypical behaviour such as hand-flapping or hand-biting. These children require the more intensive behavioural interventions that address autism, in addition to those for fragile X. Children who also have autism have lower cognitive abilities than those with fragile X alone. Why some children have more severe deficits causing autism is not known. Most children with fragile X, however, are not autistic, because they are interested in people and enjoy social interactions, although poor eye contact, hand-flapping, and hand-biting are seen in 50–90 per cent of children with fragile X even without autism (Table 1.1).

AD/HD, hyperarousal and anxiety

The behavioural problems in fragile X include hyperactivity or Attention Deficit/Hyperactivity Disorder (AD/HD) in 70–90 per cent of boys, and 30–50 per cent of girls. These children are usually easily aroused by excessive sensory stimuli such as a crowded market or a concert. Sometimes this hyperarousal leads to irritability or tantrum behaviour, hand-biting or hand-flapping. This can cause significant problem for parents and teachers if it happens in public.

Other behaviours related to sensory processing problems include tactile defensiveness or pulling away from light touch, covering their ears when sirens or alarms are sounding, occasional vomiting at strange smells, or disliking foods with an unusual texture. Anxiety frequently occurs when the child is hyperaroused. This leads to behaviour difficulties such as tantrums in new situations, with new people or even with the transition from one activity to another in school. The combination of hyperarousal and anxiety can lead to outbursts or even aggression. It is important for teachers to be aware of these problems and to develop calming techniques for use in the classroom and for activities outside school.

Females have less mood instability, aggression and hyperactivity than males with fragile X. More frequently shyness and social anxiety causes withdrawal or even the reluctance to talk (selective mutism), and attentional problems and disorganisation are common.

Physical features

Some physical features are seen in the majority of children with fragile X but approximately 30 per cent may not have these features, and they are not essential for diagnosis. The physical characteristics common to fragile X include prominent ears, a long face, a high palate, flat feet, and 'double jointed' (hyperextensible) fingers. These features are related to the connective tissue changes present in fragile X (Table 1.2). However, such features are very common in the general population, so most children with fragile X look normal.

Many individuals may have a long narrow face, although in early childhood this is less common. Boys often have rather prominent or large ears. The skin of people with fragile X is softer and more stretchable; their joints are generally more flexible, particularly in childhood. The looseness of the connective tissue also predisposes them to hernias, joint dislocations, oesophageal reflux, eye and vision problems, sinusitis and middle ear infections (see Table 1.3).

Recurrent ear infection problems have the greatest impact on education because they can cause even further damage to language development than is caused by fragile X alone. If the child has recurrent infections it is essential that hearing should be normalised by fitting pressure equalising tubes or grommets. Infections typically begin in the first year of life and require careful medical monitoring. Parents often comment that when grommets are fitted (typically at 2 to 3 years of age), they notice a dramatic improvement in speech and language development.

Vision can also be affected; 'wobbly eye' (strabismus) and/or squints are seen in up to 30 per cent of children. If these conditions are not treated the child may lose vision in the affected eye.

Table 1.3 Associated medical problems of males with fragile X syndrome

Problem	Per cent of patients with problem
Emesis (vomiting)	31
Failure to thrive in infancy	15
Strabismus (squint)	36
Glasses	22
Hernia	15
Joint dislocation	3
Orthopaedic intervention	21
Otitis media (middle ear infections)	85
History of sinusitis	23
Seizures	22
History of apnoea (breathing difficulties)	10
Diagnosis of AD/HD	80
Motor tics	19
Psychotic ideation	12

Adapted from Hagerman RJ (2002) The Physical and Behavioural Phenotype. In Hagerman RJ and Hagerman PJ (eds) *Fragile X Syndrome: Diagnosis, Treatment and Research*, Third Edition. The Johns Hopkins University Press, Baltimore, Maryland, pp. 3–109.

Seizures occur in approximately 20 per cent of children with fragile X, and these often begin in early childhood. They can be staring or absent episodes, partial motor or tonic-clonic fits, but these respond well to anticonvulsants. Seizures usually disappear after childhood although they may occasionally persist into adulthood.

Large testicles (macroorchidism) are a signature feature of boys with fragile X from early puberty onward. By the end of puberty the testicles can be 2–3 times normal size; teachers should be aware of the social and physical discomfort this can cause. Men with fragile X are normally fertile; the 15 per cent who are of higher intellect may father children, but most men with fragile X do not because of their cognitive limitations.

Girls with fragile X have the same features seen in boys, where appropriate, although these problems are usually less severe. Approximately 70 per cent of girls with fragile X have borderline or mild learning difficulties. They may also have attentional problems or executive function deficits, mood instability, anxiety and other behaviours (Table 1.1). As for all children, parental intellect (which represents background gene effects) and their environment also participate in how much they will be affected by fragile X.

A limited number of people with fragile X have cardiac problems, including prolapse of the mitral valve (MVP) and dilation of the base of the aorta. These problems are usually benign and often not seen until adulthood. They are related to connective tissue abnormalities, in the same way as are the child's loose joints. Rarely, a child with fragile X will have an uneven heart beat (arhythmia) or heart murmur.

Premutation carriers

Children who carry the premutation gene of fragile X usually have normal intellects. An occasional premutation carrier, particularly a male, may have learning difficulties, significant cognitive deficits or even autism. Both male and female premutation carriers may also have anxiety and occasionally this begins in childhood.

It is helpful to identify schoolage carriers because if learning or emotional problems occur they can be treated early. Psychologically most families feel that knowledge about their carrier status is easier for the child to accept in childhood, rather than being informed just prior to marriage or having children.

Summary

Children with fragile X have distinctive physical and behavioural characteristics, which combine shyness with attentional problems, impulsivity, hyperactivity, poor eye contact, stereotypical behaviour, perseverative speech and a good sense of humour. Teachers who become familiar with a child with fragile X are likely to recognise other children with the same disorder. Knowledge of the molecular cause of fragile X helps us to appreciate the variations that are seen from one child to another and to develop better treatment strategies in medicine and education. Treatment involves a multi-professional approach, which is well reviewed in this volume of work.

Acknowledgements

This work was supported by a grant from NICHD #HD36071 and the M.I.N.D. Institute at the University of California, at Davis.

References

Bailey, D.B., Hatton, D.D. and Skinner, M. (1998) Early developmental trajectories of males with fragile X syndrome. *American Journal on Mental Retardation* 103: 29–39.

Bailey, D.B., Jr., Hatton, D.D., Mesibov, G.B., Ament, N. and Skinner, M. (2000) Early development, temperament and functional impairment in autism and fragile X syndrome. *Journal of Autism and Developmental Disorders* 30: 49–59.

Bailey, D.B., Skinner, D., Hatton, D. and Roberts, J. (2000) Family experiences and factors associated with the diagnosis of fragile X syndrome. *Journal of Developmental and Behavioral Pediatrics* 21: 315–21.

Cornish, K.M., Munir, F. and Cross, G. (1999) Spatial cognition in males with fragile-X syndrome: evidence for a neuropsychological phenotype. *Cortex* 35: 263–71.

Cornish, K.M., Munir, F. and Cross, G. (2001) Differential impact of the FMR-1 full mutation on memory and attention functioning: a neuropsychological perspective. *Journal of Cognitive Neuroscience* 13: 144–50.

Greco, C., Hagerman, R.J., Tassone, F., Chudley, A., Del Bigio, M.R., Jacquemont, S., Leehey, M. and Hagerman, P.J. (2002) Neuronal intranuclear inclusions in a new cerebellar tremor/ataxia syndrome among fragile X carriers. *Brain* 125: 1,760–1,771

Hagerman, R.J. (2002) Physical and Behavioral Phenotype. In: Hagerman R.J. and Hagerman, P.J. (eds) *Fragile X Syndrome: Diagnosis, Treatment and Research*, 3rd edition. Baltimore: Johns Hopkins University Press, pp. 3–109.

Hagerman, R.J. and Hagerman, P.J. (2002) The fragile X premutation: into the phenotypic fold. *Current Opinion in Genetics & Development* 12: 278–283.

Hatton, D., Bailey, D.B., Hargett-Beck, M.Q., Skinner, M. and Clark, R.D. (1999) Behavioral style of young boys with fragile X syndrome. *Developmental Medicine and Child Neurology* 41: 625–632.

Hatton, D., Hooper, S.R., Bailey, D.B., Skinner, M.L., Sullivan, K.M. and Wheeler, A. (2002) Problem behavior in boys with fragile X syndrome. *American Journal of Medical Genetics* 108(2): 105–116.

Hills-Epstein, J., Riley, K. and Sobesky, W. (2002) The treatment of emotional and behavioral problems. In: Hagerman, R.J. and Hagerman, P.J. (eds) *Fragile X Syndrome: Diagnosis, Treatment, and Research*, 3rd Edition. Baltimore: Johns Hopkins University Press, pp. 339–362.

Miller, L.J., McIntosh, D.N., McGrath, J., Shyu, V., Lampe, M., Taylor, A.K., Tassone, F., Neitzel, K., Stackhouse, T. and Hagerman, R.J. (1999) Electrodermal responses to sensory stimuli in individuals with fragile X syndrome: a preliminary report. *American Journal of Medical Genetics* 83: 268–279.

Scharfenaker, S., O'Connor, R., Stackhouse, T. and Noble, L. (2002) An integrated approach to intervention. In: Hagerman, R.J. and Hagerman, P.J. (eds) *Fragile X Syndrome: Diagnosis, Treatment and Research*, 3rd edition. Baltimore: Johns Hopkins University Press, pp. 363–427.

Symons, F.J., Clark, R.D., Roberts, J.P. and Bailey, D.B. (2001) Classroom behavior of elementary school-age boys with fragile X syndrome. *The Journal of Special Education* 34(4): 194–202.

Tassone, F., Hagerman, R.J., Iklé, D.N., Dyer, P.N., Lampe, M., Willemsen, R., Oostra, B.A. and Taylor, A.K. (1999) FMRP expression as a potential prognostic indicator in fragile X syndrome. *American Journal of Medical Genetics* 84: 250–61.

Turk, J. (1998) Fragile X syndrome and attentional deficits. *Journal of Applied Research in Int Disab* 11: 175–191.

Turk, J. and Graham, P. (1997) Fragile X syndrome, autism, and autistic features. *Autism* 1: 175–197.

Chapter 2

The importance of diagnosis

Jeremy Turk

It is now widely acknowledged that a diagnosis, wherever possible, is of utmost importance to individuals who have developmental difficulties, for genetic reasons as well as to their families and carers. Indeed, diagnoses can take many forms, and this is a common cause of confusion for those who work with children and young people who have fragile X syndrome. An individual may have multiple diagnoses, all of which are important for different reasons, and all of which may have implications for intervention and support.

Fragile X syndrome is an example of a so-called 'aetiological' diagnosis. That is to say, it describes the cause of the individual's developmental, psychological and learning difficulties. A diagnosis may also be 'clinical', for example autism, Asperger syndrome, AD/HD and even challenging behaviour. These terms describe the actual cluster of clinical problems experienced by the individual, which may or may not present challenges to family members and others. Clinical diagnoses do not in themselves say anything about cause, although we now know that conditions such as the autistic spectrum disorders and attention deficit disorders do have substantial genetic determinants. It follows then that a clinical diagnosis has to be caused by an aetiological diagnosis – even if we are often unable to pinpoint exactly what it is. Thirdly, diagnoses may be descriptive of the general level of intellectual functioning as in the terms learning difficulties, learning disability and the now increasingly redundant phrases mental handicap, mental subnormality and mental retardation.

Diagnosis can also reflect social factors such as inadequate housing or education, other social adversities such as neglect or more general issues in society such as racism and migration. Finally the term diagnosis is often applied to unhelpful social interactions as in the phrase 'attachment disorder' and 'family dysfunction'. Not surprisingly, with such a morass of diagnostic possibilities, many of which may be applicable to one individual, confusion often reigns. For this reason, a 'multi-axial classification' is often applied in developmental clinical work. This consists of multiple axes, each of which describes a particular issue germane to the individual. The axes are:

1   Psychiatric diagnosis
2   Specific developmental difficulties
3   General level of intellectual functioning
4   Associated medical conditions
5   Family and other social issues
6   Degree of functional impairment

Hence, a theoretical multi-axial classification of a young person with fragile X syndrome may read as follows:

1   Attention deficit/hyperactivity disorder
2   Social understanding and receptive language (comprehension) difficulties
3   Mild intellectual disability
4   Fragile X syndrome, epilepsy
5   Single parenthood, inadequate living circumstances
6   Marked functional impairment.

Such an overview helps clarify all the interacting biological, psychological, educational and social issues contributing to the individual's welfare and helping or hindering the maximisation of potential. It also paves the way for a rational, integrated and individualised multi-agency intervention package. It is important to avoid the trap of 'diagnostic overshadowing'. This phrase describes people's tendencies to attribute all of an individual's difficulties to one specific aspect. Examples include the attribution of all an individual's problems to genetics, family issues or learning difficulties, rather than acknowledging the multi-faceted nature of developmental difficulties, their causes and treatments.

Diagnosis is important for many reasons.

The right of the individual and family to know

Individuals who have fragile X syndrome, and their families, have a basic right to know what the cause of the developmental difficulties is. For the majority of people with learning disability this can still not be established. These individuals and their families often remain sad, confused and uncertain. They may attribute the problems inappropriately to other causes such as family circumstances, inadequate parenting or other social adversities. They often search persistently in an attempt to find a reason for their family member's problems. They may attribute the difficulties to an event which coincided with early awareness of the person's developing challenges, for example immunisation or parental separation. Conversely, knowing the cause facilitates looking towards the future and planning for it. The earlier notion that having a label led to inertia has now been discredited. People want to know why they are the way they are. Nobody wants to learn of bad news, but it is a whole lot better than no news at all. At least you know where you stand.

Relief from uncertainty

Having a child with a developmental disability produces a chain of parental psychological reactions similar to those experienced by people who have lost a loved or otherwise emotionally close individual such as a spouse or parent. This grieving or bereavement reaction is thought to be for the anticipated 'perfect' child, which existed within the parents' minds and the need to work through this in order to adjust to the new reality of having a child with disabilities and what this means for each family member and indeed their functioning together as a family system. The stages consist often of an initial denial phase, followed sometimes by protest and anger. This may be directed towards others such as other family members or professionals who are trying to help. It can often also be directed inwards as self-blame or even depression. Following this is often a stage of searching which may manifest constructively as a desire to maximise knowledge about the difficulties. It can also present as shopping around for multiple professional opinions or trying a large number of purportedly beneficial interventions. Finally adaptation and adjustment develops with the gaining of a new individual and family identity. Individuals can become stuck at any stage in this process. There is an increased likelihood of becoming stuck (or 'fixated') when a clear cause for the problems is not apparent. Becoming stuck or fixated in a stage of grief can have enormous negative repercussions for the welfare and quality of life not only of the individual with fragile X syndrome, but also for the entire family.

Facilitation of grief resolution

Knowing the cause or diagnosis aids relief from uncertainty and facilitates this grieving process. Being denied access to knowledge about the cause is unhelpful. Indeed, far from being a distraction from focussing on the practical developmental problems and how they can best be addressed, knowing the diagnosis actually helps to move forward psychologically. It frees people from often traumatic and tormenting persistent obsessional thoughts regarding what the causes of the problems are. A genetic diagnosis may also give relief from sometimes overwhelming guilt feelings. These often arise from beliefs that the family and/or social factors were the cause of the learning disabilities or developmental and behavioural problems more generally.

Focussing on the future

It is certainly important to know as well as possible what has caused and led up to one's current predicament. If you don't know where you have come from, then it is difficult to plan fully the way ahead. But excessive and persisting emphasis on the past can hinder moving forward emotionally and practically, and looking towards the future. By completing a process of reflection on the past and its influences, as facilitated by the issues described above, one is then more able to concentrate on future possibilities and potentials. Thus the existence of a diagnostic label facilitates the bereavement process relating to having a family member with learning disability, and assists in grief resolution.

Genetic counselling

Fragile X syndrome is a genetic inherited condition. It is always the case that one gets it from one or other parent. It never develops anew without a parent having carried at least a premutation (see Chapter 20 on genetics). If you have fragile X syndrome, this means that you have a fifty–fifty chance of transmitting the condition to offspring every time a pregnancy occurs. Other family members may carry the genetic anomaly while being unaware and unaffected by it – so-called asymptomatic carriers. Most individuals and families wish to know what the risks are of having a child with developmental difficulties. Some may avoid future pregnancies and take other steps to ensure that their children do not have fragile X syndrome. Others will pursue pregnancies but with the benefit of being aware of the possible consequences and how their children can be helped best and as early as possible should they have fragile X syndrome. The issue is one of maximising knowledge and information in order to help people make as valid a choice as possible. Genetic counsellors do not tell people what to do. They give them as much information and understanding as they can to help them in their decision-making. For this reason, good genetic centres provide counselling before a genetic test as well as after.

The need for female carriers to be identified sooner rather than later is also important. There is increasing research evidence that females who have a fragile X chromosome can have important special educational and psychological needs. This may even be true for the so-called 'premutation' carriers who have a smaller abnormality on their X chromosome. Historically these individuals were thought to be free of developmental difficulties despite being at risk of passing on fragile X syndrome to their offspring. We now know that their special needs can be most debilitating, yet are often missed. Also, there is evidence for early menopause in this group of individuals, emphasising the need for early and expert genetic counselling.

Information on likely strengths and needs

There is now a large body of knowledge about the developmental and behavioural challenges likely to be faced by people who have fragile X syndrome and how these can best be helped. As in the current guidelines for good educational practice, a 'wait and see' approach is no longer tenable. Likely educational challenges can be anticipated, planned for, worked on proactively and hence minimised. Pupils' experiences of schooling can thus be made more pleasurable. They will feel more understood, will be more relaxed, will learn better and will develop greater self-esteem with more positive views of themselves and the future. They are also more likely to reach a higher level of ability ultimately.

Early instigation of appropriate interventions

Much early input will be relevant to young children generally who have learning difficulties. Other approaches will help commonly associated developmental problems that affect schooling and education. These include the autistic spectrum disorders and the attention deficit disorders. Such approaches will usually include some sort of special nursery input and provision and home-based programmes such as Portage. There should also be identification and action on specific educational and social needs, and packages of specific relevance to particular issues such as the Earlybird project for social and communicatory development in children with autism and their families. Other approaches will be more specific to the cause of the learning difficulties. In fragile X syndrome these will commonly include awareness and understanding of the language and behavioural oddities in the presence of a usually friendly and sociable yet often bashful and shy personality. The numeracy and visuo-spatial difficulties also require acknowledgement and special input as do the difficulties with direct eye contact ('gaze aversion') and the increasing problems with processing sequences of information as the individual approaches adolescence. Thus, not all people with learning disability are the same. The severity of intellectual impairment and conduciveness of social environment are certainly crucial in determining the individual's psychological adjustment and likelihood of progress. To these two factors we now need to add cause ('aetiology') as a further critical determinant of developmental progress and likely challenges to be faced.

Linking with an appropriate support network

Individuals and their families have a right to relate to and make contact with other families in similar circumstances. Knowing you have fragile X syndrome allows for the opportunity to learn from others, to share experiences and to know that you are not alone or unique. Much can be gained from others who have been through similar processes of learning, grief, and service provision. The practical as well as emotional importance of such links should never be under-estimated. Efforts should always be made to ensure that families have at least had the opportunity to establish contact with relevant support groups such as the Fragile X Society.

Chapter 3

Cognitive strengths and difficulties

Kim Cornish

In this chapter, we introduce the importance of looking beyond the concept of 'learning disability' or 'learning difficulties' per se and towards an understanding of the differing cognitive strengths and difficulties that can characterize children with fragile X syndrome. By achieving this goal we can provide information that can be used in a multidisciplinary framework to help guide and assist professionals in the timing of *early* interventions that could maximize academic potential and outcomes in affected children and adolescents. This chapter will first address the importance of the gender differences in the range of intellectual difficulties displayed in fragile X and why these occur; and then review the now well-documented profile of cognitive abilities in fragile X focusing especially on defining the strengths within the profile.

Why do boys and girls have different levels of intellectual ability?

Understanding the genetics of the syndrome is the key to understanding why boys and girls differ in degree of learning disability. Fragile X syndrome is an X-linked chromosome disorder that involves the 'turning off' of the fragile X gene (FMR1 gene) on the affected X chromosome. When this happens, a particular type of protein (FMRP) fails to be produced and it is the lack of this protein that causes fragile X (see Chapter 20). Recent research suggests that the protein is especially important during foetal brain development and that a loss of function would impact upon early information processing and developmental pathways resulting in atypical development from infancy and beyond.

Girls with fragile X usually have milder levels of intellectual difficulties because, unlike boys, they have two X chromosomes and only one has been 'turned off'. The other undamaged chromosome can usually compensate for or 'buffer' the effects of the mutated gene on the affected chromosome. Remember that the unaffected X chromosome will produce some FMR protein. In contrast, boys have only one X chromosome so there is no way to compensate for the lack of the protein and consequently boys are significantly more impaired than girls.

What is also important to recognize is that levels of development are not solely dependent upon the fragile X gene. Other family genes will also play a role in the child's development as will the immediate environment the child is raised in. It is the combination of these factors that will impact upon and guide the developmental potential of each child with fragile X.

The cognitive profile

At a global level, there is consistent evidence to indicate that both boys and girls with fragile X have better verbal skills than non-verbal, spatial skills. This discrepancy has been reported across a range of standardized IQ tests, including the Wechsler Intelligence Scale for Children (WISC). In this battery, a range of verbal and non-verbal (performance) skills is addressed including mental arithmetic, vocabulary, comprehension, picture completion and abstract reasoning. At the end of the testing session, three scores are produced: Verbal IQ, Performance IQ and a full-scale (combined) IQ score. Research has found that in children with fragile X there is a verbal–nonverbal discrepancy in the direction of better verbal IQ scores than performance IQ scores (Veenema *et al.* 1987). A similar pattern has also been confirmed on other standardized IQ measures both in the UK and in North America (e.g. Kaufman Assessment Battery (K-ABC)). What this profile strongly suggests is that children with fragile X perform best on tasks that involve *simultaneous processing* (placing information in a holistic, gestalt-like manner) rather than on tasks that involve *sequential processing* (placing information in a step-by-step order or putting things in a sequence).

At a more finer-grained level, research during the past decade has identified a profile of specific cognitive strengths and difficulties that characterise fragile X. This profile is outlined below and summarized in Table 3.1.

Cognitive strengths

Verbal skills

Commensurate with their intellectual ability, boys with fragile X will have severe delays in speech and language noticeable from pre-school upwards. However, *verbal skills* are a relative strength compared to other cognitive skills and include good expressive and receptive vocabularies alongside well-developed skills in verbal labelling and comprehension. Especially strong in boys with fragile X is their verbal long-term memory skills, in particular their ability to tap into a repertoire of acquired knowledge and vocabulary which appears to grow steadily throughout childhood. In girls with fragile X, however, relatively little is known about the range of verbal skills, but recent findings indicate a similar profile to that presented in the boys with particular strengths in verbal short-term and long-term memory.

Table 3.1 Cognitive strengths and weaknesses in children with fragile X syndrome

Cognitive strengths	Cognitive weaknesses
Verbal skills: receptive and expressive, comprehension	Language delay (perseveration, impulsive speech, poor pragmatic skills)
Short- and long-term memory for acquired, meaningful information	Short- and long-term memory for abstract information
Understanding and recognizing the emotions of others	Attention and concentration problems
Good face recognition	Arithmetic

Long and short-term memory for meaningful and learned information

Children with fragile X display a greater attentional capacity for meaningful rather than abstract information. In contrast, processing of non-complex information that requires fewer or basic attentional processes is performed at a level comparable to children of a similar developmental level, both those with and those without learning disability. Indeed, both boys and girls appear to have verbal short- and long-term memory strengths relative to their own intellectual ability levels. This can be seen in their ability to memorize places, people and events that have some meaning to them and to recall these details over a period of time. In particular, children with fragile X have a very good visual memory that enables them to recall complex details about their immediate environment – for example, the route of the school taxi home. In general, then, the pattern of strengths suggest that children with fragile X may learn most effectively when in a familiar environment and in lessons that tap into their relatively good visual and long-term memory skills, perhaps using visual cues that draw upon their repertoire of learned information.

Understanding and recognizing the emotions of others

Children with fragile X are good at recognizing basic emotional expressions in others (happy, sad, angry and puzzled) and when presented with different scenarios they can appropriately place the correct emotion into the story (Turk and Cornish 1998). Children with fragile X are also very good at recognizing faces they have just seen as well as recognizing faces that are stored in their long-term memory.

Cognitive weaknesses

Language delay

Generally, speech and language development in children with fragile X is at a level approximately 50 per cent of what would typically be expected for children of their chronological age. At a finer-grained level, core problems can include:

- elevated perseveration or the excessive repeating of a word or phrase during conversations;
- impulsive speech which is characterized by short, rapid bursts of speech;
- poor social use of language (pragmatics).

Reasons for the high rates of these problems, especially in boys with fragile X are not yet fully understood. However, it is likely that the social demands of the language environment for these children (eye contact, co-ordination of syntax, semantics and conversational pragmatics) promote hyper-arousal and anxiety, which in turn then results in a failure to properly inhibit verbal responses (see Chapter 14).

Long- and short-term memory for abstract, non-meaningful information

Children with fragile X have problems in processing abstract, non-meaningful information both within verbal and non-verbal (visuo-spatial) domains. This deficit appears to be further confounded by poor 'working memory' skills that require the temporary storage of information in mind or 'online', while processing the same or other information. Thus, any information that the child with fragile X needs to learn that is tedious or abstract in content will be extremely difficult for them to absorb. Given this difficulty, it may be more useful to organize this type of material into small-size units, given with greater clarity, that focus upon the child's strength in verbal skills and in their ability to remember information that is presented in a salient, meaningful context.

Attention and concentration problems

One of the most striking and persistent problems in children with fragile X is attention and concentration difficulty, which includes a behavioural triad of severe and persistent inattention (inability to remain on task in the face of distracting stimuli), impulsiveness and hyperactivity (although hyperactivity is less common in girls). This triad of symptoms leads to many fragile X children, especially young boys, being diagnosed with Attention Deficit/Hyperactivity Disorder (AD/HD) (see Chapter 18). Research at the cognitive level further suggests that on-line control of attention is especially poor in children with fragile X and that this profoundly impacts upon their ability to inhibit repetitious behaviour. Equally they cannot exclude attention-demanding distractions such as sudden changes, noises, and movements when attempting to maintain a focus. The nature and severity of this deficit appears to be specific to the condition (Wilding *et al.* 2002).

Arithmetic

Poor mental and basic arithmetic is a common and severe problem in both boys and girls with fragile X and is almost certainly related to their difficulties in processing sequential, abstract information and not to level of learning disability. Indeed, problems in number concepts, for example, have been identified as occurring as early as pre-school. These findings underlie the importance of *early* intervention in establishing a foundation for basic arithmetic and number concepts in children with fragile X, irrespective of their intellectual ability.

Is there an age-related decline in intelligence?

Research now consistently indicates a developmental decline in the intelligence quotient (IQ) of boys and girls with fragile X syndrome beginning in late childhood and adolescence. These findings have been confirmed in both cross-sectional studies (different age cohorts) (Dykens, *et al.* 1996) and longitudinal studies (same cohort over a period of time) (e.g. Fisch *et al.* 1991). In the Dykens *et al.* (1996) study, a cross-sectional analysis of IQ scores from 130 boys revealed that IQ declined from a mean of 55 in children aged 1–5 years to a mean IQ of 39 amongst children aged 16–20 years. Although one could interpret the pattern of these findings as suggesting an actual regression in intellectual level, a more probable explanation for this decline is that it reflects the fragile X child's increasing problems in maintaining and developing successful learning strategies that keep pace with their unaffected classmates.

Conclusions and recommendations

This brief review of the cognitive strengths and difficulties that characterize the child with fragile X, shows how important it is to move away from concentrating on the global effects of learning disability and look towards the more subtle cognitive profile, especially recognizing important strengths which can facilitate learning inside the classroom and beyond. Of these, the emerging picture is one of relatively good skills in some aspects of language, short- and long-term memory for meaningful and relevant information alongside good simultaneous information processing. In contrast, relative weaknesses include attention and concentration problems, short- and long-memory for abstract information, sequential information processing, and, especially in girls, poor arithmetic skills that include problems with basic number concepts. It is important to recognise the more subtle cognitive deficits in girls and the impact of these upon their academic potential and attainment. This is especially important given that girls with fragile X are more likely than boys to be educated within a mainstream, rather than a special, school environment.

Furthermore, cognitive difficulties in children with fragile X do not occur in isolation and are often compounded with a number of behavioural concerns (AD/HD, social anxiety, withdrawal) that can severely impact upon learning and memory. It is therefore important that teachers recognize the academic potential of the fragile X child within the context of their behavioural profile, and ensure that the learning environment facilitates availability of information in forms most compatible with their strengths.

In summary, given what we now know about the profile of children with fragile X, it is crucial that educational support and interventions are targeted to address both the cognitive strengths and difficulties associated with the syndrome, and to the differing needs of boys and girls. By addressing these issues alongside interventions that begin early in development, preferably within the pre-school years, it will be possible for all children with fragile X to achieve their academic potential.

References

Cornish, K.M. (2000) 'Neuropsychological patterns in Fragile X syndrome.' Fragile X Society National Family Conference, June 1998. Publ. *Fragile X Society Newsletter*.

Dykens, E.M., Ort, S., Cohen, I. and Finucane, B. (1996) 'Trajectories and profiles of adaptive behaviour in males with fragile X syndrome.' *Journal of Autism and Developmental Disorders* 26: 287–301.

Fisch, G.S.T, Arinami, U, Froster-Iskenius U, Fryns J.P, Curfs,L.M, Borghraef, M, Howard-Peebles, P.N, Schwatrz, C.E, Simenson, R.J. and Shapiro, L. (1991) 'Relationship between age and IQ among fragile X males: A multi-center study.' *Journal of Medical Genetics* 38: 481–487.

Turk, J. and Cornish, K. (1998). 'Face recognition and emotion perception in boys with fragile-X syndrome.' *Journal of Intellectual Disability Research* 42(6): 490–499.

Veenema, H., Veenema, T., and Geraedts, J. P. (1987) 'The fragile X syndrome in a large family: II. Psychological investigations.' *Journal of Medical Genetics* 54: 378–383.

Wilding, J., Cornish, K.M. and Munir, F. (2002) 'Further delineation of the executive deficit in males with fragile X syndrome.' *Neuropsychologia* 40(8): 1,343–9.

Chapter 4

Atypical language production of males with fragile **X** syndrome

Vicki Sudhalter and Richard C. Belser

The fragile X syndrome behavioral phenotype includes problems with language production, especially among affected males. These problems include both delayed and atypical language. *Delayed language* refers to the production of language that is characteristic of younger children, whereas *atypical language* refers to language that either is not produced by typically developing children of any age or contains excessive amounts of certain speech or language errors. Delayed language is attributable to general cognitive delay; it is not specific to fragile X and will not be discussed here. Instead, this chapter will focus on three specific forms of atypical verbal behavior that are commonly observed in this population. They are tangential language, perseverative language and repetitive speech. Although girls with fragile X tend to be less affected than boys, and most have relatively strong verbal skills, they too may exhibit these characteristics within their conversational language.

In addition to describing this atypical language, we will show how fundamental characteristics of fragile X may be responsible for it, by affecting early language acquisition processes and influencing later conversational language production. By describing what we believe are the underlying causes for this atypical language, we hope to foster a greater understanding of the factors that affect it, and promote the development of more effective intervention and remediation programs.

Early language acquisition

The ability to communicate with another person relies upon many different, although mutually dependent, skills. A speaker must be able to prepare a message, taking into account the thought he wishes to express, the conversational setting and the knowledge base of his listener. In addition, the speaker needs to choose the correct form in which to create the intended message, find the words to convey the intended meaning and develop the articulatory motor plans necessary to produce the sounds of the intended message. The acquisition of conversational and language competency is perhaps the hardest task any individual will have to do in his life. Considering that they are often exposed to very poor examples of language (such as incomplete and ungrammatical sentences), it is remarkable that most typically developing children acquire their language without explicit instruction, and in a relatively short period of time. Most 4-year old children cannot tie their shoelaces but they can form a question to ask someone to help them tie their shoes. Thus, within a mere four years, a child can acquire rather sophisticated linguistic competency.

This chapter cannot deliver an extensive review of child language acquisition, but will review briefly two of the earliest stages of language acquisition, and show how fundamental phenotypic characteristics of fragile X interfere with the normal course of these stages.

Stage 1: sound–environment mapping

In order for language to be acquired, an infant must be able to associate or 'map' specific sound patterns with observed objects. Initially, he must distinguish the sounds of language from other sounds within his environment (car horns, hair dryers) that do not represent objects. He must learn to select sounds made by human mouths. This requires the ability to distinguish people from other 'things' in the environment; to localize and focus on a speaker's mouth, and to identify what the sound being produced by that speaker is referring to.

One of the major feats of this earliest stage of language acquisition is the infant's ability to extract individual words from the array of sounds confronting him. If his mother says, 'Look at the cat,' the child must relate the sound /K-A-T/ to the small furry feline purring at his feet. Exactly how an infant is able to accomplish this at such an early age is not well understood. It has been suggested that infants become sensitive to 'clues of meaning', such as stressed syllables and word ordering, in their language, and that these clues help them parse streams of sound such as 'Look at the cat', and recognize that the most important sound is /K-A-T/. In addition, parents and their infant children interact in ways that promote language acquisition. Parents will draw attention to objects in the environment while the infant smiles, looks at the objects and babbles.

How fragile X syndrome interferes with noun acquisition

In order to map auditory to visual stimuli, infants must be able to hear sounds and have the cognitive skill to integrate auditory and visual sensory input. Infants usually require multiple exposures to each auditory-visual pairing to perceive the associations, and thus learn the meanings of words. Infants with cognitive delays require additional unambiguous, consistent exposure to this kind of input in order to learn from such auditory-visual pairings.

Children with fragile X are prone to recurrent ear infections such as otitis media or glue ear. Although research on long-term effects of recurrent ear infections on language performance is not conclusive, there is evidence from non-delayed children to suggest that early otitis media is related to a poorer ability to process the sounds of language. Recurrent ear infections have also been associated with poorer language performance and impaired listening and articulation ability. Thus, children with fragile X who also have recurrent ear infections would be expected to exhibit delayed acquisition of nouns, and also experience greater difficulty with the perception of speech sounds.

In addition, many children with fragile X have sensory integration problems that make it difficult for them to integrate two or more sensory inputs (such as visual and auditory stimuli). When integration cannot occur, the stimuli in their environment become a buzzing whirr without meaning. The sensory-integration difficulties that are an inherent characteristic of fragile X can further interfere with the acquisition of the sound–sight pairing.

Stage 2: Babbling

The emergence of a child's own vocal output occurs concurrently with his mapping of mouth sounds to specific environmental stimuli. Stoel-Gammon (1998) eloquently expressed how important a child's own vocal output is to his subsequent production of words:

> Children must recognize the links between their own oral-motor movements and the resulting acoustic signal. Thus, the 6-month old who frequently produces [ba] becomes

aware of the tie between the tactual and kinesthetic sensations associated with this syllable and the auditory signal that occurs. . . . Infants must learn that their production of [ba] resembles the adult words ball, bottle and Bob. When these two types of learning have occurred, the prelinguistic form [ba] can serve as a basis for production of words from the target language.

(p. 27)

There is considerable research suggesting that infant babbling is strongly related to the acquisition of articulatory competence. Studies have reported significant correlations between early word usage and rehearsed consonant–vowel babbled syllables (Vihman, 1992); between the onset of babbling and the onset of meaningful speech (Stoel-Gammon, 1998); between the number of vocalizations produced at three months and vocabulary size at 27 months (Kagan, 1971); between the number of consonant–vowel syllables produced at one year of age and the age of first word usage (Menyuk et al., 1986); and between the diversity of syllables and sound types produced between the ages 6 and 14 months and performance on speech and language tests at 5 years of age (Jensen et al., 1988). There is clearly an important relationship between infants' babbling and their acquisition of articulatory competence.

How fragile X syndrome disrupts babbling

Many individuals with fragile X syndrome are born with low tone, or hypotonia. Children with hypotonia may not acquire their motor milestones on time, and this failure often leads parents of children with fragile X to consult their pediatrician before any cognitive delay becomes apparent. In addition to motor milestone delays, children with fragile X may experience oral-motor delays that prevent them from feeding effectively. An infant may have difficulty latching onto his mother's nipple, and older children may have very specific food preferences (such as disliking cold or hot foods, soupy or hard-to-chew foods) or may stuff their mouth because they cannot feel that it is full. Feeding problems are among the earliest indicators that a child may develop speech motor planning difficulties that can impair his ability to produce language sounds.

It is easy to see how oral-motor planning difficulties can interfere with the onset of babbling, and the subsequent production of syllables. Because impaired or delayed babbling interferes with a child's ability to learn how his vocal output relates to word meanings, oral-motor planning may be a contributing factor to delays in the onset of productive language skill. Additionally, once a child does learn to talk, oral-motor planning difficulties may continue to affect his speech articulation.

Social anxiety, reluctance to talk and hyperarousal

In addition to the physical characteristics described above, males with fragile X exhibit certain behavioral tendencies, including social avoidance. This is reflected in such behaviors as gaze aversion, overt turning of the body away during face-to-face social interaction, and stylized, highly ritualistic forms of greeting. Hagerman (2002) has reported that males with fragile X exhibit normal eye contact throughout their first year but gradually develop an aversion to eye contact, accompanied by social anxiety, by the time they are 4 years old.

The establishment of eye contact is a well-known non-verbal signal used between conversational partners to convey a desire to initiate communication. Whenever one makes eye contact with another person in a social or conversational setting, the person being looked at recognizes an expectation to make a verbal response. For this reason, it has been suggested that gaze avoidance by males with fragile X may reflect their reluctance to interact verbally with others. Because children are not expected to interact verbally during their first year of life, there is no reason for them to avoid eye contact. By 3 years of age, however, children are expected to engage in verbal interactions and short conversations with their family and friends. For children with fragile X, this means confronting their difficulties with motor planning, auditory processing and language comprehension. Recognizing that their own language is poor and disfluent, males with fragile X probably learn early in life that they can avoid the anxiety and embarrassment of speaking by avoiding eye contact with potential conversational partners. Thus, the same problems that interfered with their ability to acquire language could later cause individuals with fragile X to become reluctant conversationalists.

Fear of revealing poor speech and language ability is not the only source of social anxiety among males with fragile X. More important is a pervasive impairment in their ability to normally regulate arousal. The term *arousal* refers to a general state of nervous system activation that is reflected in behavior, physiological activity and emotional experience. Males with fragile X react more strongly than those without fragile X to many forms of environmental and social stimuli, and the hyperarousal that results can take an unusually long time to abate. As a result, individuals with fragile X are prone to long periods of sustained hyperarousal, especially during social interactions. We suggest that physical discomfort accompanies this hyperarousal, and that many of the symptoms of social anxiety and withdrawal, commonly seen in people with fragile X, can be interpreted as attempts to cope with this discomfort, and with the fear of experiencing even greater discomfort in socially charged situations. Restricting the number and length of one's conversations would be one way to reduce the uncomfortable anxiety associated with social interaction. Despite the use of such social avoidance strategies, there are times when males with fragile X are required to talk and otherwise actively interact with their social environment. Under such circumstances, specific types of atypical language are commonly observed.

Arousal, inhibitory control and atypical language

The types of atypical language that are produced most often by males with fragile X include tangential language, perseverative language and repetitive speech. *Tangential language* refers to off-topic questions, responses or comments that do not logically follow the preceding conversational thread. They usually disrupt a conversation by causing the conversational partner to either ask questions in an effort to discover the associational link, or to restate the previous point in order to preserve and appropriately advance the conversation. *Perseverative language* refers to the reintroduction of favorite topics over and over, even in the presence of conflicting conversational demands. *Repetitive speech* refers to the repetition of sounds, words or phrases within an utterance or conversational turn.

Tangential and perseverative language

Hyperarousal, in conjunction with diminished inhibitory control, leads to the perseverative and tangential language seen in individuals with fragile X. Ordinarily, excitatory and inhibitory processes exist in balance within the nervous system, resulting in stable, well-controlled behavior. Either increased excitatory activity or decreased inhibitory activity causes an imbalance between these systems that results in impulsive forms of behavior. Because both hyperarousal and impaired inhibitory control are characteristic of individuals with fragile X, such imbalance is easily triggered by either physical or social stimulation within their environment. When this occurs, the effect upon language production is to release impulsive tendencies to talk about favorite or highly associated topics regardless of the conversational demands. Tangential language occurs when associations between previous and current utterances are personal or otherwise unknown to the conversational partner. Perseverative language occurs when favorite topics are impulsively reintroduced into a conversation, independently of the current context, presumably because they are well rehearsed and their use provokes less social anxiety than new unfamiliar information. Additionally, perseverative topics may have been initially reinforced, thus encouraging their frequent introduction.

In many cases, hyperarousal can be triggered by events within the conversation, rather than from stimulation originating in one's external environment. Different types of conversational language carry different task demands for the speaker. For example, when an individual is asked a question, he is expected to produce a unique response that adds new information. This task can be particularly difficult for several reasons. In addition to having to attend to what is being asked, the speaker must have the confidence to create sentences that can add information, and be able to inhibit the more comfortable alternative of talking about a favorite or tangentially related topic.

Repetitive speech

In addition to the atypical types of language described above, another common linguistic characteristic of males with fragile X is repetitive speech. Once an individual has acquired some language he must learn how to communicate fluently (with appropriate rate, rhythm and articulation) within a social setting. The Neuropsycholinguistic Theory of Language Production (Perkins *et al.*, 1991) is one of many theories that describe how speakers do this. According to this theory, fluent speech requires the coordination of two independently operating neural systems: one that controls linguistic processes, such as selecting the appropriate vocabulary and syntax to convey a desired thought; and another that controls paralinguistic process, such as generating the appropriate facial expression, intonation and rhythm to indicate the speaker's emotion and intent. Disfluent speech is thought to occur when the coordination between these systems becomes impaired, causing them to become dyssynchronized.

We believe that the hyperarousal experienced by individuals with fragile X creates the conditions required for repetitive speech to occur. Anxiety triggered by the expectations of conversational participation may cause a child to develop rapid speech (Belser and Sudhalter, 2001). Rapid speech is associated with heightened anxiety and arousal and is a recognized phenotypic characteristic of individuals with fragile X. Rapid speech may result in the individual beginning an utterance prematurely, causing the linguistic elements of that utterance to lead the paralinguistic elements. When the neuropsycholinguistic system senses that this occurs, it causes the speaker to stall for time by repeating a selected phoneme, word or phrase until the associated paralinguistic elements have had a chance to catch up, and synchrony is restored.

As with the production of atypical language, the hyperarousal that leads to disfluent repetitive speech may be triggered by either environmental stimulation or conversational demands. Although simple 'yes' or 'no' answers are not difficult for males with fragile X to produce, we have found that attempts to elaborate on answers by volunteering additional unprompted information can heighten their arousal, and accordingly these utterances tend to contain more repetitive disfluencies.

Summary

This chapter has described some of the ways that fundamental phenotypic characteristics of fragile X affect the early acquisition of language, as well as later language production. These include physical considerations such as recurrent ear infections and sensory integration difficulties, which may interfere with the child's ability to learn early word meanings, as well as hypotonia and poor oral-motor coordination, which may interfere with early speech development and affect the fluency of acquired speech.

We have also described how hyperarousal and impaired inhibitory control can affect language in several important ways. By making it difficult to block impulsive verbal behavior, these problems lead to language that is inappropriately perseverative and tangential. Hyperarousal also promotes rapid speech, which can lead to the production of repetitive disfluencies.

Males with fragile X are often described as being friendly, funny, helpful, charming and curious. They express a desire to interact with their peers, but are prevented from doing so because of excessive social anxiety. We believe that the self-awareness of their atypical language and disfluent speech contributes to their social anxiety, and causes them to deliberately curtail their use of language.

Almost all children with fragile X can benefit from remedial language training to help them with syntax, semantics and conversational interchange skills. To be effective, any language intervention program must also address the underlying causes of atypical language and disfluent speech. This means that in addition to presenting exercises to improve poor oral-motor tone and coordination, they must also be helped to reduce their anxiety and arousal, for example by eliminating unnecessary sources of sensory stimulation and incorporating relaxation and stress reduction techniques.

References

Belser, R.C. and Sudhalter, V. (2001) Conversational characteristics of children with fragile X syndrome: repetitive speech. *American Journal of Mental Retardation* 106: 28–38.

Hagerman, R. J. (2002) Medical follow-up and pharmacology. In: Hagerman, R.J. and Hagerman, P.J. eds. *Fragile X Syndrome: Diagnosis, Treatment and Research*. Baltimore, MD: Johns Hopkins University Press. pp. 287–338.

Jensen, T.S., Boggild-Ajdersen, B., Schmidt., J., Ankerhus, J. and Hansen, E. (1988) Perinatal risk factors and first year vocalizations: Influence on preschool language and motor performance. *Developmental Medicine and Child Neurology* 30: 153–161.

Kagan, J. (1971). *Change and Continuity in Infancy*. New York: John Wiley & Sons.

Menyuk, P., Liebergott, J. and Schultz, M. (1986) Predicting phonological development. In: Lindstrom, B. and Zetterstrom, R. eds. *Precursors of Early Speech*. New York: Stockton Press. pp.70–93.

Perkins, W. H., Kent, R. D. and Curlee, R. F. (1991) A theory of neuropsycholinguistic function in stuttering. *Journal of Speech and Hearing Research* 34: 734–752.

Stoel-Gammon, C. (1998) Relationship between lexical and phonological development. In: Paul, R. ed. *Exploring the Speech–Language Connection*. Baltimore, MD: Paul H. Brookes Publishing Co. pp. 25–52.

Vihman, M.(1992) Early syllables and the construction of phonology. In: Ferguson, C.A., Menn, L. and Stoel-Gammon, C. eds. *Phonological Development: Models, Research, Implications*. Timonium, MD: York Press. pp. 393–422.

Chapter 5

Educating girls with fragile X syndrome

Lesley Powell

The findings reported in this chapter, and the strategies developed from the findings, resulted from a study in 1999 at the University of Western Australia. The study involved 80 British and Australian girls with fragile X syndrome and 80 Australian girls, matched for age and IQ, who formed the control group.

Girls with fragile X syndrome exhibit a range of academic and emotional difficulties. Parents are faced with complex educational decisions over how and where to educate their daughters. This chapter provides parents and teachers with strategies to enable these girls to reach their full academic potential, without raising their anxiety levels or leaving them with a negative attitude to school.

The strategies are specifically designed for girls who carry the full mutation but do not have an intellectual disability. Full mutation girls with a moderate to severe intellectual disability learn in a way similar to boys with fragile X. Educational strategies developed by Braden (1996) and discussed in this book are equally successful with these girls.

Girls with the premutation (or carrier only) status do not appear to have the academic difficulties experienced by full mutation girls. Nevertheless, there is evidence to suggest these girls may experience some of the emotional difficulties usually associated with a full mutation.

This chapter mainly addresses the education of girls who have the full mutation with average or below average intelligence or mild intellectual disability. They are more likely to be educated in a mainstream school setting than more severely affected girls. Notably, the difficulties exhibited by the girls in general do not necessarily apply to every girl who carries a full mutation. They may exhibit all, some or none of the following educational and emotional difficulties. The strategies regarding emotional and social development can also be used with premutation girls who exhibit social and/or emotional difficulties.

Educational and emotional difficulties

The Australian study suggests that the following areas often require remediation:

- Mathematics: basic number skills; addition; subtraction; multiplication; division; fractions; decimals; percentages; mental computation; problem solving; geometry and measurement.
- Literacy: reading; writing (transferring ideas to paper rather than handwriting); inferential comprehension.
- Emotional and social behaviour: making friends; shyness and conversation; working in a group; making decisions; sequencing and planning.

Mathematics

Many researchers, parents and teachers have commented in the past on the poor mathematical skills of girls with fragile X. It was not apparent to what extent these difficulties were due to lower academic and intellectual abilities or to the presence of fragile X. The Australian study tested 33 girls with a full mutation but no intellectual disability and compared their results with those of girls matched for age and IQ. The girls with fragile X did not perform as well as the control group on all areas of mathematics, but the differences in performance between the two groups were not statistically significant until the girls were over 9 years of age. The younger girls were able to perform simple algorithms involving addition, subtraction, and multiplication. However, many of the older girls, when presented with quite simple calculations, commented that they used to be able to do those types of sums but had forgotten the procedure. Thus, the difficulties with mathematics associated with the full mutation are not evident until the girls are aged 9 years and over. Girls younger than 9 were also confident about their mathematical ability whereas the older girls were not. Anxiety and poor self-esteem with regard to mathematics were noted constantly, despite reassurance.

Up to age 9, children learn the basics of mathematics: addition, subtraction, simple multiplication and division, mathematical signs and symbols, simple geometry, simple fractions, time, and calendar skills. It is known that once a task becomes more complex, girls with fragile X record less brain activity in the relevant areas than girls without.

After age 9, children are taught problem-solving where they must apply basic mathematical skills to abstract situations. They must tackle complex fractions, decimals and geometry. The study showed that many of the older girls had been so confused by complex mathematical concepts that they no longer retained their basic, rote maths skills. They could not tackle division and multiplication. Anxiety prevented them from attacking their mathematical problems with confidence. The logical solution is to limit mathematical learning to what is relevant to their lives. This does not mean that very able students learn only basic mathematics. It means that girls who experience mathematical difficulties should not be required to struggle with concepts that will be irrelevant to their adult lives.

Children with fragile X work better with 'concrete materials' or a visual representation but this is not always possible in real-life settings. Concrete materials can be used to teach new concepts and skills but at some stage the girls must perform addition, subtraction, multiplication and division without reliance on concrete materials or visual cues. Continued reliance often indicates that the child does not understand the underlying concept of the mathematical task.

Teaching at the primary level must concentrate on learning basic mathematical concepts related to functional mathematics. Consolidation of those skills at the secondary school level should follow. Girls with no mathematical difficulties should continue with their secondary mathematics studies. However, girls who are bewildered by higher-order mathematical concepts should not continue, especially if this results in their losing the ability to perform simple tasks needed in adult life. To continue with concepts that are too difficult guarantees failure, social anxiety and low self-esteem.

The sensible approach is to revise basic mathematics skills, concentrating on academic areas of interest and ability to promote high self-esteem and allow the student to excel or be on a par with her peers.

Strategies for parents to support teaching

- Ensure that your daughter knows the basics; continually revise them so she does not forget.
- Inform teachers of your daughter's difficulties and stress that you are not concerned if she does not understand abstract mathematical concepts, such as algebra or multiplication of fractions.
- Insist that teachers concentrate on, and continually reinforce, the basic mathematics skills.
- Involve your daughter in simple mathematical tasks at home – setting the table and shopping are functional mathematical tasks.
- Impress on your daughter that her difficulties with mathematics are not her fault; you only expect her to work to the best of her ability and achieve her highest level of expertise in the subject. If she can go further and still retain the basic knowledge then of course allow her to do so.

The basic mathematical skills listed below are guides for teachers and parents. They are followed by teaching strategies based on visual learning techniques, such as *The Easy-learn Maths* series of basic skills, (Tan *et al.*, 2000), which provides a new approach to visual mathematics. Visual representations for problem solving, and step-by-step instructions and workbooks are excellent for students who rely on visual stimuli in learning a new task or concept.

Pre-mathematical skills

1 counting
2 number recognition
3 1-to-1 correspondence
4 mathematical language (over, under, through, more than, less than, equal to, left, right, up, down)
5 sand and water play: weights, measures and estimation skills
6 sorting and grouping: sorting objects into groups by colour, shape, etc.
7 classification: sorting groups into more specific classifications; sorting a group of transportation toys into groups of buses, planes, cars, trucks and trains
8 sharing equally: sweets, cake, blocks

Hierarchy of basic mathematics skills

1 addition
2 subtraction
3 calendar skills: days of the week, months of the year, seasons, calculating dates
4 counting by twos, fives and tens.
5 measurement: centimetres, metres, kilometres, perimeter, area
6 geometry: shapes, angles, parallel lines.
7 money
8 basic multiplication
9 using a calculator for complex addition, subtraction, multiplication and division.
10 fractions: halves, quarters, thirds, eighths.
11 division: using one-digit denominators

12 simple addition of fractions with the same common denominator or denominators divisible by 2, 4, 3, 5, or 10.
13 simple problem-solving, writing algorithms relating to real-life situations: 3 people are going out to eat two hamburgers each: $3 \times 2 = 6$ hamburgers

Visual teaching strategies: multiplication

2 multiplied by 3 is the same as two groups of three

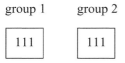

group 1   group 2

There are 3 in each group, therefore, 2 multiplied by 3 = 6

Visual teaching strategies: division

9 divided by 3 is the same as 111111111 divided into three groups

group 1   group 2   group 3

There are 3 in each group, therefore, 9 divided by 3 = 3

Visual teaching strategies: fractions

The conventional method of teaching fractions is to divide one whole shape (usually a cake) into equal pieces that represent pieces, or fractions, of the whole. Children with fragile X however, tend to see things from a different perspective – visually and holistically. The pieces of cake representing fractions are then viewed as whole pieces and not related to the original whole cake.

It is better to teach fractions using the number line method that allows whole numbers and fractions to be seen visually and in context without removing sections. For example, the following figure is a number line representing whole numbers and halves.

1   2   3   4   5

Literacy

Most girls read well and some read extremely well. If a girl does have reading difficulties the best method of instruction is to teach the four main reading strategies for word recognition, fluency and understanding. These are: sight words, phonics, context and comprehension.

Sight words

These provide a base for word recognition because they are recognised instantly by students. The more words children recognise by sight alone the more fluently they read. The Fry Instant Word Lists (1980) comprise three lists of 100 words each. The first 10 words in these lists make up approximately 24 per cent of all written material; the first 100 make up 50 per cent, and the 300 words make up 65 per cent.

These can be taught with flash cards, playing word bingo, and writing simple sentences. The words can be used to teach word families. Many simple everyday words are irregularly spelt so need to be recognised by sight rather than sounded out.

Phonics

Using phonics (association of specific sounds with specific symbols) rarely works with boys with fragile X because of their totally holistic approach to word recognition. This does not appear to be the case with the girls. Phonics instruction should include: consonant blends (bl, gr, st, str); long and short vowels and the use of mute 'e'; double consonants that create a new sound (ch, sh, ph, ck, th) and double vowel combinations (ee, ea, oa, ow and ai).

Context

Context helps the reader identify an unknown word and decide which pronunciation to use in a sentence. For example, 'I read yesterday' or 'I will read today'.

The use of context clues can be taught from a very early age by encouraging children to look for clues in the illustrations in children's books. The use of context can be promoted long before children begin formal literacy by allowing them to finish a sentence, phrase, or nursery rhyme. Making amusing errors in sentences for them to correct: 'the pig said moo!' prepares children for learning literacy through play.

Comprehension

If a child does not understand what she is reading, she is simply decoding or attacking each word in isolation. The following strategies teach children to think about the text as they read or listen. Ask very young children to:

- predict what will happen in a story;
- reassess their prediction as you read;
- retell the story;
- discuss why the characters did certain things;
- think of a different ending.

The 'Toe by Toe' reading system (Cowling, 1993), developed in Britain, works particularly well for girls with fragile X on the first two reading strategies, word recognition and phonics. It teaches a reading/spelling rule then applies it to nonsense words, real words, and finally sentences containing those words. Because it uses nonsense words to begin with, children become used to facing unknown words and applying their decoding skills. This reduces anxiety levels during reading. The sentences used are grammatically correct but the content is nonsense so the girls cannot guess what is written, they must read exactly what is on the page.

Emotional and social behaviour

Texts on inappropriate behaviour are mainly devoted to violent behaviour, disruptive classroom behaviour, and anti-social behaviour. None of these relate to the girls that I have had the pleasure of knowing. Most are passive and shy and totally puzzled by the actions of other girls.

It is well documented that many girls with fragile X, with or without learning difficulties, suffer social anxiety resulting in poor social skills. These include gaze avoidance; difficulty conversing and initiating contact with their peers; organising social outings; isolation (isolating themselves as well as exclusion by peers); understanding the use of specific language in specific social contexts, and blatant honesty – it is not always the best policy to tell the truth!

It is not known exactly what causes these social difficulties. However, in executive function tasks of strategic planning, impulse control, organised search and flexibility of thought and action, non-fragile X girls perform significantly better than girls carrying the full mutation. Also, almost all of the participants with fragile X exhibited some degree of anxiety, especially the girls who had reached puberty. I would like to offer my own theories why this might be:

- Their shyness, inflexibility of thought and action, inability to think in the abstract, impulsivity and lack of planning skills make it difficult for them to make good social judgements, and initiate, follow, and participate in complex conversation, especially with their peers.
- Often the girls do not have positive role models – especially if their brothers, sisters or mothers are affected to some degree.
- The girls seem to prefer the company and conversation of adults who accommodate their difficulties and relieve their anxiety.
- Most importantly, they appear to enjoy their own company and do not seem to crave or miss social interaction with their peers.

Parents of girls with the full mutation face a real dilemma. They want their daughters to be socially comfortable and competent, to be relaxed and enjoy social interaction, and to seek and maintain friendships. Conversely, parents realise that their daughter neither seeks social interaction nor misses the closeness of friendship. Unfortunately, these girls are expected by society to live actively in the world, gain employment, perhaps marry, raise children and be productive, successful members of society.

Do parents leave them in isolation where they feel comfortable? In many cases, yes, especially when the girl has not been diagnosed, and until she is struggling to cope with the social demands of adolescence. It is difficult to teach high-level social skills to girls and young women who are already experiencing social anxiety or bewilderment at the behaviour and multi-layered conversation skills of their peers. When a girl is diagnosed at birth, early intervention strategies can be implemented in a bid to raise a more socially confident child, who is able to interact with her peers by the time she begins her formal education.

As well as dealing with their own difficulties, girls with fragile X often have to make allowances for one or more affected siblings. Anderson (2001) identified several negative effects on siblings of boys and girls with special needs including:

- feelings of isolation;
- the burden of care taken on by siblings as children, and in adult life;
- pressure to achieve, to be the 'superchild';
- jealousy relating to the amount of attention the affected sibling receives and the unacceptable behaviour that they exhibit without punishment;
- fear of developing or passing on the gene (a very real fear for girls with fragile X);
- guilt at not having the disability. In my study, sisters who had not inherited the gene often expressed feelings of guilt.

Also participating in this study were siblings who had no disabilities. The problems of affected siblings are much worse for girls with a full mutation, and who have problems of their own. To lessen the effect of coping with severely affected siblings:

- If possible, place girls in a different school from their severely affected siblings.
- Do not expect them to take care of their affected siblings.
- Discuss the issue of guilt with all family members.
- Do not expect more from girls academically than they are capable of achieving.
- Encourage them to participate in activities away from the home environment.

Social skills

Social skills training can be started in the early years through play, and getting little girls to observe and copy each other at play. We know that anxiety increases with age, so if we train girls when they are less anxious we may avoid higher levels of anxiety later on in their lives. The following issues may need to be addressed: making friends, shyness and conversation, working in a group, making decisions, and sequencing and planning.

Making friends – strategies for parents

- Join a playgroup or activities for toddlers and observe the girl at play.
- Observe other children at play and encourage similar experiences for your child. Remember, very young children don't play together, they play alongside one another, so don't expect co-operative play. She will get used to being in a group, experiencing social interaction, listening to and participating in early conversation.
- Encourage your daughter to choose friends with similar interests or a similar personality. A shy child may not seem to be the best role model, but the most popular or the cleverest child in the class or group may overwhelm your daughter.
- Once she reaches school age you may have to take the initiative and invite girls over to play who are similar – quiet, shy and gentle. Later, you can encourage her to invite children to play.

Making friends – strategies for teachers

- Encourage the girl with fragile X to participate in class activities and contribute to discussion.
- Guide her towards friendships with other girls in the class, especially quiet, compassionate girls.
- Recruit a girl from a higher grade with similar interests to become her mentor. In Australia this has resulted in firm friendships.
- Watch for signs of creativity or interest in art, music, dance or drama and encourage areas of talent. Many girls excel in these areas where they can be 'someone else'.
- Encourage eye contact in non-threatening situations but do not insist on eye contact when a child is anxious or upset.

Shyness and conversation – strategies for parents

- Talk to your daughter about eye contact and shyness. Persevere gently, point out that there is no need to be shy with people who have proved to be trustworthy.
- Encourage her to talk to you about her feelings.
- Role-play social situations over and over again and then act them out in public. Include ordering in a restaurant, eating in public, asking for directions, buying a ticket at the cinema, shopping, using public transport, and what to do if she is lost or anxious.
- Role-play conversation for different social situations.

If the girl remains shy and anxious, and the anxiety increases with age, then medication may be required.

Working in a group

Group work at school is excellent for girls with fragile X. Students are usually set special tasks or have individual roles within the group and this enables girls to work on their own, but still work co-operatively within a group. Teachers need to be conscious of group dynamics and place the child in a group of children who will interact with her and act as positive role models without overwhelming her with their actions or personalities.

Making decisions

Girls with fragile X find it very difficult to make decisions, especially if they are in a public place and anxious about the social setting. For simple decisions, such as deciding what to order in a restaurant, she can carry a special coin to flip if she really cannot decide between two choices. Decision-making, however, is often more complicated than deciding what to order.

Always discuss a variety of options with the child and give her an alternative plan of action. If you plan to meet her at a particular time make sure she knows what to do if you don't arrive. Using a mobile phone provides security for children and young adults who find themselves in situations where things have not turned out as planned or expected, they cannot decide what to do or are anxious about decision-making.

Sequencing and Planning

Braden (1996) provides wonderful strategies for young adults but training needs to begin from a very young age. Include sequencing in everyday life situations. The following strategies will make life less stressful and provide opportunities for girls with fragile X to observe and practise practical planning and sequencing.

- Provide a written list or sequence of pictures, of tasks to be completed before school, getting ready for bed, or how to tidy her room.
- Play afternoon games of remembering and sequencing the day's events.
- Explain the day's activities each morning to reduce anxiety levels. With boys and severely affected girls, use a variety of strategies, including photographs, pictures to provide a visual plan of the day's activities. Girls as well as more severely affected boys need the security of knowing what the day's activities are and what they will be doing next.
- When planning an activity such as a picnic, ask her to help you plan the whole activity and sequence as many different actions as possible.
- Model thinking aloud (a form of metacognition). Teach the girl to talk to herself and ask herself specific questions such as: What equipment or materials do I need to do this activity? How will I go about it? What will I do first, second, and third?

Conclusion

Research, observation and anecdotal evidence strongly suggest that girls with a full mutation exhibit complex difficulties ranging from mild, moderate and severe intellectual disabilities, to educational difficulties and emotional problems. These difficulties need to be identified and addressed in the child's early years so that intervention strategies and programmes can be implemented as soon as possible. The introduction of strategies described in this chapter has led to a positive school experience and the reduction of anxiety in girls in Western Australia. It is hoped that widespread implementation of these strategies for future generations of girls will lead to a greater reduction, or even absence, of the anxiety and poor social skills associated with the inheritance of a full mutation.

References

Anderson, K. (2001) *A Lifetime of Sorrow*. Perth, Western Australia: Curtin University Press.
Braden, M. L. (1996) *Fragile Handle With Care: Understanding Fragile X Syndrome*. North Carolina: Avanta.
Broadbent, P. (2001) *Letts – Key Stage 1 Success (maths workbooks using visual teaching strategies)*. London: Letts Educational.
Cowling, H. and K. (1993) *Toe by Toe*. Staningley: Toe by Toe
Fry, Edward. (1980). The new instant word list. *The Reading Teacher* 34 (December): 284–289.
Johnston. C., Eliez, S., Dyer-Friedman, J., Hessel, D., Glaser, B., Blasey, C., Taylor, A. and Reiss, A. (2001). Neurobehavioral phenotype in carriers of the premutation. *American Journal of Medical Genetics* 103(4): 314–19.
Powell, L.J. (1998). An investigation of etiology-specific cognitive functioning profiles for schoolgirls with fragile X syndrome. Doctoral Thesis: University of Western Australia.
Tan, J., Howard, P. and Coroneos, J. (2000). *Easy-learn Maths*. Rose Bay, NSW, Australia: Coroneos Publishing.

Part II

Education issues

Chapter 6

The effects of fragile X syndrome on learning

Marcia Braden

Although each child with fragile X syndrome is an individual, there are similar processing styles that need to be accounted for when developing appropriate remediation and accommodations. As discussed in Chapter 3, the cognitive strengths and weaknesses are specific and warrant attention so that a successful educational plan can be implemented.

It is critical for the parent, teacher and support staff to understand this processing style so that the best educational strategies can be adopted. At this point, clinical evidence suggests that fragile X has the following effects on learning (Braden, 2000).

Performance

Children with fragile X perform better on achievement tests than cognitive tests (Hodapp *et al.*, 1992). It is often assumed that cognitive ability determines achievement, but children with fragile X outperform predictions based on cognitive test scores. This is most likely due to strengths in long-term memory and the effect of repeated exposure to academic material. Familiar tasks that have been taught within a context are often better remembered than those that are novel and unrelated.

Inflexibility

Children with fragile X tend to be inflexible in their thinking, and like children with autism, may become over-selective about the stimuli they attend to. They may want to use a certain type of pencil or paper. They may need to sit in a certain seat or prefer others to sit in certain places. This learning characteristic may promote perseverative thinking about unrelated aspects of a task. In other words, it is easy for them to get stuck on something that is extraneous and unrelated to the task being taught.

Executive functioning

Children with fragile X show a lack of executive function, that is: the ability to forumlate a plan in total and to execute it. Executive function involves planning, working memory, inhibition and flexibility of thought processes (especially in problem-solving). It requires goal-directed and structured behaviour, usually in novel contexts. The child with fragile X may understand the goal, but fails to accomplish it due to perseveration, lack of persistence, intrusions of task completion, irrelevant behaviour and lack of initiative.'

Closure

It is well documented (Braden, 2000b) that children with fragile X need completion or closure. It is not uncommon to observe a child finishing a puzzle or filling in a blank before being able to move on. This sense of completion can become a compulsion that may interfere with daily functioning. Rather than focusing on the negative aspects of the compulsive behaviour, educators are now using the trait to elicit more complete verbal and written communication. For example, if a child is upset about an experience at school and is unable to verbalize the sequence of the event, one may use a closure technique to gain additional information. Instead of asking, 'Who hit you?' or 'Where did this happen?' one might begin with a story line such as, 'Today on the playground you got (hit). When you were hit, you (told the teacher).' As the incident is pieced together, it is possible gradually to add more specific information to the story and to better understand the child's perspective about what happened.

Simultaneous processing

Rather than learning one step at a time, children with fragile X tend to learn by taking in a whole image (Dykens *et al.*, 1987). For example, when learning to read, children may use a combination of strategies, such as phonics, whole-word recognition, picture and contextual cues, but they still follow a sequential route from sounds and letters to whole words, phrases and sentences, and, eventually, whole books. The learning of maths is even more sequential, with one numerical concept building on another. By contrast, simultaneous processing uses a gestalt or whole image to organize information. In other words, children with fragile X learn concepts by taking in multiple stimuli that offer them more information or related parts for forming an image in order to solve a problem. A child with fragile X is more likely to correctly identify a missing part from a whole image than he is to identify a whole image from the individual parts. This style clearly requires a different teaching approach, one very different from traditional teaching methodology.

Associative learning

As a result of the simultaneous learning style, it is easier for children with fragile X to recall information if it is related to or associated with a bigger whole. A child with fragile X will, for example, learn the rhythm of a song long before being able to sing specific lyrics. Because individuals with fragile X often demonstrate attentional deficits and hyperactivity, information that is presented in isolation without association may get lost or confused. It is important to weave high-interest materials into the fabric of the child's school programming. In order to develop high-interest materials, the use of an interest inventory can be helpful. Such an inventory can be completed by parents, teachers, and primary caregivers. It provides educators with a variety of ideas from which to create teaching materials. For example, one student interested in television weather maps used the maps to learn geographical locations, states, and capitals. Another, who was interested in wildlife, learned to associate a particular indigenous animal with a specific world location.

Direct questioning

It is not uncommon for children with fragile X to become stymied by a direct question. A direct question in isolation may force a response without the benefit of contextual information. The same question asked in an informal setting will be more likely to result in spontaneous recall. School performance often differs considerably from that at home due to performance anxiety created by the school environment and expectations.

Long-term memory

Generally, children with fragile X have good long-term memory skills (Kemper *et al.*, 1988). Simultaneous processing contributes to long-term memory through repeated exposure. In addition, long-term memory can be triggered by an association. Showing the child a map may conjure up questions about a relative living in another region, or seeing an old friend may prompt dialogue about an experience that happened several years earlier with that friend.

Providing an appropriate educational programme changes from one age group to another. As the child matures and learns new skills, other challenges emerge. The sections below list those developmental levels, discussing specific challenges along with a variety of strategies to promote successful learning.

Early education

One of the more difficult tasks for young children with fragile X is that of attending to a specific stimulus. Very often young children hear and understand instruction incidentally but it is difficult to judge the extent to which they actually attend to instruction. Assessing just how much has been understood and how much will be generalized from the information can be accomplished by observing behaviour in varied environments and noting responses (Braden, 2000b).

Sometimes, it is absolutely necessary for the child with fragile X to attend. When attending behaviour is forced in a direct way, there is a risk that anxiety will become so overwhelming that the child may choose to avoid the task. A number of avoidance behaviours may result, such as acting out, becoming non-compliant or demonstrating escape. For this reason it is necessary to develop attention through a specific desensitization programme. As the child becomes more accustomed to the interaction with the adult authority figure, the child begins to habituate the behaviours and responds naturally to the attending demands.

Early education placements may include or integrate children with fragile X with mainstream peers. In other placements, children are homogeneously grouped. It is usually more productive to employ intensive therapies at this early stage of academic development, such as occupational, speech and language, cognitive training and behavioural intervention. As the child acquires formative skills, socialization can be encouraged.

Elementary education

During the elementary school years, individuals with fragile X often experience significant academic growth, especially if intensive early intervention programs have been provided. At this point, it is common for school systems to explore inclusive educational opportunities.

This model provides a stronger foundation for successful social skill development and academic achievement within the school environment.

Including (integrating) students with fragile X with typically developing peers allows access to high-interest curricula. It is common for elementary age children with fragile X to proclaim an interest in science, history or other content areas. Exposure to content-based information may sustain enough interest and motivation to stay focused while engaged in less interesting academic tasks.

Junior school or middle school

During this time in the life cycle, individuals with fragile X become more aware of their challenges. Typical peers are also grappling with social issues related to sexual relationships. The transition from childhood to adolescence is commonly turbulent. Peer relationships provide a feeling of affiliation and social skills become as important as other academic tasks. Becoming part of a group is paramount to this stage of development and the adolescent with fragile X is no exception. Feelings of rejection are often poorly verbalized and instead replaced by anger or behavioural outbursts. Talking about feelings at an early age helps the adolescent work through social issues in a more appropriate way. Addressing feelings related to individual differences, academic failures and social rejection is often helpful to both males and females.

In middle school, the academic environment expands to include more space and people. The physical facility is much larger and more difficult to navigate. The noise level increases and it feels more impersonal, which can be intimidating. Including an orientation period prior to school starting is often prescribed. Using videotaped school previews through the holiday months prior to the start of school has been effective in clinical trials. An album of photographs or a yearbook of teachers, classrooms and familiar students can provide a method to familiarize the student with the new school environment and people in it.

High school or senior school

At this point in the academic development of young people with fragile X, two distinct areas gain momentum: becoming socially acceptable and engaging in meaningful employment.

Although academics may supplement the school day, the curricular focus shifts from academics to a more functional learning application. In other words, academics serve a more functional purpose than before. Reading now provides the vehicle to access charts, recipes, labels and directions. Likewise, maths concepts are applied to making a purchase, managing money and telling time.

The focus now diverts from a traditional curriculum to one that includes daily living skills, sex education and vocational interests. Community access, living options, leisure skills and vocational interests claim the foundation for teaching objectives.

Just like middle school, the physical site of a high school requires movement many times during the day. The change in classroom routine and settings may be disruptive and difficult at first. Teaching style and class size may differ significantly among classes. Additionally, the community may be used to augment a traditional instructional placement. Specific programming to learn to tolerate this type of change is critical because it lights the path for future real life adjustments. Assigning a mentor to accompany the student with fragile X will provide comfort and build confidence. As the student becomes desensitized to a much bigger and more complicated school environment, the support can be reduced.

Conclusion

In summary, it is important to realize the effect fragile X has on learning and to understand the learner's cognitive profile to accommodate them successfully. Providing learning strategies that are conducive to a particular learning style and incorporating them into the curriculum will increase the likelihood of success without frustration or discouragement. Identification of cognitive strengths should be the focus of any educational remedy. While it is important to isolate the disability and relative weakness, the strengths provide a vehicle through which successful intervention can occur.

References

Bennetto, L., and B. F. Pennington (2002) The neuropsychology of fragile X syndrome. In R. J. Hagerman and P. J. Hagerman (eds), *Fragile X Syndrome: Diagnosis, Treatment and Research*, 3rd ed. Baltimore: Johns Hopkins University Press, pp. 238–239.

Braden, M. (2000a) Education. In J.D. Weber (ed.), *Children with Fragile X Syndrome: A Parent's Guide*. Bethesda, Md.: Woodbine House, pp. 243–305.

Braden, M. (2000b) *Fragile: Handle with Care, More About Fragile X Syndrome – Adolescents and Adults*. Dillon, CO: Spectra Publishing Co.

Dykens, E.M., R. M. Hodapp, and J. F. Leckman (1987) Strengths and weaknesses in the intellectual functioning of males with fragile X syndrome. *American Journal of Medical Genetics* 28: 13–15.

Hodapp, R. M., J. F. Leckman, E. M. Dykens, S. Sparrow, D. Zelinsky and S. Ort (1992) K-ABC profiles in children with fragile X syndrome, Down syndrome, and nonspecific mental retardation. *American Journal of Mental Retardation* 97: 39–46.

Kemper, M. B., R. J. Hagerman, and D. Altshul-Stark (1988) Cognitive profiles of boys with the fragile X syndrome. *American Journal of Medical Genetics* 30: 191–200.

Chapter 7

Educational placement and provision

Denise Dew-Hughes

All parents want their children to receive a varied and sound education suited to their needs and skills, and to be happy in school. They want access to a broad-based and relevant curriculum, which celebrates individual contributions and will empower their children eventually to play a self-determined role in the wider social world. They usually prefer a local school with strong community links, where children can socialise with a peer group who have interests and experiences in common. It is the same for parents of children with special educational needs, although the type and number of schools able to deliver this may well differ.

The Education Reform Act (1988) endorsed the educational entitlement of all pupils to a coherent, balanced and broad-based curriculum, appropriately differentiated to their needs. This should be delivered within the community, alongside peer groups and in the least restrictive environment. For pupils with the most complex or severe learning difficulties, these objectives might seem on the surface to be unlikely, or at least to require highly specialised approaches outside the commonality of mainstream teaching.

Nevertheless, the movement from segregated, specialist provision to mainstream inclusion, impelled by a continuum of legislation, is set fair to become the educational norm. What the Education (Handicapped Children) Act of 1970 began in abolishing the concept of ineducability, the Special Educational Needs Act (1981) endorsed by introducing a wider definition of special needs and establishing a structure of support and entitlement. By 1988 all pupils, including those in special schools, became entitled to a National Curriculum for learning. The Education Act (1993) and the Code of Practice (DfEE, 1994) made every teacher responsible for identifying and meeting special educational needs (SEN), and initial training in SEN for all teachers was increased (DfEE, Circulars 9/92, 10/97). In 1997 the DfEE Green Paper 'Excellence for all Children' defined inclusive education as the ultimate purpose of special provision. This succession of legislative measures reaffirmed the entitlement of all pupils to knowledge, attitudes and skills in the teacher, to curriculum access, management support systems and shared values. Pupils with special needs had a further entitlement to value-added enhancement of their learning, or to more specialised approaches where these were appropriate.

The education of children with special educational needs – by definition, needs that require something over and above the ordinary provision of a mainstream school – has become focused around a number of issues. Each of these constitutes an ongoing debate, with arguments polarised or subject to educational ideologies. This complexity can result in confusion, and parental choice can become a burden instead of entitlement. Balancing a child's needs with the choice or provision offered to parents by a school or Local Education

Authority (LEA) can lead to conflict, a successful outcome, or merely a 'good enough' education. With so many variables involved, decisions over school placement can only be well founded when they rest on the suitability of a school and the education it provides in meeting each individual child's needs.

Questions asked by parents commonly concern the type of school – mainstream or special, day school or residential, state-aided or privately funded? They ask about the expertise and experience of the teachers, the number of learning support assistants (LSAs) and the availability of ancillary therapies. All of these issues relate to levels of funding or suitably trained practitioners to support a child's special needs.

Mainstream or special school?

As long as they were confident that the education provided was suitable and accessible, most parents would want their child to attend the local mainstream school. Excluding a child from being educated alongside their natural peer group in a community school may present risks to the grown child's future membership of society. Mainstream schools offer wider choices of curriculum, friends and experiences. By being educated alongside everyone else, the child with special needs will not be disqualified by their learning difficulties from full membership of the local community. They will form friendships and relationships with young people who do not have learning difficulties and their social development will parallel that of mainstream peers. With appropriate levels of support, they will have opportunities to imitate or slipstream normally developing children, make their own decisions and eventually plan their own life.

Special schools offer individual learning programmes, tailored specifically to the child's needs and delivered through appropriate methods. Their smaller size suits children who have difficulties with complex communities, higher noise levels and social anxiety. Specialist teaching and equipment, smaller classes, more LSAs and a family atmosphere are advantages comparable with the most exclusive private schools. Special schools are usually free from the mainstream constraints of teaching to national standards of pupil development and examinations. Above all, special schools understand and value the child with learning difficulties. They celebrate personal, rather than norm-referenced, levels of achievement. However, they are segregated from mainstream education, and cannot offer the same opportunities for social development (Dew-Hughes, 2001)

These distinctions between types of school are not clear cut. Many mainstream schools have special units or departments and can offer advantages from both worlds – a special curriculum with mainstream socialisation. Some mainstream schools are themselves specialists, centres of excellence in offering expertise and support to the pupil with learning difficulties. Some special schools specialise further by accepting children with a single diagnosis, such as autism or visual impairment. Residential special schools offer 24-hour education programmes, an extended and enriched curriculum, or the capacity to adopt a holistic approach to behavioural problems.

Transition

The majority of children, including those with fragile X syndrome, begin their education in a local playgroup or nursery school. Most of these will transfer naturally to the local primary school. It is at this early point of transfer that decisions over school placement begin. A child who played happily in a local nursery may not be able to cope with formal learning in a mainstream primary. Statements of educational need and extra non-teaching support can help narrow the gap, but as the child matures their learning and development may proceed at a shallower angle than that of their peers.

This consideration returns at later points of transfer, most notably that between primary and secondary school. After the age of 11, the gap in learning between slowly developing children and their peers widens. This is due as much to the nature of the secondary school curriculum and teaching methods, as to slower development. The more integrated child-centred approach of primary schools gives way to subject-based pedagogy in the secondary school. The larger sites and higher numbers of pupils, staff and subjects add further difficulties. Increasing the level of support in order to cope with social, geographical and curriculum complexity may result in over-reliance on a non-teaching assistant.

The educational placement of pupils with fragile X syndrome

In order to give a clearer picture of the issues surrounding school placement for the child with fragile X syndrome, a national survey was conducted through the UK Fragile X Society. This collected information about 398 young people aged between 3 and 25 years. Parents detailed their children's school history and placement, extra support and ancillary therapies. They also evaluated the adequacy of the education received, and gave the result of any contest of provision.

More than two-thirds of the young people in the survey had been diagnosed with fragile X before starting school and the remainder before they left primary school. Apart from 20 pre-school children, all had a Statement of Special Educational Needs. The large number of young people diagnosed before starting school suggests that diagnosis of conditions such as fragile X takes place at an early age. This may result from factors related to fragile X, such as:

•   the availability of accurate testing since 1991, especially for girls;
•   the learning and developmental difficulties associated with fragile X being apparent at an early age.

Or more general factors:

•   the Code of Practice for special educational needs imposing statutory responsibility on schools to identify children's learning needs;
•   the raised awareness of mainstream teachers, who have to implement the Code of Practice at classroom level.

The provision for young people with fragile X syndrome was considered in each of four categories, related to the main phases of education: 0–5 years: pre-school or early years; 6–11: juniors; 12–16: seniors; 17–25: post-school or further education.

These phases apply to most UK schools, including special schools, which are generally constructed in parallel with mainstream progression. The points of transfer between these phases are the most active time for assessment, placement and provision. Young people in the survey usually received help from allocated or shared LSAs at each phase of their education. This help was provided in special schools as a matter of course and in mainstream according to need. Once begun, LSA help was likely to continue at the same level. Where levels of support were high, parents usually assessed their children's needs as being met very well.

The type of educational provision described by parents was very diffuse, but all the schools answered one of the following descriptions :

1   Mainstream schools: local playgroups, nurseries, primary and secondary schools and general colleges, where teachers and LSAs offer some extra support.
2   'Enhanced mainstream' schools: predominantly mainstream but supportive to children with fragile X, or schools with a speciality (Montessori, Steiner) These schools had fully integrated support systems for SEN, specially trained staff, and features which made them particularly flexible, such as delayed entry or repeated years.
3   'Special units attached to mainstream': included those for autism or speech and language, and schools with separate special needs units.
4   Special schools: all-age schools for all learning difficulties. This category included schools specialising in MLD (mild or moderate learning difficulties and SLD (severe learning difficulties).
5   Home education: full-time provision of tuition at home, children withdrawn from the school system being educated by their parents, and full-time, specialist home-teaching approaches such as TEACCH (Schopler and Mesibov, 1984) and Lovaas (1981).

The percentage of young people surveyed who were in each of these five different types of provision is shown in Table 7.1.

Table 7.1 shows that the percentage of young people attending mainstream schooling decreases as they progress through the different educational phases. Although more than one-third (34 per cent) of children in the pre-school (0–5 years) phase are attending mainstream school, this percentage decreases steadily, through 24 per cent and 18 per cent, to one in eight (12 per cent) of young people in the 17–25 age group.

This decrease in percentage of children attending mainstream schools is reflected in a similar increase in the percentage of children attending special schools as they progress through their school career. Less than half (44 per cent) start their school life in special schools. During their junior years (ages 6–11) more than half (55.6 per cent) are attending special school. In the secondary phase (12–16 years) more than two-thirds of children (69 per cent) are attending special school, and more than three-quarters (77.3 per cent) of the 17–25 year olds are in special school. The percentages of the 17–25 group are more complicated because educational provision for this age group is more varied. However, by the age of 17, only one in eight young people in the survey was attending a mainstream school or college.

Table 7.1 Educational provision (per cent)

	0–5yrs	6–11yrs	12–16yrs	17–25yrs
Mainstream	34	24	18	12
Enhanced mainstream	2.4	7.7	6	–
Special unit attached to mainstream	12	10.5	7	11.5
Special only	44	55.6	69.8	77.3
Home education	7.3	2.1	–	–

Although the developmental gap with mainstream peers widens, not all of the learning difficulties of young people with fragile X increase as they get older. In fact, some of their difficulties, especially those linked to behaviour, actually decrease (see Chapter 21). This movement away from mainstream education suggests that some other factor is at work, perhaps the nature of secondary education itself. For whatever reason, the increase in young people moving to special schools indicates that mainstream provision is less suited to the complex learning needs of young people with fragile X as they enter the secondary and tertiary phases of education.

Whereas the child-centred and developmentally focussed nursery and primary schools meet the needs of many young people with fragile X, the larger secondary and tertiary schools and colleges are less accommodating. Many mainstream schools and colleges go to great lengths to meet the special needs of their students, but their subject-centred teaching, vocation focus and large size make them less suitable for the young person with complex educational needs.

The survey's findings formed a pattern, where progression through the four educational phases indicated the likelihood of a move from mainstream to special school as young people with fragile X syndrome got older. They are steady learners, but the nature and provision of mainstream schools and colleges becomes significantly less suited to their needs.

Contesting provision

Many parents had contested their children's provision. Some had contested provision within the school, but others had argued their case with the LEA or at a tribunal hearing. As a result, provision had been changed and improved for some children, but not for others. Some parents were still awaiting the outcomes of their contest. The number of parents contesting provision within each of the four educational phases is shown in Table 7.2.

Parents' assessment of educational provision

The parents of young people with fragile X in the national survey evaluated and commented on each phase of their child's educational provision. The majority thought this was adequate; more than half said their child's needs had been well met for some part of their education.

Table 7.2 Parents contesting provision of education

	0–5yrs	6–11yrs	12–16yrs	17–25yrs
% in each group contesting	27	28	39	44.5
Contested at school	5	19	23	19
Contested at LEA	8	33	27	27
Contested at tribunal	2	9	6	4
Resulted in change	7	28	31	24
Resulted in no change	2	5	6	14
Resulted in improvement	7	29	29	24
Resulted in no improvement	1	7	8	12

These figures also show that the percentage of parents who contested provision rose as the child progressed through their school years. Just over one in four parents contested their child's pre- and junior school placement, more than one in three the secondary school and approaching half protested about colleges.

A substantial majority, however, were less pleased and recorded that their child's provision had been inadequate. More parents recorded dissatisfaction with secondary and tertiary education than with early years provision. Dissatisfaction was lowest for the youngest age group (9.5 per cent, or less than one in ten). More than twice as many parents of young people in tertiary education recorded that their needs were not being met. As with school placements, this rise in parental dissatisfaction focuses attention on the nature of provision as children move through the education system.

Parents added comments about their children's individual circumstances. They commented on the same educational issues that concern all other parents: the child's needs met by suitable provision within a local school, with support to access a mainstream curriculum if possible, or an appropriate programme in a special school.

Suitability of provision was determined by an appropriate placement, with sensitive management and well-informed teaching:

> We are extremely pleased that we sent our daughter to the local High School. She is included in every lesson – she works really hard, best of all she is really achieving.

Understanding the child's needs was necessary in order to deliver an appropriate education matched to the child's needs:

> There is a need for better guidance as to the suitability of schools and more help when a school is not meeting the child's needs.

> The teacher in number 3 school had previous experience with children like our son and understood his needs. She gave us back our happy, controllable son.

> An autistic unit was opened . . . it met his needs very well and the ethos suited him.

> There was little understanding of what motivated him to learn. Consequently he was not given the opportunity to use the skills he has to best effects.

> My son was treated as 'dyslexic' despite my protests that he was fragile X (after diagnosis!).

> I think my son's secondary school have been at a loss as to how to deal with him.

> MLD High School appears unaware of our son's needs and has made no provision for his classroom support.

> He was excluded for two years for behaviour outbursts that he couldn't control. Nobody would help him.

Integration in the local school had been advantageous for some and unsuitable for others. Social development was rated highly by some parents:

> My son started in mainstream and coped very well. At the end of Year 3 the teachers felt he would benefit from going to a special school, but I felt that the social skills were more important at that stage. They agreed to let him do Year 4 and he did really well.

> Because my son is in mainstream school he fits in with all the normal activities. He still cannot do a lot but his social skills are really good.

My son spent the entire year in the computer room. This is integration – small units which everyone forgets about.

His playground is a tiny yard and he runs around the flowerpot. He will have six years of running around the flowerpot. I supported integration 5 years ago – I wish I hadn't.

Parents entered the debate over mainstream and special schooling, and were well aware of the merits and drawbacks of both:

There is too much emphasis on integration into mainstream schools by some parents . . . those who do not dare opt for special schools are made to feel they are failing their child, when in reality the special schools are doing an excellent job.

I work as an LSA myself and I know there is no way that he could have coped in mainstream, even with support, beyond a certain stage. I see children who even with mild learning difficulties cannot cope in a large group.

Whilst I acknowledge in ideal circumstances in the perfect world, inclusion would be a great thing, at present the special school system offers the best educational provision for my child. In the current educational climate with cutbacks, staff stress and shortages, in a mainstream situation he would be isolated in a crowd and 'the kid who is different'.

The mainstream education system is very lacking in the knowledge to educate to the best standard a child with fragile X, through lack of information available to teachers.

We received support and understanding in all aspects of his mainstream education; we haven't had to contest or fight for our son to have the same schooling opportunities as our daughter.

There had been difficulties and delays in statementing procedures and in attaining suitable provision:

I had to agree to a special school because the LEA wouldn't give more support in mainstream. I felt very demoralised.

The LEA took almost a year to prepare a draft (statement) and refused to consider changes.

The paediatrician felt that statementing wasn't necessary but my son couldn't get help at school without a statement.

Where additional non-teaching support levels had been high, parents were more likely to record satisfaction with their child's needs being well met. Parents were sensitive to a lack of suitable support:

We feel (LSA support) has to be evidence-based, not 'tariff' based.

I am only in favour of mainstream should adequate help and support be made available.

I believe he could have gained more by having more support when he first started school.

18 months after starting school he was given 5 hours support a week. It was too little too late.

Emphasis was laid on the importance of quality teaching:

> It is the teachers who matter. If they are not able to understand the needs of the child, then all the statementing and the school's reputation are worthless.

> All the professionals we have met with have positively contributed to his development. Their investment will enable him to achieve his maximum potential.

> Our experiences have been positive and rewarding and we're grateful to the professionals involved with us.

> The local primary school totally embraced him and his challenging behavioural difficulties. The teachers accepted their lack of experience and sought advice.

For young people with fragile X in the national survey, issues surrounding educational placement and provision were the same as those of their peers. Parents were aware of the range of provision available and the difficulties inherent in making choices. Overall, they wanted their child to be happy in a local school within the community, and to develop socially alongside other children, sharing their interests and experiences. They also wanted their child's special needs to be understood, and for skilled teachers to deliver an education suited to their needs and skills, and for the school to celebrate their contributions and progress. As far as possible, they wanted access to a broad-based and relevant curriculum to prepare their children to be independent in the wider social world.

References

DES (1970) *Education (Handicapped Children) Act.* London: HMSO.
DES (1981) *Education Act. Special Educational Needs.* London: HMSO.
Dew-Hughes, D.M. (2001) 'The Social Development of Pupils with Severe Learning Difficulties. *Early Child Development and Care* 167: 63–76.
DfEE (1993) *Education Act.* London: HMSO.
DfEE (1994) *The Code of Practice on the Identification and Assessment of Special Educational Needs.* London: HMSO.
DfEE (1992) *Initial Teacher Training (Secondary Phase)* (Circular 9/92). London: HMSO.
DfEE (1997) *Teaching: High Status, High Standards* (Circular 10/97). London: HMSO.
DfEE (1997) 'Excellence for all Children' (Green Paper). London: HMSO.
Lovaas, I. (1981) *Teaching Developmentally Disabled Children.* Tunbridge Wells: Costello Educational.
Schopler, E. and Mesibov, G.B. (1984) 'Helping autistic children through their parents: the TEACCH model', in E. Schopler and E. Mesibov (eds) *The Effects of Autism on the Family.* London: Plenum.

Chapter 8

Key issues in assessment

Charles Gibb

Children with fragile X syndrome are first and foremost children. Some will want to be footballers when they grow up, and some will want to be pop stars. Some of them will be brighter than others. They'll laugh at things they find funny, and cry when hurt. Many girls will be fond of Post-its and other stationery, and many boys will climb trees or do wheelies on their bikes. There will be the typical sex differences, just are there are in children who do not have fragile X. So, on average, the girls will develop more quickly and they'll do better in school. They will endure puberty and all that it entails. Sooner or later most of them will acquire a fancy for the opposite sex, their chosen suitors sometimes inducing dismay in their parents.

Children with fragile X, like all other people, begin life with a particular biological endowment. This is what makes babies cry when they are hungry and sleep when they are tired. It brings with it too a range of individual predispositions, such as the capacity to be more or less impulsive, or moody, or sociable. It is these latter items that are significantly changed by experience and learning. Nobody comes into the world able to read or knowing the current standards of good behaviour. They are born with more or less capacity to learn these things. Irrespective of those capacities it is unlikely that a child who is not taught to read will ever learn it. The same goes for learning acceptable standards of behaviour. All of this applies to children with fragile X in exactly the same way as it applies to all other children.

Fragile X brings with it a unique biological endowment. Compared with the average of all children, the average child with fragile X is likely to be more impulsive. They will find it harder to maintain concentration, and be more prone to social anxiety. They will like routines more and engage in more repetitive behaviours, particularly when anxious. In terms of classroom learning, they will be slower to learn and will show a relative strength in reading over arithmetic. They will have delayed speech and language development with particular features evident. The average girl will be significantly more able than the average boy. However, differences such are these are present in any group of children and adults who do not have fragile X. They are human characteristics that range from mild at one end to extreme at the other end. The biological endowment of fragile X is to move the average individual further towards one end of that range.

The key word in the above is 'average'. No individual child might actually be like that, just as no child without fragile X might be like the average child. Some children without fragile X might show more fragile X characteristics than some children with fragile X. Just as no two children are the same, no two children with fragile X are the same. It is not possible to tell from a diagnosis and a list of fragile X characteristics what an individual child will be like. They could have effects ranging from the barely discernible to severe and profound learning difficulties, or they could have anything in between. In other words, assessment by diagnosis is not possible. Still less is it possible to intervene by diagnosis.

It would be much easier if all children with fragile X were broadly the same and we could therefore assess and intervene by diagnosis. As things are, the matter is filled with uncertainty. Human beings are uncomfortable with uncertainty, and they sometimes try to create some where none exists. Thus, for example, we have Internet Addiction Syndrome, whose devotees might favour an elaborate psychiatric intervention instead of simply cutting the cable between the computer and the phone socket. It is only a matter of time before someone invents Footwear Demand Syndrome in which children demand shatteringly expensive trainers. It will be many years, many conferences and many research papers before someone comes up with the idea of saying 'no'.

The process of medicalising normal human problems is conveniently exculpatory. It lets adults off the hook. To say 'no' to a child we have to have the kind of relationship with them that allows us to discuss reasons without them resorting to the leverage of a tantrum. Without such a relationship it is easier to say 'yes' and then locate the resultant problems as something wrong with the child. The same thing applies to classroom learning. There are many learning problems where it is easier to look for a fault in the child than to do something about them.

Fragile X should be different. It is after all an indisputable organic phenomenon, indisputably related to how children perform. Moreover, it brings with it important heritability issues. There is real science in the biological and genetic investigation of fragile X, and there is no need to resort to the kind of explanatory fictions contained in the examples given above.

As it happens, there can still be flights of fancy and over-professionalisation of simple, if very difficult, problems. This may be precisely because the children have an organic medical condition. Set against a list of features said to be characteristic of fragile X, individual children can be seen in terms of the list rather than as they really are. Features may suddenly be noticed in a child for whom up to then such behaviours were not previously evident or regarded as particularly worrying. What is essentially a social and educational matter becomes primarily a medical problem, even though children with fragile X generally have no more day-to-day medical needs than other children. This is how we convert people who are first and foremost children into people who are first and foremost an expression of fragile X.

Fragile X syndrome and the internet example contain easily identifiable core problems. In the case of fragile X it is a faulty gene. In the case of the internet it is a child who has been allowed to get away with it. Nothing can be done to fix either in a laboratory or consulting room. Faced with this fact, and imbued with a wish to be seen to be doing something, adults resort to inventing apparently more manageable, and glamorous, things to think and do. The thicker the scientific veneer the better. It is at this point that some people part company with common sense. We would rather give children a scientific-looking scale than look at them to find out what they are like. Huge inferences can be made about individual children with fragile X on the basis of how they perform on particular tests or scales. It would be as well to read tea leaves. Both require only one thing: a person to believe in them. Such bogus science merely raises the questions it purports to answer.

Unfortunately, this is more than just an interesting phenomenon. It does not always simply exist alongside more useful information, it often supplants it. It also creates the illusion that making a diagnosis or administering tests and scales is the same as doing something about the problem. Actually, a great deal can be done about fragile X to bring about change, but in order to do it we need to be careful not to obscure straightforward thinking. Children with fragile X can have Footwear Demand Syndrome too. But it won't be a result of having fragile X, although the manner in which they go about it might be.

To find out what a child with fragile X is like, you have to look at him or her in realistic situations, and listen to people who know them. It is not necessary to be an expert in fragile X to carry out educational assessment; only to be an expert in education, such as a teacher. Teachers should not be de-skilled into passivity by believing that they have to know everything about fragile X. If they have confidence in their own expertise, teachers can easily assimilate information about fragile X as it relates to a particular child. The individual child in context is the central consideration for educational assessment, not fragile X.

Not all teachers are good at having confidence in their own expertise; some even deny it. 'I don't want you to think of me as an expert,' a teacher might say to a parent. Such denials of expertise compound a problem that bedevils the teaching profession: that everybody thinks it is easy. Teachers can be bombarded from all quarters outside education with advice and even instructions on how to do their job. It is invariably ill-informed. This is not a recommendation for teachers to go about claiming to be experts. It is however a plea for them not to deny it.

No assessment of educational needs takes place in a vacuum. The background will colour, in subtle but significant ways, any process applied to an individual child. It is not science, it is life with all its inescapable uncertainties. In education we must embrace that uncertainty and work with it in the interests of each child. Uncertainty is not unique to education. It is characteristic of all disciplines where there are no absolutes. To work with it effectively, all concerned must reach a range of core understandings.

The first of these is the purpose of educational assessment. Contrary to the beliefs of some, it is not to find out what a particular child is like, what they do or do not know, can or cannot do, or how they learn. If this is not already known for a child who has been attending school for some time, something is seriously wrong with the education they have been getting. Let us assume that an assessment of what the child is like is already in place. If the process stops at that, nothing is achieved. We have only a snapshot of the child, perhaps saying that they have a key word sight vocabulary of 100 words, or a tendency to wander around. We have also the prospect of an interminable cycle of pointless reviews at which everybody says what the child is like.

The purpose of an educational assessment should be to use what is known about a child in order to establish what needs to be done next. Educational reviews should not so much review the child as the adults who were supposed to be doing something, and the usefulness of what they were supposed to be doing. Responsibility for progress lies not with the child, but with the adults. There is a crucial difference between, 'Dorothy is easily distracted and over-sensitive to perceived criticism' and, 'Dorothy needs to be taught to add up.'

Our understanding of special educational needs is crucial in this. No-one has ever decided formally what a special educational need is. All children have educational needs of some sort or another. In any classroom, at any age, there will be a wide range of abilities and attainments. Teachers and schools manage this as a matter of course. What makes an educational need special is that it is outside the range that can be managed within existing planning and support. That is to say a special educational need is something requiring more than that which is normally available. But how can we get to this point given that there is no definition of a special educational need? Well, there is a definition that can be applied for each individual child. A special educational need exists when the key people concerned – parents, school, LEA, and, where feasible, the child – agree on it. Although this is sometimes not easy, it is what working together means. The problems that arise with it are not there because there is no definition. They are there because despite the rhetoric we are not very good at working together.

In doing this we need to understand the connection between fragile X and special educational needs. The fact of having fragile X does not mean children will automatically have special educational needs. Nevertheless it is likely that most will, in the terms described above. Some of these children will have extensive educational needs, while the needs of others can be met within the normal course of classroom events. For individual children who have special educational needs as well as fragile X, having fragile X will not reveal what the educational needs are. It is important to remember that we are dealing with individual children who are constitutionally distinct as well having been brought up and educated in widely differing circumstances.

If we do not remain aware of that, we are that much more likely to confuse special educational needs with the resources proposed to meet them. No child with fragile X, even if they do have special educational needs, ever had an educational need for an extra teacher, a non-teaching assistant, a particular school, or any other additional resource. There is a significant difference between a need and the resource proposed to meet it. 'To learn to buy items in a shop' may be an educational need for a particular child. 'Fifteen hours of one-to-one specialist teaching per week' is not; it is a measure proposed to meet a need. More of something, or different something, does not in itself achieve anything. We need to be able to say what it is for. When we do that, an LEA is more likely to provide it. Any LEA would be foolish, or in dereliction of its duty, to provide a resource without a clear expression of what it is supposed to achieve.

Not all of the needs defined for a child with fragile X will fall within the competence or power of an LEA. Schools are about education. Teachers and education authorities should not claim expertise in areas outside their competence. Nor should others attempt to foist it upon them. 'Regular speech therapy' is not an educational need, even though the two are clearly related. Neither is 'Therapy at the local clinic to tackle her excessive sensitivity to criticism.' The child might well benefit from such a thing, but it is not within the competence of an LEA. Educational needs should only refer to items that an LEA has the competence and wherewithal to deliver. We do not want teachers prescribing medicine for our children, nor should we want medics specifying education for them. Apart from the obvious pitfalls, this diverts responsibility for resourcing and accountability away from the person proposing the intervention.

Multidisciplinary working means people working in different areas of competence and knowledge finding ways of meshing their particular expertise in a child's best interests. Few people would argue with this, given that no child exists as a set of discrete bits. Conditions like fragile X that are accompanied by lists of characteristics, attract the assumption of an automatic need for everybody who might conceivably be involved, actually to be involved. This can result in meetings of twenty or more professionals, most of whom may never have seen the child or met the parents. All of them will probably say something specific to that child, none of it particularly illuminating, and most of it concerned with someone else's area of competence. Multidisciplinary working is sometimes practised as an open invitation to try to do everyone else's job. Over-much professional involvement can also come about through inappropriate advocacy. Sometimes parents encourage this, prompting one professional to put pressure on another even though they have limited or no competence in the area in question. This can be seriously damaging. Useful multidisciplinary work in fragile X results when all concerned focus on their own expertise, take responsibility for it and its costs, and work at integrating it with the expertise of others, including parents.

There is also an issue here concerning children's privacy. Most of the things that children do and say, and the things they think are not analysed and agonised over by adults. Children with fragile X are particularly vulnerable in this respect. They can be frisked for deeper meaning in their most mundane activities. They are taken away by strangers and examined in little rooms. Things are said about them that cut across their desires to be like other children. It can be easy to forget we are dealing with human beings, irrespective of their level of need, and not exhibits for whom normal standards of respect have been suspended.

Effective assessment and intervention with fragile X in education has six fundamental criteria.

- The aim is to inform the teaching and learning process for the child to whom it is applied.
- The assessment and intervention are carried out in the context in which the child learns, that is, normally, the classroom.
- Assessment and intervention are not separate. They are both an integral part of the teaching and learning cycle.
- Assessment and intervention are led by the people who have the responsibility for implementing them.
- Parents and teachers work together.
- The process aims for the least intrusive way of achieving its purposes.

In essence this amounts to curriculum-referenced assessment. In this, a teaching and learning goal is established, based on what it is believed a child should and can learn as a matter of priority. For one child, that priority – or educational need – might be to learn unit number bonds. For another it might be to make an unaccompanied bus journey. For any individual at any one time, this can cover a range of needs. The next step is to assess by observation and by doing. One child may be able to get on a bus and pay the fare, but another might be able only to get on the bus. One child might complete number bonds to within five while another may be unable to match a written number with a physical quantity of objects. Although the goal for these children is the same, their starting points are different. This approach can be applied to any area of a child's learning.

In the end we always come back to the fact that children with fragile X are first and foremost children. Because of their biological endowment we have certain expectations of them. But that does not mean we have to accept these expectations. No child with fragile X ever had a learning difficulty except in the presence of someone trying to teach them something. And no child with fragile X ever had a behaviour problem except in the presence of someone trying to control them. In other words, promoting the learning and development of children with fragile X syndrome is more about what adults do and think than it is about the children themselves.

Chapter 9

Formal assessment and constructing an individual education programme

Marcia Braden

The process of obtaining an assessment begins with a concern that the child may not be progressing normally. An evaluation can be requested by a parent, classroom teacher, therapist or advocate. A family physician, paediatrician or other specialist may also initiate the evaluation process. With a young child, the first step is to inquire about the necessary requirements and the local school district (or education authority's) special education services. The results of the evaluation may lead to a formal statement of the child's need for special services and support.

A screening or multidisciplinary evaluation is usually the first step in accessing services. A screening is a routine check to see if a child has a disability or is at risk of developmental delay. A more in-depth assessment may result from this screening. Generally, children with genetic conditions like fragile X syndrome qualify for services. Developmental skills that may be assessed include cognitive, sensory, physical and motor skills, communication and adaptive ability. Children with fragile X often experience delays in these areas sometimes even before fragile X is diagnosed.

In order to assess all dimensions of a child's functioning, a multidisciplinary approach is used. The child is observed and tested by professionals, who may all observe the child performing a task or participating in an activity. Following this, professional teams and parents meet to discuss their findings.

When the child qualifies for early intervention or special education services, parents and the professional team meet to identify the needs of the child. The child's development is viewed as resting on the family and community, and the family is empowered to help direct the services instead of relying on professional diagnoses and suggestions for treatment. After the eligibility for services is determined, an Individual Learning Programme is developed and should include the following components:

- The child's present level of development, listing skills the child has already demonstrated, along with strengths, interests, and weaknesses.
- The family's resources, priorities, and challenges, including the need for additional money, community resources and emotional support.
- Goals for the family, both long-term goals and short-term objectives.
- Supports and services needed to reach these goals.
- Designation of a case manager to oversee all that is going on with the family. This person may be assigned or chosen by the family. The case manager helps the family by:

  - procuring an evaluation if needed;

- facilitating the development and yearly review of the Individual Education Programme;
- helping to identify resources within the community;
- coordinating the delivery of support services;
- coordinating medical services;
- facilitating the development of transition into elementary or primary school.

Qualifying for services after preschool

Similar to the requirements for a preschooler, children of school age must also qualify for special education services. The local school district (or LEA) is responsible for conducting an evaluation to determine eligibility for educational support. If the child is eligible then a plan for services, called an Individual Education Programme (IEP), is developed.

The evaluation team should include, but not be limited to, the following:

- the parents;
- a regular education teacher;
- a special education teacher;
- a representative from the school district;
- individuals who can interpret the results of the evaluations (to include private evaluations);
- the student, when appropriate;
- anyone else the parents want to include.

As before, a variety of testing methods may be used to determine the child's needs. Ideally testing should be done by observing the child in a natural context, rather than by formal tests. Eligibility for support is determined following discussion of specific information from the diagnostic data. Some eligibility requirements vary between regions, as do the resources available to meet children's needs.

Evaluation should assess the child's current level of functioning in the following areas: cognitive; behavioural (social and emotional); physical (vision and hearing); and developmental (speech and language development, fine and gross motor development). This will provide a starting point for instruction and the creation of goals and objectives to be included in the IEP (Appendix).

It is as important to determine every child's unique strengths as well as their weaknesses. Assessing what is difficult to learn and what is easy will help formulate an effective educational programme. Weaknesses form the basis for goals and objectives. Strengths are just as important because they can be used to help the child compensate for his weaknesses. For example, if counting and maths are difficult, find strength around which to centre the teaching. High-interest materials, such as money, building and construction or calculators, can be the focus of maths instruction to make it interesting.

The child's rate of learning will assist in setting goals and objectives that are realistic and attainable. Depending on their rate of learning, it may be more appropriate to expect the child to learn to recognise his printed name than it is to be reading within a year.

Test results not only provide a specific level of functioning, but can also provide important diagnostic information. It is possible to discover from the testing process how the child learns and what motivates them. In addition, special accommodations such as regular movement and routines, a quiet workspace or the positioning of furniture and materials, may be essential for the child to succeed. This information should be included in the IEP. It is prudent to review existing evaluation data, including reports from the regular education classroom, private therapists and community resources. This allows the team to look at the child's behaviour outside a specific environment and to suggest appropriate methods to augment services within the classroom.

After analyzing the assessment data, the next step is to determine what supports and services are needed to meet the goals and objectives in the IEP. Any support should focus on enabling the child to participate and function in the least restrictive educational environment. Support may be drawn from a wide range of professional services, and may include such varied items as a full-time para-professional, speech therapy, voice-activated word processing, a sensory menu, or even a sensory integration therapist's recommendation of a weighted vest.

Two types of evaluation are generally provided; the initial evaluation for eligibility and ongoing evaluations after placement. Both kinds serve important roles in the success of the child's special education placement and programming. The initial evaluation is performed when the child is first placed into the special education system. Both standardized testing and informal observations are used, and the parents' views are also presented. Testing specialists, such as educational psychologists and the early years special needs team, meet with the parents to discuss test results and determine the best ways to meet the child's educational needs.

Follow-up evaluations usually take place every year after the initial evaluation and will involve staffing teams similar to those involved in initial evaluations. The purpose of the follow-up is to review and provide an update relating to the child's current level of functioning as well as the progress made during the year. The education programme and need for related services are adjusted, according to the progress made by the child and the effectiveness of support and services received. A request can be made for testing at any time during the school year if the parent or teacher feels that it is needed. There must be an evaluation or review of progress before determining that the child is no longer eligible for or benefiting from special education services.

Even though specialists provide most testing, it should be remembered that although professionals have an expert point of view, no one knows the child better than a parent. It is important to be sure that the professionals' views assimilate the parent's perspective.

Evaluation should take into account the child's unique characteristics. Typically, standardized testing requires the child to withstand intense and direct interaction with the examiner. This testing experience may provoke anxiety in the child with fragile X, prompting a flight or fight reaction which can affect the reliability of any test results. It is difficult to view the results with complete confidence, unless the examiner is an expert in testing children with fragile X.

Private evaluations

It may be necessary for parents to seek an independent evaluation in order to assess the child's ability level and address treatment methods. Some parents choose to do this because they disagree with the school district's evaluation, or they want the evaluation to be conducted by a professional with specific expertise in fragile X. Because fragile X is still comparatively under-diagnosed, it has had a low prevalence rate. Consequently, there may be few professionals who have extensive experience of working with children with fragile X. Professionals provided by the school district to perform an evaluation might not have the necessary level of expertise to render accurate results for children with these specific difficulties.

A parent may opt for private psychological, speech and language, occupational, or educational testing. If the school district or LEA sanctions this, the cost will be paid directly by them. Often due to monetary constraints, a school district will prefer to use their own staff. In that case, parents can accept the test results or attempt to show that the LEA professional evaluating the child lacks the expertise to evaluate their child accurately. Parents who choose to bear the costs of a private evaluation may find that the school district or LEA may not accept or act upon the results. Parents may wish the private evaluator to attend the IEP meeting to make sure they provide input into the IEP process. Most school districts and LEAs welcome additional information provided by members of the private sector. There are a number of standardized tests on the commercial market. It is important for parents to become familiar with the pros or cons of each so that an informed consent can be given.

Behaviour intervention plans

Because children with fragile X often exhibit behaviour that interferes with learning, it is important to develop and include a behaviour management plan in their IEP. If the child's behaviour interferes with learning, a Behaviour Intervention or Modification Plan (BIP or BMP) is essential. This plan encourages educators to address behaviour by understanding the function of it before developing intervention strategies.

Most behaviours, even disruptive behaviours, persist only while serving a purpose. For example, infants learn that when they cry, they get attention either by being fed, changed, or played with. The behaviour continues as long as it gets the desired attention. When children learn to communicate their needs using gestures or verbal language, it is no longer necessary to cry. If the verbal attempts to get the necessary attention fail, the child reverts back to disruptive and noisy behaviour to get the desired response. Children learn over time that their behaviour leads to something called a consequence, and that this can be positive or negative.

Educators working with children with fragile X have also learned that sometimes a behaviour results from something that has just happened. For example, a child who begins to flap his hands may be reacting to excessive noises or a large crowd of people causing arousal and overstimulation. When this happens, the event before the behaviour is the antecedent. After extensive study and clinical experience of both the causes and function of behaviour (Maurice et al., 1996; Sobesky et al., 1996; Braden, 2000b; Hagerman, 2000), educators and therapists have learned effective methods to help change negative or disruptive behaviour.

It is important to analyze antecedents when identifying the behaviour to be reduced or increased. In addition, there are ways to observe and analyze the function of a behaviour (Maurice et al., 1996; Braden, 2000a; Myles et al., 1998). A behaviour may serve as an avoidance or escape mechanism. Children may prefer punishment (time out, loss of privilege) to continuing a task they dislike. Because there are numerous factors contributing to behavioural episodes, it is important to observe the child over several days and in various settings. This gives the observer a better idea of what function the behaviour serves and under what conditions.

Myles and Simpson (1998) have developed a functional assessment tool that qualifies the behaviour. This approach not only notes when the behaviour occurs, but under what conditions (structured activities, group, playing with others or alone, during times of transitions, in the morning or afternoon, and within certain environments such as the classroom, gym or library). The following are examples of behaviour plans used with students with fragile X.

Functional Assessment and Behaviour Intervention Plans

Presenting problem

*   Jan is an eighth grader at St Mary's Middle School.
*   Jan has fragile X syndrome with a full mutation.
*   Jan is very shy and tends to avoid social interaction.

She has recently developed excessive picking behaviours. She began picking scabs from insect bites, scrapes and cuts this summer. Now that school has begun, she is picking more often and seems to engage in this behaviour in times of stress. She is picking scabs at night and puts Band-Aids over bleeding scabs when she goes to school because she becomes embarrassed.

Frequency

Jan picks at herself approximately 15 times a day.

Function of behaviour

It appears that Jan is inept at coping with high stress created by social interaction at school.

Behaviour Intervention Plan
Baseline: 15 times a day

Antecedent	Behaviour	Consequence
Jan becomes anxious about a social interaction	Jan picks at a wound	Jan puts a Band-Aid over her wound

Antecedent	Behaviour	Consequence
Jan engages in deep relaxation exercises when anxious	Jan becomes relaxed Jan practices deep relaxation exercises when she's in speech class or before going to lunch each day at school	Jan does not pick at her skin

Discussion of function and conditions

Because the target behaviour has increased since school began, the school environment may provoke anxiety. The analysis revealed that Jan's behaviour escalated during speech class most likely because Jan anticipated speaking in front of the class. The behaviour also escalated during lunch time and unstructured situations when Jan may have become stressed about social expectations.

Behaviour Intervention Plan for David: no 1

Target behaviour: cursing at School
Baseline: multiple days, averages 10 times a day

Functional behaviour assessment

David was observed at school from 9 a.m. until 3 p.m. He was observed in his regular education classroom, playground, cafeteria, special education classroom, auditorium and gym class. (See Table 9.1.) The assessment clearly implicates transition and anticipation of large-group activities either in the gym or auditorium. The cursing seems to be a function of his anxiety and decreases when the pressure to go into a crowded and noisy environment is removed. The behaviour plan should incorporate that knowledge into managing David's behaviour.

Behaviour Intervention Plan for David: no. 2

Level I

1 David anticipates transition to loud, crowded environment
2 Teacher presents him with three forced choice picture cards

   • stay in classroom
   • go to PE or any other environment that is loud and crowded
   • help with a school job

3 Teacher ignores cursing and reinforces adaptive behaviour

Level II

1 David anticipates the transition and tells teacher he cannot go to the auditorium, gym, etc. (he refrains from cursing)
2 David is given forced choice cards to desensitize reaction

   • go to auditorium, gym, etc. for 2 minutes in the beginning of the class
   • go to auditorium, gym, etc. for 2 minutes at the end of the class

3 Teacher reinforces his choice and success in not cursing

The most important element to any plan is data collection. If a plan is working it can be substantiated through the test of frequency and change from the baseline. The baseline data

Table 9.1 Diary of David's behaviour

Time	Antecedent	Behaviour	Consequence
9:35	Lining up in regular education classroom to go to PE class	Curses	Teacher redirects to sit down and wait
9:40	David is sitting and class has left	Cursing decreases	Teacher walks David to the gym for PE
9:45	David is walking to PE with teacher	Cursing increases	David is removed from PE and returns to classroom
9:55	David is in the classroom	Cursing stops	Teacher gives David positive reinforcement
12:00	David lines up to go to the cafeteria for lunch	Curses	David stays in the classroom to eat and isn't allowed to join his class in the lunchroom
12:15	David eats his lunch alone in the classroom with teaching assistant	Cursing stops	David goes out to recess
12:30	Teacher discusses procedure to leave classroom and go into the auditorium for a presentation	Curses	David is ignored
12:35	Cursing is ignored and the classmates line up	Cursing increases	David is asked to take a note to the office instead of following his class to the auditorium

is always gathered before a behaviour programme ensues and continues throughout the intervention phase. When a predetermined pass criteria is met, the programme can be faded and data taken once a week.

(Taken from *Fragile, Handle with care, more about fragile X*, Braden, 2000a)

Example of Behaviour Intervention Plan for Tim: no. 1

Target behaviour: bites index finger (school only)
Baseline: averages 20 times a day (school only)

Functional behaviour assessment

Tim was observed at his school placement from 9 to 12 on Monday and from 12 to 3 on Wednesday. He was observed in all included and special education classes. (See Table 9.2.)

Table 9.2 Diary of Tim's behaviour

Time	Antecedent	Behaviour	Consequence
9:20	Watching cartoon video in home room	Bites and pushes with teeth against index finger	Ignored
10:15	Waiting to take a turn playing bongo drum in music	Bites index finger	Told he couldn't have a turn
11:45	Waiting in line for turn on relay team in PE	Pushes against index finger with teeth	Peers on team tell him to stop

Discussion of function

An analysis indicates Tim bites his finger or pushes against his finger whenever he is excited or amused. Consequences have not effectively reduced the behaviour. The function of the behaviour appears to be used as a way to calm down an autonomic reaction to a pleasurable or excitable condition. Because it is a non-voluntary reaction, completely eliminating the behaviour by punishing Tim would prove non-productive. An important component of this behaviour programme is to provide Tim with an alternative behaviour to replace his finger biting. For example, he may be conditioned to push his hands together, squeeze his hands together or fold his hands when he becomes excited.

Behaviour Intervention Plan for Tim: no. 2

Targeted behaviour: bites index finger (school only)
Frequency: averages 20 times a day (school only)
Consequences/interventions attempted: verbal reminders, wearing gloves, keeping hands busy, redirection

Functional behaviour assessment

Antecedent is anticipation of an exciting or humorous event. Function of behaviour is to calm himself in some way, bringing deep pressure to his sensory system (see Table 9.3).

Table 9.3 Tim's functional behaviour assessment

Antecedent	Behaviour	Consequence
Tim becomes overstimulated (watches video, becomes excited, or amused)	Bites finger – pushes finger against teeth	When Tim begins to bring his finger to his mouth, immediately hand him a squeeze ball, or other apparatus to push on instead of his finger. The trainer reinforces the use of the replacement behaviour and ignores the biting or pushing on finger.

Source: Braden 2000a

Appendix

Examples of goals and objectives

Present level of performance (PLOP)

Case no. 1

Jake is 4 years old. He attends an integrated preschool and has adjusted well to the preschool placement. There are times when Jake gets excited and chews on his shirt collar. He has destroyed many shirts and the other preschoolers have begun to imitate him. The staff praise him for not chewing his collar, but he replaces this with chewing a sleeve or his hand. The chewing seems to be correlated with anxiety.

Goal: Jake will develop adaptive behaviours

Dates observed: 2/6; 7/6; 10/6

Baseline: Jake averages 17 episodes of chewing in 2½ hours

1 STO: (specific teaching objective) During the first hour in school, Jake will reduce his chewing on his shirt by 15 per cent. Remind him every 30 seconds.
2 STO: During the morning Jake will reduce chewing on his shirt by 50 per cent.

Present level of performance (PLOP)

Case no. 2

Sean is a pre-schooler attending morning kindergarten classes. Although he is able to read 10 basic sight words, he struggles with writing. He is able to copy a circle, square and cross from a model. He is currently unable to copy his first or last name from a model. Sean has been referred for an occupational therapy evaluation to assess his motor planning ability.

Goal: Sean will improve his written language ability

Dates observed: 20/10; 21/10; 22/10

Baseline: writing his name – 0 per cent with model and 0 per cent without model

1 STO: (specific teaching objective) Sean will be given a model (name writing worksheet) with his first name dotted out. He will trace his first name staying on the dotted line with no more than 2 errors.
2 STO: Sean will complete without error the letter S in his first name beginning with a dot and no other prompts. He will trace the rest of his first name without errors.
3 STO: Sean will free-write the letter S without dotted line and without errors. He will increase this sequentially, adding one more letter each time.

Present level of performance (PLOP)

Case no. 3

Joe is a 16-year-old high school student. He is included for two periods of the day, but mostly he has special education and community-based learning. Joe can read some fast food logos and signs, but has a limited sight vocabulary. He is interested in sports and wants to learn to read the sports page or sports magazines.

Goal: Joe will improve his sight reading ability

Date observed: 12/2

Baseline: Joe reads 8 sight words and 10 fast food logos without assistance 100 per cent of the time.

1 STO: (specific learning objective) Joe will identify any words he can read on the sports page and highlight them. Joe will read back the words he has highlighted with 100 per cent accuracy.
2 STO: Joe will identify unfamiliar words on the sports page through associations and context 80 per cent of the time.
3 STO: Joe will study 10 sight words and read them from a juniors' sports magazine with 100 per cent accuracy.

Present level of performance (PLOP)

Case no. 4

Jon identifies numbers both expressively and receptively to 100. He understands basic operations, but lacks accuracy in computation skills. He knows the value of numbers into the teens and skip counts by 2, 5 and 10. He can tell time to the hour on a face clock and most times by a digital clock. Maths appears to be his most challenging academic area.

Goal: Jon will increase maths skills

1 STO: (specific teaching objective) Jon will copy legibly from a model each number from 1 to 20 in random presentation with 80 per cent accuracy.
2 STO: Using a calculator, Jon will add and subtract a variety of one and two digit number combinations with 80 per cent accuracy.
3 STO: Jon will correctly identify combinations of coins to one dollar, pound or euro with 70 per cent accuracy.
4 STO: Jon will place in sequence number cards given to him in random order, with minimal prompts leading to 100 per cent accuracy.

Present level of performance (PLOP)

Case no. 5

Steven finds spelling difficult due to fine motor planning and visual memory deficits. He is able to spell simple words orally. He performs best when he is given a visual presentation using cloze techniques such as spin s __ i __ or cat ca __.

Goal: Steven will improve spelling skills

1 STO: (specific teaching objective) Steven will spell from word families (gnat, bat, sat,) using cloze techniques and backward chaining 20 per cent above baseline.

2 STO: Steven will take a spelling test of familiar words and pass with 70 per cent accuracy.

3 STO: Using a word processor, Steven will spell correctly his full name, phone number, address and school name with 70 per cent accuracy.

Present level of performance (PLOP)

Case no. 6

Alex is included in a second grade (Year 3) classroom. His interests are age appropriate and he has a full time educational assistant. Although he participates in most classroom activities, it is necessary to adapt the curriculum or offer alternative strategies. Alex has difficulty sustaining attention during instruction that does not engage his interest and he does not complete work without prompting.

To help Alex to be successfully included in his mainstream placement, his Individual Educational Plan should aim to:

- differentiate curriculum and teaching methods;
- employ alternative testing measures;
- use a multi-sensory approach to written language activities;
- contain a Behaviour Intervention Plan;
- base approaches on observed data and functional behaviour assessments;
- make direct 1:1 adult support available throughout the day;
- reduce the number of transitions between activities and classrooms;
- break down multiple step tasks into single components;
- identify antecedents that produce maladaptive behaviours such as smell, taste, shoes off, perseverative/non-meaningful speech;
- ignore perseverative verbal interaction;
- use a whole-day picture schedule;
- use tokens of high-interest materials;
- practise 'time out' breaks when he is 'over the edge';
- combine verbal instruction with demonstration for new motor tasks;
- use occupational therapy fine motor activities and a sensory integration menu;
- maximise attention and language responses by using frequent sensory interventions, such as tactile or deep pressure;
- communicate between home and school on a daily basis;
- site him near a supportive adult during large group activities;
- pre-teach academic, language and social skills in 1:1 setting, using direct instruction;
- give clear find consistent guidelines and expectations for all school environments, including common classroom behaviours, such as lining up and raising hand.

Goal: Alex will participate successfully in his included, mainstream environment

1 STO: (specific teaching objective) Alex will follow multi-modal instructions in 30-minute group settings, without additional prompts 70 per cent of the time.

2 STO: Alex will consistently comply with instructional cues when prompted 80 per cent of the time.

3 STO: Alex will successfully change activity or classroom five times during the day without prompts 60 per cent of the time.

4 STO: Alex will attend to a teacher-directed activity, 15 minutes in length in the general classroom without assistance.

5 STO: Alex will spontaneously express his wants to adults, using words, signs or pictures, without assistance 80 per cent of the time.

6 STO: Alex will leave the playound with his peers when summoned by bell or whistle, without additional prompting 100 per cent of the time.

7 STO: Alex will identify and locate common places around the school (library, playground, office, lunchroom, music room) with 100 per cent accuracy.

8 STO: Alex will interact appropriately with helpers 80 per cent of the time.

9 STO: Alex will sign 100 per cent of the time that he needs help from adults when he doesn't understand tasks or verbal requests.

References

Braden, M. (2002) In R. J. Hagerman and P. J. Hagerman (eds), *Fragile X Syndrome: Diagnosis, Treatment and Research,* 3rd ed. Baltimore: Johns Hopkins University Press, pp. 428–462.

Braden, M. (2000a) *Fragile: Handle with Care; More About Fragile X Syndrome – Adolescents and Adults.* Dillon, CO: Spectra Publishing Co.

Braden, M. (2000b) Education. In J. D. Weber (ed.) *Children with Fragile X Syndrome: A Parent's Guide.* Bethesda, MD: Woodbine House, pp. 243–305.

Hagerman, R. J. (2000) Treatment of aggression in children and adults with fragile X syndrome, *Foundation Q,* Winter 2000.

Individuals with Disabilities Education Act of 1997, 20 U.S.C. 1400 *et seq.*

Maurice, C., G. Green, and S. C. Luce (1996) *Behavioural Intervention for Young Children with Autism.* Austin, Tex.: PRO-ED.

Myles, B. S., and R. L. Simpson (1998) *Asperger Syndrome: A Guide for Educators and Parents.* Austin, Tex.: PRO-ED.

Sobesky, W. E. (1996) The treatment of emotional and behavioural problems in fragile X. In R. J. Hagerman and A. Cronister (eds), *Fragile X Syndrome: Diagnosis, Treatment, and Research,* 2nd ed. Baltimore: Johns Hopkins University Press, pp. 332–348.

Chapter 10

Obtaining educational support for a child with special needs

A structured approach for parents and teachers

Kate Schnelling and Denise Dew-Hughes

Children with special needs require a level of support throughout their years in school. As in all cases where an individual requires a central provider with limited funds to fulfil a perceived need, application for support can become an issue. When the procedures for obtaining support are imperfectly understood or administered by parents, school and the Local Education Authority (LEA) or school district, it is more difficult for all to reach a satisfactory outcome.

The role played by professional teams in evaluating children with learning difficulties or slow development has been explained earlier (see Chapter 8). The importance of parents' views about their own child cannot be over-emphasised. They know the child better than any assessor and can give valuable help to the professional teams who will determine the child's needs. Quite naturally, parents want the best possible educational support for their child. Schools want to provide this, and the LEA wants to balance the needs of all the children in its care and use its funds effectively. This is more likely to be achieved if all the parties understand the procedures and can work towards establishing a co-operative working relationship.

Teachers and LEA officers become familiar with the complex procedures of obtaining LEA help for individual pupils; parents meeting these procedures for the first time need to have them explained in straightforward terms. Having a child with special needs can be a cause of confusion, but obtaining the right level of help often depends on a structured and organised approach. Such an approach to the procedures is described below for parents and teachers who are embarking on the process. This works as effectively for pupils with complex or severe learning difficulties, as it does for those who may not need a formal statement of needs, but still need extra help.

All children in education are individuals, whether or not they require special help. Those who do have learning difficulties are no less individualistic, although their differences may be more acute. All children with learning difficulties are said to have 'special educational needs' under the terms of the 1981 Education Act. These needs can take many forms, and the term covers the entire range of children, including those gifted or exceptionally talented, those with specific physical or health requirements, and those with complex, profound and severe learning difficulties. The educational needs of most children could and should be met by their local mainstream school and LEA, following the stages of the Code of Practice. Other children will need the more specialised help available from a special school or support unit, or even home tuition. The Code of Practice (DfEE, 2001) recommends three stages for meeting children's special educational needs, the first two of which are the responsibility of the school. Although not legally enforced, this approach is followed by all LEAs.

Children who are diagnosed with a condition associated with learning difficulties will usually be issued with a Statement of their educational needs. This is so for most children with fragile X, even though the condition covers the range of provision normally available in a mainstream school, as well as a wide variety of special needs. A recent national survey of children diagnosed with fragile X (Dew-Hughes, 2002), showed that more than 90 per cent had been issued with a formal Statement of special educational needs before they finished their reception year in school. Most of the remaining 10 per cent were pre-school age children who had not yet completed the process of assessment, evaluation and provision.

Some LEAs do not issue Statements of special needs before the child starts school at the age of 5, unless they anticipate a significant level of difficulties. This 'wait and see' approach may account for the fact that just under half the pre-school children in the national survey had no Statement. Nevertheless, a high number of these very young children were formally assessed before the age of 3, and the rest in the year before starting primary school.

Very few children in the survey had been issued with a Statement after starting primary school. Of those who had received their Statement later, most were girls who in general exhibit subtler learning difficulties. With a genetic condition such as fragile X, there is always the possibility of retrospective diagnosis and Statementing. This occurs when a younger sibling has learning difficulties and tests positive for fragile X. Brothers and sisters are then tested, often after they have started school. The diagnosis of one sibling sponsors the investigation of older children whose learning and developmental difficulties are less severe. In the national survey, most of the children who were diagnosed while at primary or secondary school had a younger sibling with fragile X.

The age at which a child is diagnosed with fragile X is closely related to their age when issued with a Statement of needs; diagnosis and Statement go hand in hand. Figure 10.1 shows this close relationship. Children are grouped into each of the four educational phases, pre-school, junior, senior and post-17, according to their age at the time of diagnosis and being issued with a Statement. Figure 10.1 shows that, whatever the current age of young people in the survey, most had been diagnosed and issued with a Statement in their pre-school years.

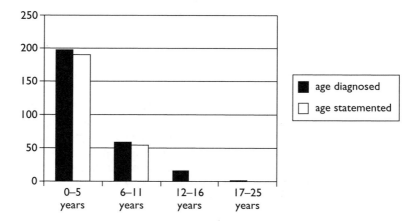

Figure 10.1 The age at which children in the 2002 national survey were diagnosed with fragile X syndrome compared with their age when they received a Statement of Special Educational Needs.

For children without a diagnosis of a specific condition, the picture is less clear cut. The term 'special educational needs' covers a very wide range of difficulties and specific skills. This also applies to those with fragile X, where levels of learning difficulties and the resultant educational need can be very different even within the same family. Because the needs of individual children are so varied, it is important for all concerned in the Statementing process to have an accurate, individual profile of the child's skills, strengths and weaknesses, and to know the implications for teaching, learning and the type of school. It is particularly important that children without a Statement should have their needs listed in detail, because these will not be enforced by a legal document.

The first stages of assessment

When a child has more complex and long-term difficulties, the parent, carer or school may ask for a statutory assessment to identify more clearly the child's needs and any necessary provision. The parent or guardian must give permission before a statutory assessment can begin. The LEA will ask advice of parents and professionals, including those who may already be helping the child, and they may then draw up a statement of the child's special educational needs.

Parents going through this process with their child should know what the school is already doing and what they plan to do next. Teachers should provide this information, explaining the stages of the Code of Practice and the details of the child's individual education plan (IEP). Children identified as being 'on the Code of Practice' should have an IEP, which describes their needs. It should also state how these needs will be met and when the plan is to be reviewed. The SENCOs (special educational needs co-ordinators) in mainstream school are responsible for monitoring special needs among its pupils. They also assist and inform parents and liaise with LEA officers and support services.

It is advisable for parents to have support from a friend or relative in the early stages of assessment. The name of the education officer responsible for the child's support is given on any correspondence with the LEA. He or she will have a list of trained volunteers called Named Persons who can offer support when parents need it and help them to make their views clear. It may be helpful to meet and talk to the named education officer who can explain what type of support is available and how the system works.

The statutory assessment

A child may have a statutory assessment made to determine more precisely his or her educational needs and level of support required. It is important that parents and teachers give their opinion on their child's difficulties and what they feel is needed. The parents' opinion is extremely important. How they present their child's strengths and difficulties will influence both the type of provision and the resources that will support the child in school.

In order to present the fullest and most accurate picture of the child as an individual learner, parents and early years teachers should prepare in advance for the statutory assessment procedure. They could collect a folder of useful information, medical records or other documents about the child so that the details are to hand when needed. The folder should contain details about what the child does at school and at home. Parents and teachers should work together in collecting this information, and agree on the contents. Not only does this reinforce the accuracy of the information, it also encourages adults to pool their expertise and operate as a team. Discussing different views, and different behaviour at school and home, can result in a much clearer picture of the child's learning and development. The following guidelines could form a structure for those involved in preparing their folder.

A structured approach

The early years

- What do you remember about the early years that might help?
- What was the child like as a young baby, in the nursery or playgroup?
- Were you happy about progress at the time?
- When did you first feel that things were not right?
- What happened?
- What advice and help was available or offered, and from whom?

The present situation

- Describe the child's general health.
- Note down minor ailments, serious illnesses or periods in hospital.
- Record special diets, allergies or medicine.
- Describe their general alertness or tiredness, does this have a pattern?
- Detail absences from school – how many absences and for how long?

Physical skills

- Describe the child's activities such as walking, running, climbing, riding a bike, doing jigsaws, drawing pictures, sewing, football, construction kits.
- Are there any favourite activities, any skills or particular difficulties?

Self-help

What level of independence has the child reached?

- Can they do up buttons and fastenings when dressing?
- Can they manage the toilet independently; how much help is needed?
- Can they help to make the bed or set the table, tidy up toys or their room?
- Can they cope with daily routines or adapt to changes?
- How do they get out and about?

Communication

- Does the child speak, or prefer to use signs, pointing or carrying your hands to what they want?
- Explain the level of the child's speech. How do they tell you things, describe events or relate messages?

- Can they join in a conversation, is the speech repetitive, do they echo what others say?
- Are there any particular features of the child's speech which are unusual, such as uneven phrasing or difficulty in forming their words?

Playing and learning at home and outside

- What does the child enjoy doing at home?
- Do they watch TV, read, pursue hobbies?
- How long can they concentrate?
- Do they play with others, share, join in games?
- Do they enjoy sporting activities, go to a club, in a group or alone?

Relationships

- What social relationships does the child have at home and outside in the community?
- Are they a joiner-in or a loner?
- Does the child co-operate at home, share, listen, help with jobs, fit in with family routines and rules?
- Are they very affectionate, sulky, have temper tantrums or outbursts?

At school

- Does the child generally enjoy school?
- Has the school helped in any particular way?
- How are relationships with other children and the teacher?
- What progress has the child made at school?
- Detail the child's progress in formal subjects like reading, writing and numbers.
- Does the child need extra help with school work, in which activities, subjects or areas?
- What does the child find easy and difficult?

Your general views

- What do you think the child's special needs are?
- How best do you think these can be met?
- How do you compare this child with others of the same age, or siblings?
- What is the child good at?
- What are the worries and concerns about the child's development and learning?

Is there any other information you would like to add, for example about significant events in the child's life that may have affected them? How do the child's needs affect the rest of the family or class group? Do you have reports from other people or professionals, which could enhance what you say and reinforce the request for support? Would you like more contact with or advice from other professionals – if so, what and why?

Support

Teachers and others can deal more effectively and confidently with a child with learning difficulties if they have had appropriate training, and understand the implications of the child's condition, and the learning difficulties associated with this. Support for the child should be flexible and capable of changes over time; there should also be co-operation between education, social services and health departments.

Provision

This can take a number of forms:

- identifying and meeting a pupil's needs within mainstream provision;
- giving extra support to a pupil in mainstream;
- supporting a pupil in mainstream with resources from a special school, unit or service;
- educating the pupil in a special school.

Successful provision will cover a continuum of learning abilities across the age range. It will be linked to other agencies and professionals. Most importantly it will involve consultation with parents and be based on positive attitudes to children. Its key aims should be to promote understanding of the whole child, and also understanding of any diagnosed condition such as fragile X syndrome, hearing impairment or epilepsy. A flexible approach is important because not all conventional teaching methods are the best for a particular child. Provision should take care that individual support does not encourage over-dependence on a supporting adult, such as the 'Velcro approach' where the adult becomes a permanent fixture, thereby damaging the child's independence and social interaction with peers. Support provision should reduce stressful situations, gradually exposing the child to new experiences or schools. Care should be taken to encourage social development, perhaps by a 'buddy' system, or close links with mainstream peers or schools. Links are particularly important for those teachers and pupils in mainstream, who require ready access to knowledge about the child with special needs, and to those who can help explain and advise.

It is impossible to over-stress the importance of establishing a good, co-operative relationship with the LEA, remembering that staff are there to help. Not all LEAs are the same; they have different budgets, policies and priorities. Parents should be firm and consistent when asking for support, while remembering that the LEA's funds are limited, and that the schools and help staff available may not be exactly what they want. The main focus for all involved in these procedures must be what is best for the child. Sometimes we all have to settle for the best fit.

References

DfEE (1997) *Excellence for all Children*. London: HMSO.
DfEE (2001) *The Code of Practice*. London: HMSO.
Dew-Hughes, D.M. (2002) *Educational Placement and Young People with Fragile X Syndrome: A National Survey*. Hastings: Fragile X Society.
Spencer, C. and Schnelling, K. (2002) *A Handbook for Pre-school Provision: The Code of Practice in Relation to the Early Years*. London: Fulton.

Recommended reading

Special Educational Needs – A Guide for Parents, is published by the DfEE and is available from Orderline, P.O. Box 5050, Sudbury, Suffolk. CO10 6ZQ. Tel. 0845 602260.

Part III

Education strategies

Chapter 11

Classroom adaptations
Good practice and work habits

Marcia Braden

Learning can be difficult for people with fragile X syndrome, especially for those most significantly affected. Exactly how the FMR-1 protein affects brain functioning is still being investigated; scientific data available to test specific educational methods is limited. Several studies, however, have given rise to the identification of a cognitive phenotype with a subsequent characterisation of relative strengths and weaknesses in those affected by fragile X syndrome.

Cognitive foundations for academic strategies

Because people with fragile X are being diagnosed at an earlier age there is a greater awareness of their overall deficits. Physical, behavioural and processing deficits all have impact on the cognitive style of those affected. Cognitive development requires the ability to pay attention, solve problems and recall information (Sobesky *et al.*, 1994, Sudhalter *et al.*, 1991, Scharfenaker *et al.*, 1996). These areas of deficit clearly affect performance in the classroom.

The most important research leading to a definition of a cognitive phenotype was that of Kemper *et al.* (1988), subsequently replicated by Hodapp *et al.* (1992), which evolved as the standard for defining learning strengths and weaknesses. These, and consequent studies, identified a particular processing style for males with fragile X on which intervention strategies have been built.

The cognitive profile initially defined by Kemper *et al.* (1988) describes a learning style that is unique. Males with fragile X perform better on tasks that include a simultaneous approach to understanding information, and clinical experience has proven that people with fragile X best understand information that is presented within that format (Braden, 2000). Information presented using a simultaneous approach resembles a 'visual whole'. The use of pictures, diagrams and visual associations supply the glue to solidify long-term memory of novel tasks. Long-term memory has been noted by several investigators as a relative strength in males with fragile X (Dykens, 1987; Kemper *et al.*, 1988 and Hodapp *et al.*, 1991).

Matching processing style with teaching methods

The Kemper (1988) study also provided evidence for academic treatment methods. People with fragile X process the sum of parts rather than the individual parts themselves: this style of information processing is counter to most traditional teaching methods.

Educational curricula most often include a scope and sequence of skills. Each skill is presented and learned in order as a prerequisite for the next. In addition, teaching methods usually include a sequential presentation. For example, teaching reading involves the acquisition of sounds, blended together in a sequential manner from left to right, which ultimately results in the reading of a whole word. This phonetic process requires the learner to utilise cognitive processes that are commonly deficient in males with fragile X. When the reading method utilises a phonetic approach, the child is required to:

- attend to the stimuli;
- recall the symbol;
- pair the symbol with a sound;
- recall the sound with the symbol;
- hold the sound/symbol while moving on to the next symbol;
- attend to the next symbol;
- repeat the earlier steps and blend the sound-symbols to form a word.

In addition to the cognitive components, Kemper *et al.* (1988) showed that people with fragile X seem to perform best with familiar and repetitive tasks. Novel and unrelated tasks are more difficult for them because they require flexible thinking, impulse control and reduced performance anxiety. Deficits in these areas affect performance on intelligence testing, because test material is intended to be unfamiliar in order to preserve the integrity of the test. People with fragile X perform better on achievement testing because the outcome is predictable, and this familiarity reduces anxiety.

Suggested teaching strategies

Suggested strategies for mathematics

- Use concrete manipulative materials to teach concepts and mathematical operations.
- Use visual cues whenever possible to reinforce mathematical operations.
- Allow additional time to reduce the possibility of provoking performance anxiety.
- Minimise auditory distractions during time periods when concentration is required (computation, problem-solving).
- Use diagrams, illustrations, and visual patterns whenever teaching a new concept.
- Use repetition and patterning whenever rote memory tasks are required.

Suggested strategies for auditory memory

- Give specific instructions in a slow, simple, and concrete manner.
- Place the student close to the instructor to ensure attention and concentration.
- Structure the environment to eliminate auditory distractions – use earphones, carrels, or seating arrangements.
- Vary presentation to include frequent breaks to avoid attention difficulties and lack of concentration.

Suggested strategies for visual organization

- Limit amount to be copied from printed or written materials.
- Simplify visually presented materials to eliminate a cluttered or excessively stimulating format.
- Provide visual cues – such as colour coding, numbering, and arrows – to organise written tasks.
- Give specific concrete cues when giving oral directions that require an organised format.
- Give additional time for written assignments, when needed.

Students with fragile X in the classroom

Because children spend much of their day at school, it is incumbent on teachers to understand their needs. The classroom environment is typically busy, fast-paced, noisy and includes a variety of transitions. A number of adults and peers interface daily with a variety of social interaction patterns. The cognitive and behavioural profile defined above may make this environment frustrating for the child with fragile X.

During the elementary school years, people with fragile X often experience significant academic growth, especially if intensive early intervention programmes are provided. At this early stage, schools usually provide inclusive educational opportunities. Although some preschool placements educate children with fragile X alongside their peers, it is more productive to employ intensive therapies (occupational therapy, Speech/language, cognitive training, behavioural intervention) at an early age and then transfer into inclusive education. This provides a stronger foundation for successful academic achievement and social development in the primary school.

Attentional problems also affect the acquisition of learning. Early intervention usually increases attention, and it is important to continue making this an educational goal because it is required by many learning activities in the primary school. Classroom rules require attending behaviours such as waiting in line, raising a hand and waiting until called upon. Cooperation through turn-taking is also important in an integrated placement.

Environment

The environment *in which* one learns can be as important as *what* is learned for children with fragile X. Because they exhibit behaviours that can appear reactionary, it is good educational practice to control the environment as much as possible in order to minimise these behaviours and foster learning.

A number of variables have been observed to affect academic outcome. Braden (1991) identified changes of routine to be more difficult for people with fragile X. Normal classrooms involve numerous transitions throughout the day – subject changes, physical transitions and classroom movement. The student with fragile X requires a consistent and predictable learning environment; for example, using a visual timetable promotes predictability while reducing anxiety.

Specific placement within the classroom may also be advisable. Often the student with fragile X demonstrates hypervigilance, which competes with focus and concentration. If the student is positioned in the front of the class with clear access to a door or exit, attending behaviours improve.

The size of the classroom and group are also important; smaller groups are more conducive to learning, especially for novel tasks. Classroom size is correlated with the noise level. People with fragile X are sensitive to noise, and often cover their ears if too loud noise levels become overwhelming. Motor excesses such as hand-flapping, moving and rocking may increase if the environment is particularly busy and overstimulating. Every attempt to reduce classroom noise level should be made, especially for younger children whose coping skills are not well developed.

People with fragile X are averse to noisy environments such as cafeterias, gymnasia and theatres. Supporting the student to attend part of a presentation, game or lunchtime will provide opportunities to become desensitised, gradually reducing anxiety in larger and more crowded environments.

What to teach

In general, most parents want their child's education to enhance ability and maximise their potential. Academic acquisition for children with fragile X is varied and generally tied to the severity of affectedness. Specific standards of what should be taught at what age are difficult to determine. Clinical experience, however, suggests it is beneficial to follow standard objectives.

Identifying strengths and weaknesses as the child develops can help formulate a learning rate. As this process continues, the challenge to find the right balance between teaching academic skills and functional skills (self-help and independence) ensues. Some academic knowledge is necessary in order to teach most functional skills. For example, to follow a written recipe, one must read and follow a sequence of directions. To measure ingredients, one must recognise numerals and fractions and match these to the amount given.

At an early age the child must be provided with knowledge that will foster independent functioning without restrictive supports. It is more natural for the adult with fragile X to live independent of family, within a multi-level support system based on need. This goal should be addressed early and supported throughout the school years.

Formulating a curriculum involves examining learning traits unique to people with fragile X and making any necessary adaptations to access the curriculum. Behavioural traits that may compete with the natural acquisition of skills must also modified. Braden (2000) presents a Suggested Curriculum Guide appropriate for this purpose, including a systematic presentation of necessary skills. The sequence is projected through four levels of academic development: preschool, elementary school, middle school and high school. Targeted skill areas include attending behaviours, language, problem-solving, social/sexual development and academics.

Mathematics

Deficits in mathematics, especially with reasoning and conceptual skills, have been reported (Kemper *et al.*, 1986; Mazzocco *et al.*, 1992; Miezejeski and Hinton, 1992). Providing cognitive restructuring about the execution of mathematics has strong implications for remediation. Teaching models should include a component to address faulty cognitions, which may contribute to phobic reactions or mathematics anxiety.

The ability to learn and apply mathematics has a strong impact on functional life skills. Effective teaching is essential and occurs only if strategies are multimodal and systematic.

Introducing concepts using concrete, 'hands on' materials will set the stage for higher-order learning. Because mathematics is sequential and requires the learner to build systematically from one step to the next, the curriculum used in regular education classrooms will most likely need to be adapted. Instruction must include demonstration, practice and positive reinforcement. It may be necessary to review the skills expected and focus on those that are functional, discarding those that are superfluous. This method of curricular adaptation is called 'skill streaming'. Adapting the curriculum requires assistance from a special educator familiar with fragile X and the child, along with the parent and classroom teacher.

Mathematics as a functional skill should be considered carefully when developing an educational plan. Basic skills, such as number identification, value, money, time telling, reading tables and recipes, should be taught.

People with fragile X syndrome have difficulty generalising mathematical concepts into situations for future problem-solving. Teaching should include patterns and visual gestalt whenever possible to reinforce complex mathematical processes.

Mathematics goals

1 Develop one-to-one correspondence/number value.
2 Identify and write whole numbers.
3 Use numbers in problem-solving situations.
4 Recognise geometry in classroom and community.
5 Improve functional understanding of maths skills in measurement and money.

Mathematics strategies

- Number lines/omit numbers in the line
- Teach maths patterns: $6 + 3 = 9 / 3 = 6 = 9 / 9 - 3 = 6$, etc.
- Coins matched to dots to teach value
- Use playing cards to sort by number
- Add using coins and objects
- Rulers and yardsticks
- Dot mathematics – superimposing dots onto the numeral to show value and configuration
- 1:1 correspondence with money + bank
- Use playing cards to arrange sequence
- Identifying more or less by cost and money

Reading

Reading is less contingent on sequential processing. It can be acquired using a variety of methods including a simultaneous approach where the configuration of word and contextual meaning can provide enough information for the learner to read.

Teaching children with fragile X to read is more successful if a high-interest, whole-language-based approach is used. They often lose interest and experience failure with phonetic or sequential approaches. Reading for various purposes is necessary to meet instructional goals. Teaching the specific vocabulary necessary to read a grocery list, follow directions, cook from a recipe or read a daily planner is essential for independence.

If the student's ability level is higher, simple word recognition can be used for general information, such as reading forms, newspapers or TV schedules. As the reading programme progresses, understanding factual information transcends into more abstract verbal reasoning. The student begins to understand inferences, predict outcomes and draw conclusions.

Sequential deficits may also interfere with comprehension of complex and abstract concepts. Using a cloze technique often works well to help increase general comprehension. This technique is similar to that described above for remediation of executive functioning deficits. Cloze technique presents a paragraph with beginning and ending sentences intact. Words are then systematically omitted throughout the passage. The reader fills in the blanks to make sense of the passage's content, which provides information necessary to understand the whole passage.

People with fragile X can and do learn to read, some quite successfully. The most successful reading programmes use a visual approach and linked computer activities to aid comprehension and conceptual orientation. Programmes based on the child's interests are particularly successful, such as The Logo Reading System (Braden, 1989), which uses well-known fast food logos to teach word recognition. Words are generalised into families and ultimately sentence strips. This programme readies the reader to move on to a more traditional reading curriculum.

Reading goals

- Develop reading readiness skills.
- Listen to acquire information – who, what, where?
- Read at first grade level.
- Read to acquire information – who, what where?
- Listen and read critically – what if? Why?
- Respond to a variety of written information such as recipes, schedules, newspapers.

Reading strategies

- sight words
- visual approach with patterns
- word configurations
- words with pictures
- rebus pictures and words
- labels on objects – whole word
- phrase cards of familiar greetings, sayings,
- story pictures with words

Written language

People with fragile X syndrome vary in written language ability. Usually, we write what we can say. Because males with fragile X are often tangential in spontaneous oral language, their written language may be the same.

Fine motor deficits and motor planning also affect writing. People with fragile X may have difficulty copying or writing down information. Assigning a scribe or using a keyboard can decrease the frustration caused by poor motor planning and lack of fine motor control. The chart below identifies written language goals and strategies.

Writing goals

- Trace and then write letters.
- Copy sentences.
- Express a thought in writing.
- Compose a story.

Writing strategies

- Pencil adaptations/grips
- Following lines and dotted lines
- Scrabble letters to form words
- Models and dotted line models
- Word puzzles with fill in squares
- Tactilely defined lined paper
- Connecting dot to dot to form a line
- Connecting numbers to numbers (dot to dot)
- Templates of letters and words (name, phone number, etc.)
- Fill in blanks in words (like hangman)

Curricular adaptations

It may be necessary to decide what is most important to teach at different educational stages. A common goal is to advance the learner to the greatest possible level of independence. Placement options may need to be discussed at various junctures. For example, it may be more prudent to place a young child in a special school, with undisturbed access to intensive individual therapies and instruction. As the child develops skills to tolerate a wider group, they can be included with mainstream peers, with special academic support. Children with fragile X included into mainstream schools may need curriculum evaluation and/or adaptations.

Table 11.1 illustrates curriculum design variables.

It may be too difficult at times to adapt the mainstream curriculum enough to be meaningful. If the student with fragile X does not have sufficient reading skills to benefit from an existing lesson, the support staff may develop a parallel curriculum, differentiated according to instructional complexity.

Prevocational and vocational education

During the middle school years, vocational interests are generally explored in a variety of environments. Time is spent assessing prerequisite work behaviours such as attending, asking for help, indicating when a job has been completed and working under supervision. Environmental work conditions, job content, skill requirements, staff ratio, acceptable behaviour and production rates are all explored during these middle years. Results from this ongoing process are shared with the high school staff and used to match students to job placements.

Table 11.1 Decision tree for curricular adaptations

Can the student with fragile X understand and interact with the mainstream curriculum?	
No	Yes
If functioning level is minimally delayed, curricular expectations are adapted based on functioning level; for example, the reading level is lower, but understanding of content is within normal limits	No adaptations are necessary. May require time adjustments or other accommodations such as skill streaming existing curricula to include only those skills that are important to maintaining competency in the classroom/course.
If the functioning level is moderately delayed, curricular adaptations include a parallel curriculum in which the same content is taught but with less volume and complexity of content.	
If the functioning level is significantly delayed and curricular adaptations cannot be provided due to level of cognitive functioning and delayed academic skills, a differentiated curriculum is used. This curriculum is different from the one presented in the regular education placement.	

A variety of vocational experiences have proven successful for those with fragile X. School programmes should provide a rotation of job placements to assess individuals' interests and competence. In high school, work experience studies can enhance academic credit while providing environments to practise appropriate work behaviours. Providing a flexible programme allows the student with fragile X to experience a variety of jobs and work settings.

Social development

Even though people with fragile X demonstrate a desire to interact with others, they often lack the necessary skills. Providing the vehicle for social development to evolve is as critical as teaching academic skills.

Social skills are correlated with speech and language development, but are not mutually exclusive. It is a mistake to wait until speech develops before teaching social skills or developing social interactions, such as sharing and taking turns. These can be expanded later into verbal exchanges as language develops. Good family and personal interaction patterns in the adult depend on early acquisition of social skills.

In the early years, children with fragile X are usually included with normally developing peers through most of the day. Even for those more seriously affected, there are times when group work, experiential activities and cooperative learning can maximise social experiences rather than academic instruction. Elementary classroom environments are more flexible in accepting individual differences. Elementary school teachers are more aware of developmental models, learning style and individualised instruction, making inclusion more effective at this age.

The role of a teaching assistant (or LSA) assigned to provide support should be defined so that it does not interfere with the principles of inclusion. Access to support should be provided without developing 'prompt dependency' in the child with fragile X, or interrupting their natural initiation of inquiry. The LSA can direct calming activities and sensory integration support when the child is stressed, or facilitate social interaction within a group of children.

Children at this age tend to accept individual differences and are less aware of academic deficits. Children with fragile X are relatively easily integrated because they are socially engaging and fun to be with. They should be encouraged to participate in social activities, lessons, sports or church groups during this time. Imitating peers and learning socially appropriate behaviours through repeated exposure will promote skill development of enormous benefit to future life. (Sobesky, 1996).

The social skills training described in Table 11.2 can be used by LSAs, teachers, school counselors or social workers. This model can be used to acquire interactive skills within a natural environment at school and in social activities.

The social behaviour of those with fragile X typically manifested during the middle school years is immature, even though their physical development is normal. This paradox presents a dilemma because society expects age-appropriate behaviour. People with fragile X respond well to rules, so it is effective to respond to immature social behaviours by emphasising their immaturity: 'That is what your little sister would do.' 'Now that you are 14 and wearing a rugby jersey, you don't chew with your mouth open anymore.'

Socio-sexual behaviours also require advance programme planning. Although the prerequisite social behaviours are reinforced during preschool and elementary school, a number of new challenges emerge when the preadolescent enters the middle-school years. A normal interest in sexual relationships intensifies, and the adolescent with fragile X may become obsessed with male/female relationships. Looking at magazine advertisements, or surfing television channels for romantic and intimate interaction, is a common way to gain access to the dating experience. Sex education at this point of development should include open discussion about curiosity. If it is not discussed, the adolescent may feel ashamed and try to hide his interest. If this voyeuristic behaviour is not addressed openly, it takes on a repressed quality that feeds obsessive-compulsive behaviour and could result in misunderstood motivation.

Developing social behaviours is imperative because, just like everyone else, people with fragile X need to be accepted in a wider social setting, to build competence and credibility in the world of work. During the middle- and high-school years, mainstream peers will model social relationships, such as dating, school dances and extracurricular activities. Students with fragile X will be exposed to those behaviours at school. Appropriate participation can be successful if adequate social behaviours have been learned.

Sex education is an area of great importance during the years of adolescence, but has typically been one of the most difficult to discuss. Schools should aim for honest and open discussions about sexual relationships and health with all students, including those with learning difficulties. Many mainstream peers are sexually active, others may wish to be, or may be hesitant, depending on their stage of social development. The lack of appropriate social skills can create complex and far-reaching problems for the young person with fragile X syndrome. It is not only possible but also essential to educate young people with fragile X about privacy, exploitation, voyeurism and sexual conduct. Many teaching programmes are available to help with socio-sexual development and behaviour for young people with a wide range of learning difficulties. These encourage learning through role-play, behaviour modeling, and discussion of issues based on media stories and real-life situations.

Table 11.2 Social skills training model

Level I

Turn taking with an adult

- Parent/teacher chooses a toy or activity of high interest.
- Adult verbally models 'my turn' or if the individual is non-verbal, points to self and takes a turn.
- Adult gives the individual game piece, toy, etc. and says 'your turn', pointing to him and shaping the pointing to self

- Individual indicates desired object, toy or activity.
- Individual waits his turn and imitates the role model.
- Individual points to himself, picks up toy, game piece and takes a turn.

This process continues for at least five exchanges.

Variations: Pegs, lego building, drawing a person (hangman), drawing cards from a deck, passing objects back and forth, etc.

Turn taking with another child

- Adult acts as facilitator and prompts whenever necessary.

- Individuals wait and take turns, pointing or verbalising when it is their turn.

Level II

Verbal exchange with an adult while developing spontaneously initiated verbal interaction

- Adult gives individual a compliment – 'I like your shirt'.
- Individual repeats – 'I like your shirt'.

- Individual responds with 'thank you'.
- Adult responds with 'thank you'.

As the interaction becomes spontaneous and the individual initiates the compliment without prompts from the facilitator, the adult begins the generalisation step.

Generalisation step: This step can be facilitated by a visual cue such as pegs, photograph, icon, rebus symbol or sentence strip.

Trainer holds up visual cue to prompt a broader array of complimentary statements. For example, picture of a face to prompt facial features, or a sentence strip to cue, 'I like your lego space ship', 'I like your drawing', etc.

Level III

Verbal exchange using facts of personal information already mastered in isolation

- Adult asks (from a list of personal information questions)
  'Do you have a brother?'
  'What is his name?'
  'Do you have a pet?'
  'Where do you live?'

- Individual answers the question and asks the same question.

Generalisation step: Adult facilitates this interaction between two students and prompts whenever necessary.

Table 11.2 continued

Level IV

Taking turns talking to an adult

This level is facilitated by a travelling notebook provided by parents to teacher/therapist. The parent includes information related to an experience, event, book read, movie, trip taken, etc. This information forms the basis for discussion. It is later replaced by a chart that the child fills in and uses in place of a sentence strip.

• Adult says 'Talk to me' and passes talking stick to the individual. If necessary prompts discussion about an event discussed in the notebook.	• Individual responds with information about a specific event, movie, or experience.
• Adult asks questions related to the information shared and begins to count the number of reciprocal exchanges dealing out cards.	• Individual responds to the question and offers a reciprocal response. A card is given after each appropriate exchange.

At the end of the discussion, cards are counted and tallied on personal interaction sheets.

Taking turns talking to another group member

• Adult facilitates interaction between two individuals within a group milieu.	• Members pass the talking stick back and forth. The stick cues the turn and reinforces waiting a turn.
• Adult begins the discussion with 'Talk to (other group member) about your trip to the zoo (or any other event noted in the traveling notebook)'.	• Individual responds to other group member, but waits his turn.

Level V

Taking turns talking and listening

This level is to reinforce the importance of sharing talking time and listening. Questioning after listening is prompted verbally or with a visual icon or symbol. Formulating questions appropriate to the discussion is also reinforced. The use of cards and the talking stick can also be employed to signal the speaker.

• Adult holds up visual icon, current event from a newspaper or presents an idea to be discussed	• Group member responds with appropriate verbal exchange.
	• Group member passes talking stick to group member of his choice and listens.
• Group member formulates a question about the subject discussed.	• Group member answers the questions and listens.

Variation: Discussions can be based on newspaper events (can use weekly readers or children's sections of the newspaper), sports events (males with fragile X syndrome usually love sports), contrived scenarios about taking a trip to Disney World, a local amusement park, TV game show, etc.

(Taken with permission, Braden, 2000)

Conclusion

The process of educating a child with fragile X is arduous and ongoing. It requires much commitment from parents and professionals. It is now clear that there are specific educational strategies that used appropriately will enhance overall achievement and functional independence.

In the past, parents negotiated their way through an educational maze towards disappointing outcomes. Many were told that their children were ineducable and incapable of living independent lives. With advances in research and clinical experience, there is today greater promise and direction for these children. The Statement of Special Educational Needs and Individual Education Programmes protect their rights and ensure appropriate educational intervention. Although some practitioners promote a non-categorical philosophy of educational delivery, many others disagree. The unique learning style of people with fragile X syndrome needs to be addressed specifically; one size does not fit all. It is important to continue working towards a better understanding of this unique learning style, while at the same time striving to match educational strategies and teaching techniques. In this way, people with fragile X will be confident of achieving their full learning potential.

References

Braden, M. (1989) *The Logo Reading System*, 100 E. Street, Vrain #200, Colorado Springs, CO 80903.

Braden, M. (1991) 'Screening Instrument for FRA-X Males', unpublished dissertation.

Braden, M. (2000) *Fragile: Handle with Care; More About Fragile X Syndrome – Adolescents and Adults*, Spectra Publishing Co., Dillon, CO., pp. 30, 90, 103. 108.

Dykens, E.M., Hodapp, R.M. and Leckman, J.F. (1987) 'Strengths and weaknesses in the intellectual functioning of males with fragile X syndrome.' *American Journal of Medical Genetics* 28(1): 13–15.

Hodapp, R.M., Dykens, E.M., Ort, W.I., Zelinsky, D.G. and Leckman, J.F. (1991) 'Changing patterns of intellectual strengths and weaknesses in males with fragile X syndrome.' *Journal of Autism and Developmental Disorder* 21: 503–516.

Hodapp, R.M., Leckman, J.F. Dykens, E.M., Sparrow, S., Zelinsky, D. and Ort, S. (1992) 'K-ABC profiles in children with fragile X syndrome, Down syndrome and nonspecific mental retardation.' *American Journal of Mental Retardation* 97: 39–46.

Kemper, M.B., Hagerman, R.J., Ahmad, R.S. and Mariner, R. (1986) 'Cognitive profiles and the spectrum of clinical manifestations in heterozygous fragile (X) females.' *American Journal of Medical Genetics* 23: 139–156.

Kemper, M.B., Hagerman, and Altshul-Stark, D. (1988) 'Cognitive profiles of boys with the fragile X syndrome.' *American Journal of Medical Genetics* 30, 1–2: 191–200.

Mazzocco, M.M., Hagerman, R.J. and Pennington, B.F. (1992) 'Problem solving limitations among cytogenetically expressing fragile X syndrome women.' *American Journal of Medical Genetics,* 43: 1/2, 78–86.

Miezejeski and Hinton (1992) *International Fragile X Syndrome Conference Proceedings*. Spectra Publishing Co., Dillon, CO.

Scharfenaker, S., O'Connor, R., Stackhouse, T., Braden, M., Hickman, L. and Gray, K. (1996). 'An integrated approach to intervention.' in R.J. Hagerman and A. Cronister (eds) *Fragile X Syndrome: Diagnosis, Treatment and Research,* 2nd edition. Johns Hopkins University Press, Baltimore, MD, pp. 349–402.

Sobesky, W.E. (1996) 'The treatment of emotional and behavioral problems in fragile X.' in R.J. Hagerman and A. Cronister (eds) *Fragile X Syndrome: Diagnosis, Treatment and Research*, 2nd edition. Johns Hopkins University Press, Baltimore, MD, pp. 332–348.

Sobesky, W.E., Pennington, B.F., Porter, C., Hull, C.E. and Hagerman, R.J. (1994) 'Emotional and neurocognitive deficits in fragile X.' *American Journal of Medical Genetics,* 51: 378–385.

Sudhalter, V., Scarborough H.S. and Cohen, I. C. (1991) Syntactic delay and pragmatic deviance in the language of fragile X males. *American Journal of Medical Genetics* 38:493–497.

Sudhalter, V. (1992) 'The language system of males with fragile X syndrome.' In R. J. Hagerman and P. McKenzie (eds), *1992 International Fragile X Conference Proceedings.* Spectra Publishing, Dillon, CO: pp. 165–166.

Further reading

Bennetto, L. and Pennington, B.F. (1996) 'The Neuropsychology of Fragile X Syndrome,' in R. J. Hagerman and A. Cronister (eds) *Fragile X Syndrome: Diagnosis, Treatment and Research.* 2nd Edition. Johns Hopkins University Press, Baltimore, MD, pp. 210–241.

Bourne, E. J., (1995). *The Anxiety and Phobias Workbook.* New Harbinger Publications, Inc. Oakland, CA.

Braden, M., (1999) 'Sex Education for Children with Disabilities: A beginning conversation.' *The New Hampshire Challenge,* PO Box 579, Dover, NH 03821–0579.

Braden, M. (2000a) 'Education,' in J.D. Weber, (ed.) *Children with Fragile X Syndrome: A Parent's Guide,* Woodbine House, Bethesda, MD.

Braden, M. (2000b) 'Treatment of aggression in children and adults with fragile X syndrome.' *The Foundation Quarterly,* Spring 2000.

Freund, L. and Reiss, A.L. (1991) 'Cognitive profiles associated with the FraX syndrome in males and females.' *American Journal of Medical Genetics* 38: 542–547.

Gibb, C. (1992) 'The most common cause of learning difficulties: a profile of Fragile X Syndrome and its implications for education', *Educational Research* 34(3).

Graham, P.J., Turk, J. and Verhulst, F. (1999) 'Behavioral and cognitive psychotherapies' in *Child Psychiatry: A Developmental Approach.* Oxford: Oxford University Press, pp. 401–420.

Grigsby, J., Kemper, M.B. and Hagerman, R.J. (1992) ' Verbal learning and memory among heterozygous fragile X females.' *American Journal of Medical Genetics* 43: 111–115.

Hagerman, R. J. (1987) 'Fragile X syndrome.' *Curr. Probl. Pediatr.* 11: 627–674.

Hagerman, R.J. (1996) 'Physical and behavioral phenotype' in R.J. Hagerman and A. Cronister (eds) *Fragile X Syndrome: Diagnosis, Treatment and Research.* 2nd Ed. Johns Hopkins University Press, Baltimore, MD, pp. 3–87.

Hagerman, R. J. (2000) 'Treatment of aggression in children and adults with fragile X syndrome.' *The Foundation Quarterly,* Winter.

Maccini, P. and Hughes, C.A. (1997) 'Mathematics interventions for adolescents with learning disabilities.' *Learning Disabilities Research & Practice* 12(3): 168–176. Lawrence Erlbaum Associates, Inc.

Maurice, C., Green, G. and Luce, S.C. (1996) *Behavioral Intervention for Young Children with Autism.* Pro-Ed, Inc. San Antonio, TX.

Mazzocco, M.M. and O'Connor, R. (1993) 'Fragile X Syndrome; a guide for teachers of young children', *Young Children,* November: 73–77.

Mercer, D.D., and Miller, S.P. (1992) 'Teaching students with learning problems in mathematics to acquire, understand, and apply basic mathematics facts.' *Remedial and Special Education* 13(3): 19–35.

Myles, B.S., and Simpson, R.L. (1998) *Asperger Syndrome, A Guide for Educators and Parents.* Pro-Ed, Inc., San Antonio, TX.

Papolos, D.F., and Papolos, J. (1999) *The Bipolar Child,* Random House, Inc., New York, NY.

Schopmeyer, B.B. and Lowe, F. (1992). *The Fragile X Child.* Singular Publishing, San Diego, CA.

Spiridigliozzi, G., Lachiewicz, A., MacMordo, C., Vizoso, C.A., O'Donnell, C., McConkie-Rosell, A., and Burgess D. (1994) *Educating Boys with Fragile X Syndrome: A Guide for Parents and Professionals.* Durham, NC: Duke University Medical Center.

Sudhalter,V., Cohen, I.L., Silverman W.P. and Wolf-Schein, E.G. (1990) 'Conversational analyses of males with fragile X, Down syndrome and autism: a comparison of the emergence of deviant language.' *American Journal of Mental Retardation* 94: 431–441. *The New Hampshire Challenge,* Fall. PO Box 579, Dover, NH 038210579.

Tranfaglia, M.R. (1995) *A Parent's Guide to Drug Treatment of Fragile X Syndrome.* FRAXA Research Foundation, West Newbury, MA.

Chapter 12

Classroom strategies for fragile X and autism

Julie Taylor

Our specialist school educates children with fragile X syndrome and autistic spectrum disorders (ASD). Over the years we have built up a bank of strategies that have achieved good results; the children learn, develop and gain control over their individual difficulties. Some of our practices are based on off-the shelf approaches, but mostly they were gleaned from parents, professionals, literature, past experience and the 'try it and see what works' approach.

We have a few golden rules for all children, but each of our strategies is adapted and adjusted to suit the needs of the individual child. Our golden rules are:

* stay calm;
* mean what you say and say what you mean;
* aim to raise the child's self-esteem;
* stand back, wait and avoid prompt dependency;
* smile and have fun!

These apply to all children – whatever their difficulties, ages or level of development. They form the basis of good teaching practice, and are even more essential to teaching both children with fragile X syndrome and those on the autistic spectrum.

The strategies we have found successful can be divided into five categories: speech and language; social skills; cognitive functioning classroom management and behaviour.

Speech and language

Remember to praise when the speech is good. Don't criticise or correct all the time. With perseverative speech say, 'You can say that three times and then I won't listen any more.' Make sure the target is reachable and praise when they stop themselves. Teach the child a phrase to say when he doesn't understand something or he needs help. This will reduce anxiety – but only if an adult attends to him straight away. If a child has difficulty understanding instructions then try breaking them down and give one at a time not a sequence.

Group instructions may be a problem; always bear in mind that the child may not realise that, 'Everyone come here', means them too. Use their names and give individual instructions. However, you will need to point out that everyone does mean them as well. Responding appropriately to group instructions is an excellent teaching target. Some children can take up to ten seconds to process and respond to what has been said, so always give them time. If you repeat the instruction too soon they may have to start all over again.

Snack times and lunchtimes are ideal opportunities for promoting good language. Our aim is for all our children to ask for what they want without being prompted. It is vital that each child learns to initiate the communication. Food times are often the most motivating and much progress is made. Keep all facial expressions and gestures clear and consistent and make sure they match what you are saying. Remember, just because a child chooses not to look at you does not mean that they are not listening.

In order to help with echolalia, limit the use of direct questions and instead use open-ended statements, such as 'Today the weather is . . . ' or 'After dinner we will go . . . ' rather than 'Where are we going after dinner?'

Social skills

Although many children never progress beyond parallel play, always encourage turn-taking and sharing activities. We use counting to help with turn-taking. We have a large trampoline in the garden; each child who wants a turn bounces for a count of ten and then has to get off. One family used counting to help their son overcome his fear of hand dryers in public toilets. By starting with a count of two and a promise of an ice cream afterwards he managed to stay in the toilet for two seconds. Gradually the count was increased and they would say, ' Yes – toilet for ten and then ice cream.' Eventually the family could go out for a whole day because their son was able to use public toilets.

Over-the-top praise can be very uncomfortable for our children. Think of praise as an acknowledgement and be careful about making it public unless you have the child's permission. Always praise the behaviour; praising the child can confuse them with exactly what the praise is meant for. We use simple praise and identify the behaviour, saying 'good sitting', or 'good writing'. This tells the child directly what you want and expect; it also directs the attention of other children so that they can imitate the 'praiseworthy' behaviour. Allow time for contact with normally developing peers. We join the adjacent mainstream school for playtime every morning and mainstream children come into our garden to play after lunch. Do not insist that the child with fragile X or autism plays with the other children, stand back and quietly praise any appropriate interaction.

Cognitive functioning

Identify motivators and strengths and use these throughout the day. We say, 'First we will do this and then you can do that.' The 'work first and then play' system works really well. For some children we present this pictorially; a picture of a number puzzle is placed on the left and a picture of the desired computer on the right. We say 'First puzzle (point to the puzzle) and then computer (point to the computer).' Always work left to right or top to bottom. Once the child learns they have to complete one task to gain the desired activity, increase to two or more tasks.

Encourage thinking, say 'What will happen next?' or 'He fell off his chair because . . . ?' Sometimes say, 'What do you think?' in answer to one of his questions. If a child is crying tell the others, 'He is crying because . . . ' Use every opportunity to encourage each child to think for themselves.

Try to avoid prompt dependency. Let them make mistakes and then help them to find solutions for themselves. A big problem for children with fragile X and ASD who are supported in mainstream lessons is that they are prompted all the time. By trying too hard to make inclusion successful, helpers can inadvertently discourage thinking by prompting the child through everything; when the helper withdraws the child cannot cope.

Use the child's strengths and don't dwell on what they find difficult. The most successful way to lower children's self-esteem is to make them keep practising something they find difficult. Be alert for the child with fragile X who perseveres with a failed strategy. Their persistence and industry is often exemplary, but encourage them to think of another way to do things if the first way didn't work. Discuss why the approach was unsuccessful, and try to encourage them to think of alternative strategies. This flexibility of thinking and executive functioning is very difficult for children with fragile X and autism, and therefore a skill they need to practise. Computers can be very motivating because the troublesome human element is removed and the child is completely in control. However, many computer programs for teaching early years skills have the drawback of mirroring the very inflexibility of approach you are trying to reduce. Choose a variety of programs that teach the same skill in different ways.

Classroom management

Busy cluttered environments do not suit autistic children or those with fragile X. Clearly demarcated areas and simple displays cut down on distractions. Children with high levels of distractibility learn better in rooms with minimum visual stimuli and effective sound-proofing. We use group activities primarily to teach social skills. We don't expect the children to learn anything academic in a group. They are often too anxious in close proximity to others to learn very much.

Provide clear predictable routines throughout the day. Set up a class schedule along one wall at the children's height. For the younger or less able children captioned photographic schedules are best. Use Velcro to attach it to the wall. Daily schedules should begin with 'come to school' and end with 'go home' (or to Granny's or respite). A typical schedule for the morning might be: Come to school – read books – literacy – assembly – playtime – drinks – numeracy – get ready for dinner – eat dinner – clean teeth – garden play.

Some children might need more detailed reminders such as 'toilet' or 'coat on peg' Pre-planned, visual schedules make change in the school day easier to manage. You might say, 'It's raining so play inside.' If necessary, take a child outside to see the rain, remove 'playtime' from the wall and put in its place a photograph of inside play. Some children may think they can change the day by altering the schedule. I found Colin in the classroom one morning looking very pleased; he had changed the schedule to his ideal day: Minibus – swimming – drink – playtime – walk – eat dinner – go home.

Some children have individual schedules. We place these vertically on the wall with a photograph of the child at the top and a finished pocket at the bottom. Laminated 3cm square captioned symbols are arranged from top to bottom. As the child finishes each part of the schedule they place it in the finished envelope and look for the next activity. Some children take the symbol with them, to assembly or swimming. This helps to cut down on anxiety, it also reminds them to replace the symbol in their schedule afterwards to find out what comes next. Our children are anxious when they don't know what is happening. Schedules give them the markers to help make sense of their day. When we adults attend a training course, the first thing we do is to check the programme for workshops and lunch breaks. We all feel more confident when we know what is going to happen.

For children who have problems making choices, we use a choice board for when work is finished – first work and then play, which includes computer, train, drawing, listening centre or puppets. Again we use laminated symbols and Velcro. Children make their choice and put it in the choice box. Choices are pre-selected by the teacher, and can be used to limit numbers operating the computer or encourage a child to choose a new or more suitable activity. Provide a 'finished' tray for completed work, but remember that work in the tray stays there. Don't take it out later and ask the child to do more. Finished is finished.

We use music to mark out the day and to give five-minute warnings of an activity ending. Sound a wind chime and say, 'five more minutes and then it will be numeracy time'. Encourage the children in classroom management, putting away and getting out their own equipment. Play soft music during changeover periods to keep everyone as calm as possible.

We keep captioned photograph albums of all trips and events as well as a year book. We celebrate every child's birthday – a party for Key Stage 1 and an outing for Key Stage 2. This provides a constantly updated record of what the children are doing and how they are growing and changing. These albums are kept in our front hall. The children read them before lunch and take them home as library books. Ex-pupils who visit always ask to look at the old albums. Two former pupils recently spent an afternoon looking through the albums of their time with us. One said, 'This is my life'. We use the old albums to raise a child's self-esteem. We find an album showing the child in Year 1 and say, 'Remember when you were five, you screamed and screamed and now look at you – you are big and sensible – a lovely boy!'

Some children worry about absent children or adults. We help anxious children by having photographs of everyone on the classroom door, with an appropriate caption underneath: at school, at the dentist, at a meeting.

Behaviour

Our main rule is, 'Say what you mean and mean what you say.' The children must trust you to carry out what you say. Beware of ultimatums such as, 'If you do that again then no playtime,' when you haven't the staff available to carry it out. Children with fragile X and ASD often misunderstand the more complex meaning of language, and can seem to be uncooperative or even defiant. When Bob was very young adults would shout 'Get down!' when he climbed up a fence or tree. He would keep on going up. Eventually they realised that he thought 'Get down' was what he was doing. They changed to 'Bob, feet on the floor' and he did.

Complex language forms are so frequently used by adults they can overlook the confusion these cause the child who is struggling with comprehension. What, for example, would be the literal meaning of 'stand in a line', ' fold your arms' or 'keep your hands to yourself'? Adult language contains many hidden meanings or social understandings, which are not part of the language structure of children with fragile X and ASD. We may say, 'shall we start work now?' We mean that we want and expect them to start work, but the child may interpret this as offering them the choice. Always tell the child what you want them to do, rather than ask. Say, 'sit here please' not 'would you like to sit here?' What will you do if they say 'No'?

Because of their anxiety, especially in social situations, our children try hard to control everything around them but they are unable to deal with the control. We say 'It's not up to you, so don't worry about that.' We set very clear and consistent behaviour boundaries.

We have a red chair for discipline and say, 'Sit on the red chair and count to . . . ' One boy worked out that if he counted quickly he didn't have to sit for so long! We are persistent; if a child has to sit on the chair fifteen times in a break because he keeps kicking off his shoes, we know eventually he will give up. We remain calm and asocial but consistent. When he finally keeps his shoes on then we gently praise, 'You are being sensible.' Use the words sensible and silly – not good and naughty. Naughty is an emotive label and one to avoid. If we do good work and behave appropriately, then we are sensible. Remember to praise the child who is being sensible and avoid giving lots of attention to the one who has been silly. We limit our use of the word 'No', saving it for emergencies. Children react adversely to the word 'No' particularly if they hear it frequently. We try to say 'Yes – later', as much as we can.

Tone of voice can make a big difference. We use a minibus and a car to take everyone swimming. One day a child was being silly whilst waiting for the bus. I said, 'Oh, dear. You can't go on the bus – you will have to go in my car.' A sad and sorry boy sat in the car to go swimming. At the pool his twin brother was so good getting dressed I said, 'You are such a sensible boy – you can come back to school in my car,' and showed I was pleased with him. The journey back to school was very different with a happy boy sitting in the car.

Always make sure behaviour targets are reachable and then move on gradually. Sitting for ten seconds is an achievable goal, ten minutes is not. Work up to ten minutes' sitting by praising the achievement of gradual targets. Behaviour targets are displayed in our classroom. Children must agree with their target and if possible set it themselves. A 'hot air balloon' for each child is captioned with their target. Underneath on the 'basket' is a space for smiley face stamps. When the child has accumulated ten stamps, they get a reward.

We provide areas in each class where a child can calm down if they are getting cross. Many of our children like to draw what is making them angry; they make a 'grumpy crate' containing paper, pencils and felt pens. We also offer soft music, water to drink, books to look at or an adult to listen.

All children need to feel good about themselves, especially those who find learning difficult and the world a confusing place. Think about how to raise their self-esteem. A good starting point for this is identifying what makes you feel good about yourself. Most of all, keep things simple and enjoy being with them.

Chapter 13

Home and school

Developing a genuine partnership

Claire Wolstencroft

> Don't ever give up. Every quarter inch of improvement is worth striving for.
> Keep searching for ways to teach.
>
> (Campbell, 1992)

Children are constantly moving between two very different worlds: home and school. For the child with fragile X syndrome, transition, the change between different activities is difficult. Often the greatest transitions in their lives are those between home and school. If school and home work together effectively, they can minimise the stresses of these transitions and make a real difference to the child's life. In this chapter I hope to suggest how this can be done. All the suggestions are simple, good teaching practices, easy to apply, and often applicable to the whole class.

The development of a co-ordinated, consistent approach linking home and school is essential. Many parents attempt to teach children at home using commercial workbooks, generally designed for the 'average' child, and may not realise that there are other, often better, ways to teach their child. The teacher of the special child can show parents ways to reinforce key skills at home, and explain the purpose of the exercises so that parents can understand their educational value. This way the parent can feel they are a valued member of the child's learning team and build up a good relationship with the school. It demonstrates that the school has the child's best interest at heart. If learning is real and relevant and fun for both child and parent then a great learning partnership can be formed and maintained.

Children with fragile X syndrome often have behavioural difficulties, ranging from noisy uncontrollable tantrums to being quietly and stubbornly withdrawn. This difficult behaviour is often a direct result of not knowing or understanding what is going on around them. Developing a daily calendar for use at home and school during parent/teacher meetings at the beginning of each school year will provide a steady daily rhythm for the child, and also give teacher and parent insight into the other half of the child's life. It needs to be accessible to the child by illustrating it with line drawings or photos so that they can refer to it independently. If the classroom calendar is sent to the parents they can spend time each morning discussing the school routine for the day. Transition between activities will be anticipated and thus less stressful for the child.

Of course routines change, and unexpected events happen, but it is simple to either redraw the day's schedule, or change photos to update the calendar. These changes can then be shown and discussed. The child with fragile X will feel more in control of events, which will reduce unwanted behaviours. Looking forward to events can be difficult for a child who struggles with the concept of 'next week' or 'next month'. Crossing out days on a calendar helps with this, and reinforces the days of the week and the idea of time passing.

The routine home–school diary can be turned into a great learning resource. Children with fragile X syndrome generally have communication difficulties; teachers and parents may glean little about the other part of the child's life. Although some children have no speech at all, many do. However, a typical conversation with a fragile X child often goes: 'What did you do yesterday?' 'Pooh! Rubbish you. Go away'

There is a simple technique that can focus and stimulate conversation and make home–school diary more meaningful. Parent and child sit down and choose a significant event to record. They draw pin figures (artistic skill is unimportant) and describe what they are drawing. As the child joins in, the parent records what the child says about the event. The following example shows how conversation can develop from this.

Christopher was asked what had happened one Sunday; he gave the normal expressive reply, 'Pooh . . . go away'. His mother drew some stick figures at the top of the page. 'This is Mummy and she had a fork. This is Christopher and he had . . . ' Christopher joined in. 'I had the spade, Nicky had some bulbs.' The words were recorded, as the story was written, and spoken aloud. 'Yesterday Christopher, Nicholas and Mummy planted some bulbs. Christopher dug big holes in the soil with a spade.' Christopher added 'A big heavy one!' That was excellent descriptive language and deserved to be recorded. He grabbed the pen and scribbled, rushed to the window, looked out and said, 'Oh! It's got lumps in.' He added some lumps to his scribble soil and drew green shoots. In this way, much relevant descriptive language and use of observational skills resulted from simple stick drawings.

Some children with fragile X syndrome will have less spoken language than this, but the home–school diary can still be turned into a living, relevant language resource. It can encourage children to talk about or express their feelings, a difficult thing for many children with fragile X. As their greatest strengths are in visual processing, many find it hard to deal with fantasy and abstract ideas, preferring the real and familiar. Events written, illustrated with simple drawings and discussed with the child become real and understandable and provide comforting continuity. By using photos and pictures, the home–school diary becomes an exciting journal of the child's life and a basis for language work. Also the child is communicating in a less stressful way as this activity naturally takes place side-by-side, rather than face-to-face. It capitalises on their tendency to learn by incidental observation as they sit and observe the writing process. Recording comments as the child actually expresses them provides a record of how their speech has developed over time.

This visual approach can be used to improve communication between child and carer. Children with fragile X understand information more easily when it is presented in visual form. Transition is difficult; to prepare the child for changes or a new and stressful situation, the teacher or parent can sit alongside the child and draw pictures illustrating the event as they talk about it. The child is given this to hold and refer to as the event unfolds. The desired behaviour from the child can be included in the drawing too. For example, a picture can be drawn of the child sitting quietly. This visual approach gives the child some control over events. These drawings can be incorporated into the daily journal, giving a record of situations the child faced, and their responses.

Just as a visual approach is used for daily routines and journals, a similar approach can be used for behaviour management. Again, the parent sits beside the child and draws a cartoon strip illustrating the inappropriate behaviour and the desired response. This approach was used when a child threw a stone, and it helped him to understand the consequences of his behaviour. To work effectively, the child should be quiet and calm enough to communicate with. Such behaviour management strategies will be more effective if used consistently by parents and teachers.

Homework should be imaginative and enjoyable for child and parent. It is heartbreaking when one's 11-year-old is sent home with a book the neighbour's 4-year-old is reading. It is also discouraging for the child, who may be aware of their difficulties, especially if younger siblings are streaking ahead. Developing personal and individual language resources can boost self-esteem, especially when the child contributes to them. A personalised reading book made with photos of the child, family and friends may be a better way to introduce basic vocabulary than a commercial reading scheme. If the school suggests words and language to be used, books can be made at home by the parent and child together and sent into school for reading.

A first book might have photographs of family and favourite objects with words written underneath the pictures. To encourage generalisation, a problem area for children with fragile X, the same words should be presented in many different ways. If family names are being taught, parents could help the child make place cards, napkin rings or doorplates for the home, or label their possessions. Assessing whether a child knows the words may be difficult; they may refuse to read 'mummy,' 'daddy', but may be able to label beds so the family knows where to sleep.

If parents know what topics a child is working on at school, then the associated language can be reinforced at home. If the topic is weather, the teacher could suggest the child makes a chart at home, and watches the television weather forecasts. Reading books with a vocabulary similar to the topic may be chosen from the school and local libraries. Choose books with vocabulary, situations and words familiar to the child, and pictures relating to the text, to capitalise on the child's visual learning style.

The development of writing skills is often a problem for the child with fragile X, due to hypotonia and poor fine motor control. Parents can work on this area too. The child uses the same pincer grip for jigsaws with small knobs on the pieces and for holding a pencil. Sorting out beads also develops grip. Parents might experiment with different pencil grips or writing tools to see which their child finds easiest. A fun way of practising writing at home is to do pavement art on the patio. To develop left to right movement, parents can draw on the floor roads and garages going left to right. Toy cars are lined up on the left and driven to the right, the route traced with chalk. This is putting learning skills into context. Fun activities to learn letters include drawing the letters on the outside wall with a water pistol, or covering a work surface with flour and drawing letters with a finger, or making velvet letter shapes to follow with the finger. Mobiles and posters illustrating letters, words or concepts being learnt can be made for the child's bedroom.

Besides the curriculum for each term, parents need to know and understand the school's policy on teaching key skills such as direction of letter formation, style of handwriting taught, and basic teaching vocabulary. 'Sorting, Classifying and Data Handling' sounds complicated, but is just what we do when tidying the cutlery drawer and counting knives, forks and spoons. Practical activities carried out as part of daily living at home are the child's greatest learning resource. In maths, practical activities are absolutely vital to learning key skills, because maths is an area of difficulty for the child with fragile X. If children are doing sorting activities at school, the parent can be given a worksheet with ideas for sorting activities such as sorting clothes, cutlery, or tools. Simple counting can be done while laying the dinner table. For one to one correspondence, place settings could be drawn on a paper tablecloth.

Teachers should give parents the mathematical vocabulary in use: similar, different, same, top, bottom. If the child is measuring at school, the parent should know the units being used: hand spans, centimetres, cups or litres. Parents can involve the child in any measuring task at home, whether making curtains or a cake.

Money skills should be learned in context. Children often travel to school and home in taxis, without the opportunity to visit a corner shop to buy treats. Children with fragile X often find shops noisy and distressing, so parents may avoid taking them shopping. This means that, in addition to the children's difficulty with handling money, they also often experience it less often than other children. Opportunities to handle money in real-life situations must be consciously created and encouraged. Before visiting a shop, a visual cartoon strip of the trip could be drawn. Individual shopping lists can be made by collecting labels in a folder. The child can select the labels for the required items and then help with the financial transactions.

Home school liaison is vital. It is so much less confusing for the child if the activities done at home complement the school programme. Learning needs to be real, and to be fun for the child and parent. Above all, in a working home and school partnership a parent can see that the school values their child and this creates an atmosphere in which the child can grow in independence and self-worth.

Reference

Campbell, Marta (1992) *Say it With Pictures*. Fragile X Foundation. USA.

Chapter 14

Speech and language therapy

Catherine Taylor

The child with fragile X syndrome is referred to throughout this chapter as *she*, for simplicity and as a reminder that the condition is not confined to boys.

Speech and language impairment

Fragile X syndrome is associated with a particular developmental and behavioural phenotype. Although individual children can be affected to very different degrees, they tend to share a profile of skills and weaknesses, which usually has a significant impact on communication skills.

It is clear that the child's overall developmental delay will affect, amongst other skills, her acquisition of speech and language. In fragile X the general learning disability can range from mild to profound with varied affects on speech and language acquisition. Profoundly learning disabled children may not acquire useful speech. Mildly learning disabled children will experience subtler difficulties.

In addition to the developmental delay affecting speech and language skills there are typically other difficulties of a specifically oral and linguistic nature that are characteristic of fragile X. The combination of these two factors naturally impacts directly on the individual's communication skills.

Other, non-linguistic features of fragile X influence the overall communication picture. The common deficits in attention and executive functioning and the marked degree of shyness and social anxiety tend to impact less directly, but often as significantly, on the child's ability to interact successfully.

In practice the linguistic and non-linguistic features of the fragile X phenotype interrelate to such an extent that it is often impossible to pinpoint a single origin for a particular communication difficulty. With such a complex and varied picture, speech and language therapy for children with fragile X must concern itself with a multitude of very diverse skills, all of which are necessary for effective, fluent and enjoyable communication.

General principles of therapy

Knowledge of the particular difficulties likely to be experienced in fragile X and how they might interact, will naturally inform the choice of particular therapeutic techniques. However the basic principles of speech and language therapy are the same as for any other children with communication difficulties. They must be founded on a thorough knowledge of the normal process of speech and language acquisition and the impairments caused by breakdown anywhere within the process. This expertise should be accompanied by a thorough appreciation and use of cognitive-behavioural and systemic theories.

The cognitive-behavioural approach to intervention, based on learning theory, is a highly effective model. This addresses both behaviours and thoughts as means of developing children's skills. It is problem focused, primarily concerned with the 'here and now'; it emphasises collaboration between the therapist, the individual and those closely connected with her. The behavioural viewpoint lays stress on describing and defining actions and aims, on rewarding successful attempts, and on gradually approaching the final objective through a series of small successive steps. From a cognitive point of view, learning can be consolidated by shifting the emphasis from activity-based intervention towards developing self-awareness and re-evaluating long-held thoughts and assumptions. The individual can be encouraged to appraise the evidence for holding particular beliefs, for example concerning their success with communication or with making friends. This can lead them towards a more realistic and positive self-image. The cognitive approach also stresses the active nature of learning with the individual moving through a cyclical process of perception, internalisation, generalisation and active experimentation.

Systemic approaches complement cognitive-behavioural approaches and can be used simultaneously. They emphasise the relationship between an individual's beliefs and behaviours and those of others within their system. Systems can be family groups, class groups, cultural groups, and so on. Any change in one part of a system is likely to necessitate or precipitate change in other parts of the same system. Any changes in an individual's attitude towards communication or their expectations of interaction are likely to directly affect and be affected by the actions, the attitudes and expectations of those around them.

The following framework for effective speech and language therapy derives from an integration of cognitive-behavioural and systemic perspectives.

Assessment

To ensure success, intervention must be founded on thorough assessment. Speech and language therapists should take the lead in this process. Information from many sources, from direct observation and testing, parents, carers and teaching staff, must be carefully collated. We should know the child's optimum level of understanding and quality of expression, and how these are affected by fluctuating attention levels and attitudes to different social situations. Personality traits, interests, likes and dislikes need to be taken into account as well as the particular constraints under which a home or class may operate.

Agreement of aims and strategies

Once the type and extent of difficulty a child experiences has been clarified, therapeutic goals will suggest themselves. The speech and language therapist, teacher and parents/carers should then meet and discuss which aims to establish, their order and ways of realising them. Without full agreement between parents/carers and professionals on these issues, the child's progress is likely to be slow and haphazard.

The focus of therapy will vary for each individual and family, according to differing priorities at home and school. Realistic goals should be negotiated and compromises may be necessary in the interests of obtaining agreement.

Strategies for achieving these aims also need to be discussed and agreed. All parties must be sensitive to the needs of the child and those around her in different situations. Once a strategy or approach is agreed it should be used in the same way at home and at school. Everyone should be clear about exactly how to manage or get the best out of a particular situation. Everyone should use the same types of cues and reinforcements. Not only will the child learn more quickly from a consistent approach, but it is easier to identify an unsuccessful strategy, an aim set too high or one no longer appropriate.

Review and evaluation

To ensure that therapy continues successfully, it requires continual review. Open communication between home, school and therapist is essential. Progress, lack of progress or changes in circumstances will necessitate changing or refining aims or devising compensations. Metaphorically, as goals are scored, the goal posts must be moved or the game becomes stale, the players giving up and going home. It is vital for effective therapy to maintain a sense of interest and achievement.

Implementation

Communication is essentially a social and functional activity. It is meaningful only when occurring between people, spontaneously and in response to surroundings. Despite this, there is a persistent belief that only the child receiving regular one-to-one therapy from a speech and language therapist is having her communication needs met, and if not, she isn't.

What this model fails to address is that there are several stages in the learning process. Undoubtedly, many new skills or concepts are most effectively introduced one-to-one in a quiet place free without distractions. However once a skill has been learnt in a one-to-one situation, it needs to be *practised* and *reinforced* in many other situations. This, the most time-consuming part of therapy, is vital if the new skill is to become a useful part of the child's communicative repertoire.

The speech and language therapist is most experienced at devising and implementing the initial teaching of specific communication skills. Teachers, classroom assistants and family members, supported by the therapist, are better placed to enable the child to generalise skills. This requires frequent contact with the child and an ability to respond and adapt to changing circumstances. Naturally this model of teaching and rehearsal requires a high level of commitment from all those 'therapists' directly concerned with the child. However, the resultant rewards make the effort extremely worthwhile.

Development trajectory

The normal developmental trajectory should be followed wherever possible. If this pattern is adhered to, and the steps between tasks are carefully graded, the child will have the best possible chance of success. It is here that the knowledge of a speech and language therapist is particularly valuable. They know the developmental order in which concepts, sounds and grammatical structures are usually acquired. They will advise tackling relatively concrete concepts, such as 'big', 'soft' and 'heavy', before more abstract concepts, such as 'different', 'forward' or 'last'. They will encourage babbling, simple gesture and active eye-gaze before speech, bilabial sounds, such as 'm' and 'b' before sounds such as 'sh', 'l' and 'v', the pronoun 'your' well before 'our'. They know that understanding passive sentences and the ability to make judgements about degrees of politeness begin to develop after the age of four years. All this is particularly relevant to the child with a learning disability who may have a developmental age substantially behind their chronological age.

Enjoyment

Communicating effectively is enjoyable. For many of us communicating is our chief recreational activity. Sadly, children with communication difficulties may find the process frustrating or demoralising rather than enjoyable. Our most important task as therapists may well be changing this perception.

For this to happen, appropriate interaction needs to be a positive experience in itself or at least to lead to an immediate positive outcome for the child. It is essential that we plan ahead for pleasant, reinforcing interactions. For this we must be clear about the child's particular skills, interests, likes and dislikes.

The most obvious activity for fostering enjoyable and effective interaction is co-operative play. With activities that are less intrinsically rewarding the therapist must consciously supply reinforcement. For one child, conveying pleasure and approval through facial expression and praise will be sufficient. For another, reinforcement must be more tangible: a favourite activity, song, toy, food or enjoyable physical contact.

Playing to strengths

A child's strengths are as important as their weaknesses. Skills already emerged can be harnessed to develop weaker areas. For example, children with poor verbal comprehension often have far better developed visual understanding; the parallel use of visual cues, photographs, symbols or signs can both mitigate and improve poor verbal understanding. Similarly, children with speech difficulties can use music, rhythm and physical activity to develop their expressive skills.

Acknowledging a child's competence in one area will enhance her self-esteem and confidence. This is essential when tackling the very real challenges presented by communication difficulties.

Specific approaches to specific difficulties

There is a wide range of techniques within the framework described above. The choice of a specific intervention will depend on understanding the underlying cause of a difficulty as well as its current presentation. Certain types of intervention are particularly suited to certain types of problem. The specific communication problems found in fragile X concern:

- processing or understanding speech
- articulation of speech sounds
- fluency or rhythm of speech
- selection of vocabulary
- effective social use of language
- avoidance of eye-contact.

Poor verbal comprehension

Confusion caused by poor comprehension can cause a host of secondary problems. The child may become anxious, 'switch off' or develop distracting behaviours that mask the underlying difficulty.

Poor verbal comprehension has a multitude of potential causes. If a child suffers from repeated upper respiratory tract infections (coughs, colds, ear infections) a fluctuating conductive hearing loss may be suspected and a referral made for an audiological assessment and perhaps the fitting of grommets. These allow the middle ear, which can fill up with secretions, to dry out thoroughly. The child should avoid swimming for a prescribed length of time.

Attentional difficulties are a common cause of processing difficulties in children with fragile X. Many children have diagnoses of ADD or ADHD. They have a limited attention span, are easily distracted, squirmy or fidgety. They will be impulsive, unable to wait to take their turn and thus miss much of what is said to them. If so, ensure that you have the child's full attention before asking questions, making requests or giving information. Frequent changes of task, interspersed with physical activity will also be necessary. Imitation games, gradually building up to a series of actions, are excellent for developing attention skills.

Sentences should be kept short and clear with pauses in between to allow the child more time for processing. The child's attention can be maintained by adding visual cues, pictures, symbols or written words, that remain once the spoken words have gone. Signing can be useful to arrest and maintain attention; signing 'and' can indicate she should listen for more information. Signing is a more concrete medium than speech, which is too abstract for some children.

Whatever modes of communication are used it is necessary to identify key words. These *information-carrying words* convey important information not conveyed by the situation itself. Words in an utterance that constitute key words will change depending on particular situations. When a child is told at snack time to 'Put the biscuits on the plate', the word 'on' is redundant; it is clarified by the actual situation. It becomes a key word when a child is asked to fetch the box 'on', as opposed to 'inside', the cupboard. When children respond to being told 'Collect your things and go to the bus' at the end of the school day, they are most likely responding more to the situational cues of movement in the classroom than to the spoken words.

During day-to-day situations, ensure that the child has extra cues to help her understand what is said. Emphasise key words through other means, such as pointing, prompting, showing, signing or providing symbol or picture cues. It is also necessary to establish situations to test and stretch verbal processing skills. Non-verbal cues or prompts can be systematically reduced and single key word phrases built up slowly to longer utterances in a careful and controlled manner, so the child is not confused or misses vital information.

Underlying or non-literal meaning

Non-literal or idiomatic language abounds in our society. We 'rein ourselves in' or 'let it all hang out', 'lie low' or 'lend a hand'. The ability to deal with these abstractions opens the door to verbal humour, irony and the subtleties and nuances of social language.

It is common for children even mildly affected by fragile X to struggle with the non-literal interpretation of language. They do not automatically differentiate between underlying intended meanings and surface or literal meaning; consequently they become confused or distressed.

It is not practical or useful in these cases to completely avoid the colourful use of language; however the child must always be made aware of alternative non-literal meanings. Using humour to teach intended ambiguity is often highly successful. Children enjoy matching punch lines to first lines, and formulating their own jokes and puns.

Poor articulation

There are various possible causes for articulation difficulties in fragile X:

- early or persisting middle ear infections and subsequent hearing loss;
- children with fragile X typically have highly arched palates, dental overcrowding and weak muscle tone. Their particular oral structure means they must work relatively harder to produce precise articulation

Speech and language therapists can suggest chewing and/or sucking activities to strengthen oral and facial muscles. These activities, combined with oral massage, may be needed to reduce the oral hypersensitivity of some children with fragile X. These features may well be compounded by:

- immature phonological (speech sound) system;
- and/or articulatory dyspraxia (difficulty with planning and executing the complex sequence of movements required for speaking).

Whatever the cause of poor articulation, the child learns to monitor her own speech intelligibility. This awareness can be developed through games involving rhyming words. The words need to be carefully matched to the child's working vocabulary, the particular sounds you wish the child's attention drawn towards, and the sounds' position in the word. It is easier to start with pairs of words and pictures where the first sound in the word changes. For a child experiencing difficulty articulating different sounds made with the lips, choose 'box/fox', 'ball/fall', 'bin/fin'. Alternatively, for a child commonly substituting 'k' for 't' as the last sound in a word, collect rhyming words or pictures such as 'dark/dart', 'bike/bite', 'fork/fort'. The child should only be encouraged to articulate these sounds once she has learnt to hear the differences. It is essential that this type of programme be devised by a speech and language therapist. They are aware of the developmental sequence in which sounds are usually acquired and the oral movements necessary for articulation.

The term articulatory dyspraxia describes cases where the child can articulate speech sounds in short words but has difficulty with the same sounds in connected speech. Sounds may be repeated or articulated in different ways on different occasions. The child's speech may be characterised by uneven rhythm with fast rushes interspersed with longer pauses. This child has to learn to slow down their rate of speech, to become aware of how words break into syllables, of how phrases are formed and where to place emphasis. Music and rhyme can be particularly helpful in establishing a rhythm for useful phrases.

Perseveration

Children with fragile X may repeat, or *perseverate on*, whole words and phrases. This is self-repetition, as opposed to the echoing of others which is characteristic of autism. Different reasons have been suggested for perseveration. One theory relates it to the executive function deficits experienced in fragile X. Executive functioning is the ability to organise tasks logically, to stop and think or to stop and wait. Alternatively, perseveration may relate to the child's impulsivity, their difficulty with inhibiting responses, their word-finding or vocabulary problems, or the presence of anxiety. It is likely to be a combination of several of these factors.

Whatever the cause of perseveration, self-awareness is the key to self-monitoring and control. In addition the suspected underlying cause of the perseveration must be tackled. The child may need to be taught ways of retrieving vocabulary or compensating for 'lost' words. Where anxiety is seen to play a part the child should be helped to build self-confidence and esteem; the speaking environment may need to be modified to help her do this.

Vocabulary difficulties

Vocabulary development is directly linked to concept formation. Children with learning disability typically acquire abstract concepts and their linguistic terms (for example, space and time) well behind their acquisition of concrete concepts. These terms often need specific teaching. This linguistic knowledge must also be maintained, as a reduction in cognitive function may occur during adolescence in fragile X.

The usual prescriptive method for doing this involves simultaneously providing an item or event along with its label, whether visual, verbal or both. An approach requiring more from the child but which develops their general contextual inferencing skills, involves incorporating new vocabulary, within a structured and contextually cued activity, without specifically teaching that vocabulary. The child may be shown three objects, two familiar and one new. When asked for the unfamiliar object, she must select it by deduction. A combination of both approaches is usually successful.

Sometimes children cannot reliably retrieve vocabulary for expressive purposes. These children can improve their word retrieval skills by formulating definitions of occupations, objects or places, in terms of their particular characteristics. They benefit from classification activities, listing words in categories such as vehicles, sounds, or feelings, or selecting the 'odd word out' in a group. Completing cued but unfinished sentences, as in 'worms wriggle, rabbits . . . ', or 'wake up in the morning, go to bed at . . . ', can be extremely useful.

Tangential speech

Children with fragile X often have a disorganised style of speech where the conversation wanders frequently off-topic. They have difficulty conveying relevant information, and switch topics unexpectedly.

As with perseveration, this tendency towards a rambling style of conversation may be due to underlying executive function deficits and/or word-retrieval difficulties. Attentional difficulties may also contribute, with the child failing to maintain interest in a conversation.

Children with these difficulties should learn to separate key points from peripheral information. They benefit from guessing games such as 'What Am I?' or, as with vocabulary difficulties, from exercises in formulating definitions. A particularly useful intervention involves giving them, or helping them devise, a visual structure of key words or pictures to help them stay on topic, and select and organise the information they need to convey.

Difficulties with social interaction

Avoiding eye-contact in certain situations, difficulty with transitions between social situations and dislike and/or avoidance of some social situations, are common features of fragile X. The child is often described as having autistic features. Although it is quite possible for the child with fragile X to also have autism, the social interaction features described above differ from what is seen in true autism.

Autism is characterised by lack of motivation to communicate, coupled with confusion, aversion or indifference to social interaction. Fragile X children are typically interested in other people and keen to communicate, but shy and socially anxious. They are easily overwhelmed by sensory information in general and by social interaction in particular. They are socially hypersensitive, and once over-stimulated take a long time to calm down. Many children with fragile X react to the intensity of social interaction by avoiding eye-contact, biting their hands or clothes, rocking or hand-flapping. The incidence of word retrieval difficulties and of perseveration increases in line with the perceived intensity of interaction. These features become worse in adolescence, possibly as a response to this period's increased social pressures.

A high level of arousal or anxiety is unpleasant for the child, interferes with her ability to concentrate and learn, and to communicate effectively. It is extremely important to decrease this anxiety. A necessary starting point is awareness of the behaviours the child may exhibit to indicate rising stress levels. This enables adults to anticipate situations likely to be difficult for the child, and avoid, adapt and/or prepare for them.

A typically difficult situation for the child with fragile X is face-to-face teaching, where maintained eye-contact is expected. It is more useful to sit beside them, using physical prompts where necessary to reinforce verbal instructions. Face-to-face activities involving other children can be replaced by co-operative activities that require a lesser degree of eye-gaze. Signs can also decrease social pressure by encouraging the child to look at hands rather than eyes. The focus of any activity should be on joint attention rather than eye-contact.

A clear, modelled framework, often considerably lessens anxiety. Children with fragile X should have a model to imitate, perhaps provided by other children. Group games and activities where physical actions precede or take the place of speech can be extremely useful.

As the child develops, their need increases to rehearse and role-play real-life social situations. This can start with a prepared script backed up by visual prompts; perhaps asking for directions, explaining a problem, or offering a point of view. The role-plays should be followed up by supported tasks outside the classroom.

At a simpler level the child may spend time practising difficult communicative function – making requests, conveying information, or refusing politely. Situations should be devised which need particular language functions and prompt an appropriate response. The child might be 'left out' when handing out equipment or treats, employed to convey an unexpected message to a member of staff, or given something they will wish to refuse. In all these cases the child must be supported and prompted by appropriate communication.

Inevitably, the child will become socially over-stimulated in some situations in life. To help them cope, teach them to monitor their anxiety levels and practise an effective calming-down procedure. This procedure can prepare the child for social challenges as well as calming them down afterwards. It may involve listening to music, looking at a book, playing with a toy or doing some rhythmical activity, such as sitting in a rocking chair, exercising, walking or cycling. Activities that involve putting pressure on muscles and joints, such as lifting, carrying or pushing, also have a calming effect, and have the added advantage of making the child feel useful.

By age 7 children are beginning to evaluate themselves against others. Self-esteem is a necessary pre-requisite for self-confidence. All children, but particularly those with fragile X, need help in developing their sense of individuality and achievement. Provide constant reminders, whether verbal, visual or tangible, of their interests, enjoyable past experiences and successes.

Alternative means of communication

Speech may not become the primary means of communication for a severely affected child with fragile X; she may need alternative or augmentative means of communication. Developing an alternative system of communication will not inhibit the development of speech. The more effectively the child learns to communicate her thoughts and feelings by whatever means, the more motivated she will become to communicate in other modes.

Alternative means of communication vary from natural gesture (pointing, nodding, shaking the head), facial expression and posture to systematic use of signs, pictures, symbols or objects to represent concepts. A child with none of these means will nevertheless have developed some element of personal communication. Messages can be conveyed, for instance, through shouting, squealing, crying, bringing objects, grabbing, pulling, looking, walking away, biting and hugging. They may not be used intentionally, and may or may not get the child what she wants, or be appropriate to the situations. However they demonstrate what motivates or distresses; they provide a foundation upon which to build, by judicious reinforcement, anticipation and redirection, effective, intentional and appropriate communication.

In conclusion, there is a huge variation in the degree and nature of communication difficulties associated with fragile X. I have described a logical and collaborative framework for planning and implementing speech and language therapy. The activities suggested within this framework are not exhaustive. Developing children's communication skills requires constant flexibility and creative thinking. It may be exhausting but is always interesting, and potentially immensely rewarding.

Chapter 15

Occupational therapy and sensory integrative therapy for individuals with fragile X syndrome

Dido Green

Despite similarities in style of learning, behaviour and social communication, each person with fragile X syndrome will have unique characteristics that both contribute to their capabilities and the pervasiveness of functions influenced by the syndrome. Occupational therapists are concerned with the impact these features have on the acquisition of skills necessary to support competence in daily activities. The predominant features to be discussed are the specific problems with attention, sensory processing, motor coordination and emotional accommodation that are frequently reported alongside the biological and physical characteristics of fragile X. The interaction of these features may mitigate or exacerbate the difficulties experienced by individuals, necessitating ingenuity to untangle the various contributory components of presenting problems and thereby direct support appropriately.

Admittedly, the following are generalisations; it is imperative to consider individual differences alongside the context of environment and developmental experience. There can be no 'prescription' and 'quick remedy', rather our observations can guide our understanding of the rich fabric of individuals with fragile X, in order that parents and professionals learn how best to enable and empower them. It must be born in mind that there is a tendency amongst professionals to consider aspects of development that appear atypical as 'deviant' and thus 'dysfunctional'. It is humbling to remember one's own failings in the face of daily challenges and our occasional dependency on others' assistance. It is preferable to place the subsequent commentaries regarding interpretations of behaviour and intervention on a continuum of normality; that is, an extension of one's own reactions and capabilities under various constraints.

Characteristics of fragile X influencing occupational performance

Characteristic features of fragile X are described in this book and in the published literature. Amongst these, problems with attention, sensory processing, perceptual and motor difficulties and anxiety will influence learning and play behaviour. Attentional difficulties may contribute to a failure to notice that a toy has been moved slightly, requiring a partial reach to avoid knocking it over; this in turn influences the success of the game and subsequent interaction between the playmates. These problems are exacerbated by inherent anxiety and a tendency to get flustered when things do not go according to plan, for example, not picking up the toy safely.

The general effects on performance can be shown by looking at these features in turn.

Attention

Poor attention and distractibility with or without hyperactivity are commonly evident (Turk, 1998). Poor ability to focus attention may also be related to difficulty analysing visual-spatial differences between objects and to sensory processing deficits. Reduced attention and poor recognition and orientation towards relevant environmental cues may influence performance and behaviour in the following ways:

- Poor judgement of object size when reaching results in an inadequate preparation of the hand position for grasping the item: fingers over-extended or not sufficiently open.
- Failure to notice obstacles when moving around a room (especially in unfamiliar spaces) results in bumping into things or knocking items over.
- Problems determining the relative importance of various features of objects result in over-focusing attention on irrelevant aspects of an item: fixing attention on the valve or texture of a ball rather than how to kick, throw or catch it.
- Difficulties sustaining attention on a single task or sensation result in flitting between a multitude of activities and/or shifting attention between numerous environmental stimuli.
- Poor adjustment to a variety of stimuli contributes to anxiety and difficulty in accommodating changes in activities and/or stimulating environments.

Sensory processing

Various studies and clinical experience suggest that many individuals with fragile X have difficulty using and adapting to sensory information to support productive behaviour (Miller *et al.* 1999; McIntosh *et al.* 1999; Baranek *et al.* 2002). This can result in problems analysing differences between various sensory characteristics such as texture or movement speed (sensory discrimination), plus a poor tolerance and accommodation of various intensities of sensations or multiple sensory experiences (sensory modulation). From a behavioural perspective both sensory discrimination and sensory modulation are important aspects of daily life, which support our self-understanding and environmental awareness, helping us to regulate and organise responses to sensations in a graded and adaptive manner. Behaviours indicative of a defensive response to touch (tactile) stimuli and other types of sensations such as noise, smells and sights are commonly reported. The relationship between anxiety and prior knowledge to anticipate a sensory event and sensory processing itself is far more complex than previously thought and has yet to be investigated.

Changes in the activity of sweat glands and associated electrical conductance of the skin occur during positive and negative emotional events or threatening stimuli and can be measured using electrodermal responses (EDRs). Cheng's (in preparation) results using EDRs to provide a physiological marker of sensory responsivity showed that children with fragile X may accommodate and habituate to tactile (touch) stimuli when in the comfort of their own homes. This is in contrast to Miller *et al.*'s (1999) results, which suggested that children with fragile X had heightened responses (over-responded) with poor habituation to most stimuli when experimentation was undertaken in a clinical setting. It is imperative to recognise that any underlying problem in processing sensory information will be exacerbated by anxiety and poor performance. However, an individual's difficulty integrating sensory information with knowledge of the world and previous experience can affect behaviour in a number of ways:

- Poor discrimination of changes in a floor surface may reduce the likelihood of spontaneous postural adjustments required to prevent slipping or falling.
- Over-sensitivity to various sensations such as clothing texture or different types of sounds may exacerbate anxiety and feelings of discomfort and even distress.
- A failure to habituate to non-essential background stimuli may interfere with ability to focus on salient or novel stimuli resulting in distractibility and/or a need to respond to all competing stimuli.
- Difficulties regulating the degree of response to sensory stimuli influence comfortableness in daily activities such as tolerating random touch as experienced when lining up to leave a classroom.

Motor coordination

Some of the physiological characteristics evident amongst people with fragile X include excessive joint mobility (hypermobility/joint laxity) and low normal muscle tone (Hagerman and Cronister, 1996). Although competence in motor skills is often considered to be on a par with intellect this relationship is far from clear. Poor ability to conceptualise movement and plan motor sequences, frequently referred to as 'dyspraxia', affects performance of new or unfamiliar motor tasks. Although 'dyspraxia' is not a common label for children with fragile X in Europe, poor definitions of what is truly meant by 'praxis' and 'dyspraxia' may mean that this term is applied to some children who exhibit inordinate difficulties executing motor tasks.

- Hypermobile joints and low normal muscle tone may influence posture and affect ability to stabilise the trunk and maintain balance to support refined movements of the limbs required, for example, to manipulate objects with speed and dexterity or to carry a drink whilst walking.
- Poor sensory processing functions underpinning the development of body scheme and spatial awareness will also influence motor performance and may impede the acquisition of motor skills (Stackhouse, 1994).
- Despite a strength in imitation and ability to copy demonstrated movements, people with fragile X may have difficulty independently instigating the correct actions for tackling new motor tasks.
- Poor processing of movement stimuli will affect ability to adjust speed of movement and body position for success in gross motor tasks such as those required for ball games or judging speed and direction of movement to avoid accidental collisions.

Emotional accommodation

Social anxiety and fear of change are notable features of individuals with fragile X (Sobesky, 1996). Similar to the inter-relationship of sensory, attentional and motor difficulties, the extent of the impact of any one of these features on anxiety and vice versa is not known. There is an optimum level of arousal required to achieve a good standard of performance, which is dependent on the context of a given task. The ability to attend to salient sensory information and ignore (habituate) non-essential background stimuli helps an individual maintain appropriate levels of arousal. When this balance between attention and habituation is impaired (either when inherent anxiety influences the ability to interpret sensory information in a meaningful way or when inadequate sensory processing disturbs the underlying level of arousal) poor behavioural responses may ensue:

- An individual who is frequently exposed to stimuli perceived as noxious or threatening may find it difficult to orientate towards more relevant stimuli and learn from their response to effect success in a task.
- Excessive shyness and social anxiety may influence ability to maintain eye-contact and to speak clearly, on appropriate topics, which in turn affects ability to instigate and sustain relationships with peers (Sobesky, 1996).
- Feeling awkward around other children and difficulty understanding the 'rules' governing social behaviour may affect participation in group activities (Sobesky, 1996).
- The child with fragile X may not always utilise socially acceptable methods of calming themselves when distressed. Those who use chewing or rhythmic rocking as calming activities may draw negative attention to themselves, e.g. by chewing their sleeve or rocking excessively when queuing at the cinema.

Because of the complex interaction of features predominant amongst individuals with fragile X, it is helpful to look at situations in which they can succeed, and compare these with events when things have gone wrong. Individuals with fragile X require an integrated intervention programme that takes advantage of a number of different learning, behavioural and therapeutic approaches. Many daily tasks make apparent their difficulties in processing sensory information. Recruiting intervention strategies from a sensory integrative therapy approach, within educational programmes, may assist them to adapt to environmental challenges, and support greater success in learning.

Sensory Integrative Therapy (SIT)

SIT is a theory and treatment approach used by therapists to provide an understanding of the relationship between sensory processing and consequent behaviour and performance. Originated by A. J. Ayres, the key concept of SIT is 'the organisation of sensory input for use' to assist the development of adaptive responses to challenges imposed by the environment and learning (Ayres, 1979; Spitzer & Smith-Roley, 2001). The most obvious sensory experiences of sight, hearing, smell, taste and touch affect us constantly. These combine with two less apparent sensations of body position and body movement gained from our muscles, tendons and joints and head position (called proprioception and vestibular sensations). From these an individual obtains important sensory information to plan and organise emotional, behavioural and motor responses. SIT aims to address anomalies in sensory processing by enhancing sensory experiences, in a non-threatening manner, to promote more adaptive behaviour. Treatment should also help the fragile X individual acquire self-regulatory mechanisms, which maintain equilibrium between the protective and discriminative functions of the sensory systems, and sustain an adequate level of arousal for learning and success. Table 15.1 shows some behaviours that may indicate poor sensory processing.

Careful assessment and analysis of the strengths and difficulties of individuals with fragile X indicates whether sensory processing problems are contributing to deficits in performance and behaviour. Structured assessment would list all the activities and sensory experiences the individual seeks out and finds calming and in which they seem most able to learn; describe the general sensory features of these activities or objects, and finally

Table 15.1 Sensory systems and behavioural observations of people with fragile X

System	Observation
General reactions	Aversion or extreme sensitivity to touch, sound, movement or visual stimulation: • responds aggressively to any change in quality of sensory experience • shows excessive distress on changes to activities • emotional liability, becomes tearful or over-excited with minimal sensory provocation • has poor endurance and tires easily • avoids crowded or public places such as supermarkets and train stations.
Tactile (touch)	Has difficulty discriminating different textures and shapes: • cannot select coins from buttons in pocket • cannot select appropriate coin from purse or wallet without visual monitoring • does not feel difference in sock and trouser leg with the result that the trouser leg is tucked into the top of sock • does not recognise surface texture of a wet glass to adjust grip accordingly. Is hyper-sensitive to tactile stimuli: • is extremely distractible when wearing multi-layers or loose fitting clothing • is a very picky eater with respect to texture or mixtures of textures (such as fruit yogurts) or prefers chewy versus crunchy foods • responds negatively when touched lightly or unexpectedly such as touch experienced during contact sports or when standing in line • shows distress in daily tasks involving light/tickly touch such as hair cutting, nail cutting, hair washing • responds negatively or avoids messy play activities such as sand play or walking barefoot on a beach.
Movement	Finds it difficult to determine movement differences: • finds it difficult to adjust posture to avoid slipping when surface texture changes such as when stepping onto a smooth flooring from a carpeted surface • has poor posture and/or finds sports and other movement activities difficult • finds it difficult to grade movement quality and the force of grip or action is too high or too low • has difficulty manipulating objects/tools unless shown • difficulty maintaining balance when putting on trousers • bumps into doors and objects rather than adjust speed and direction of movement. Is over- or undersensitive to movement activities: • avoids climbing games • shows discomfort or distress when on escalators or when transferring from a train platform to a train • alternatively, seeks out excessive amounts of movement.
Sounds	Is oversensitive to unpredictable or excessive volumes of noise: • avoids or shows distress in crowded places, particularly shopping centres with high echo

continued . . .

Table 15.1 continued

System	Observation
Sounds *continued*	• is distractible when there is a lot of background noise • shows a negative response to particular types of noise such as vacuum cleaners, dogs barking or sirens • prefers or seeks out rhythmic tunes to more erratic musical forms.
Visual	Has poor visual-spatial analysis: • has difficulty matching objects by size or shape especially noticeable in letter recognition • misjudges the depth or height of steps • has difficulty finding a particular item amongst other similar or dissimilar forms such as sorting socks and knickers • struggles with puzzles and board games. Is hyper-sensitive to visual disarray: • finds it difficult to concentrate in cluttered spaces • avoids crowded spaces
Smell and tastes	Is hyper-sensitive to odours and flavours • shows distress or avoids centres where strong cleaning fluids are used • shows increased distractibility and/or hyperactivity in the presence of particular odours • shows aversive reactions to particular individuals whose body odour or perfume/after shave is particularly pungent • gags or shows distress with particular foods.

ascertain whether there are any similarities. For example, the child who frequently squeezes his hands together, seems to like chewy foods and appears more organised when carrying or pushing heavier items, may benefit from having additional opportunities to engage in tasks involving constant or rhythmic resistance to joints and muscles. Incorporate the concept of a 'Sensory Diet' on a daily basis to ensure that adequate amounts of the right type of stimuli are provided for self-regulation of arousal and attention (Wilbarger & Wilbarger, 1991)

Classroom strategies

• Provide a quiet, contained and uncluttered space where the child can escape when overwhelmed by the 'sensory' world or activity changes. Create a wendy house, tent or other small space/room where favourite items, textures and music are available and controlled by the child. This space should be available when arriving at home or school or following transition between environments involving unpredictable stimuli. Some classrooms have a large cardboard box or small shop in a corner for all children to use if needed.
• Provide regular opportunities to escape the bustle of a busy classroom by having the child carry a box of books or push a computer trolley to another classroom, or take the register to the head teacher.
• reduce the amount of visual and auditory distraction by careful arrangement of classroom furniture and wall displays. Minimise the amount of colour and texture contrast on walls and window shades; place classroom tables and chairs to reduce background bustle as

children move about the room. Place the child with fragile X with their back to the wall and away from corridors where other children move about regularly. Avoid flickering and bright neon lights where possible.

- Carpeted surfaces and rubber ferrules on chair legs reduce background noise.
- Provide supportive seating with arm rests for fine motor activities.
- When seating children on the floor, ensure the fragile X child has their own space, not jostled by others or irritated by carpet texture. A rocking chair to provide rhythmic movement may help some children, whilst the contained space of a bean bag chair may be comforting for others.
- Encourage the child with fragile X to wait at the end of a line/queue or hold the door open for others to avoid random tactile contact.
- Be aware of background smells; have naturally scented plants in the classroom rather than the more intrusive and pungent artificial sprays.
- Preparation for change is important. Use 'objects of reference' (transitional objects) or visual cue cards to help the child plan and look forward to the next activity or event rather than be confronted with a 'fait accompli'. Hickman (2001) provides some examples of the use of music to support transitions and develop confidence in group activities. Maintain a regular schedule for learning something new, and predictable break times following activities the child finds most difficult, such as P.E.
- Sign-post transition times with red, yellow and green giant lollipops stuck into a flowerpot:

  - Red = stay at desk and work quietly
  - Yellow = listen out for change
  - Green = free activity time or a change is required

- Utilise the child's imitative strengths to model behaviour or when providing instructions.
- Provide additional visual-spatial experiences such as climbing over, under and through objects.
- Avoid surprising a child from behind; approach from the front using a calm, steady and unobtrusive manner; avoid erratic arm gestures.
- Adapt the sensory characteristics of tasks to make them more predictable and rhythmic; include constant rather than erratic tactile stimuli. For example, rather than the child carrying a bag that may jostle his legs, use a snugly fitting rucksack.
- Chewing non-food items and foods such as fruit rolls or squeezing items such as 'stress' balls may be calming and organising. If so, provide appropriate snacks mid morning and/or mid afternoon. A small stress 'squeezy' in a pocket may help maintain focus and attention.
- Deep pressure contact tends to be more calming and modulating. When holding or touching the child to assist with dressing, try to maintain constant, firm pressure rather than erratic contact. Don't rumple hair, as one might for a child without defensive responses to tactile input.

Dressing and changing

- Certain clothing textures may irritate and cause distress; be guided by the individual. Some prefer long, tighter fitting sleeves; others prefer short ones. Avoid disparate layers of clothing, such as T-shirts under long sleeved shirts; use a tighter fitting vest under a shirt if needed for warmth. Some may need to wear tighter fitting garments such as lycra cycle shorts or leotards. Be alert for the child being uncomfortable with over-heating or excessive sweating. Children who are anxious or suffer tactile defensiveness may feel temperatures differently; be guided by the child and not by one's own interpretation of what is warm.

- Cut the labels out of shirts and underwear.
- Prepare those children who need help with dressing for each successive item; use 'hand over hand' guidance where possible. They may need 'escape' time following dressing, as the light tactile stimulation occurring during dressing can be invasive in nature.
- A visual sequencing board, numbered with appropriate pictures, may encourage the child to select items of clothing in the correct sequence.

It is hoped that the above suggestions will stimulate those working with people with fragile X to be sensitive to their sensory requirements. The strategies should be incorporated into other approaches discussed in this book rather than be seen as an exclusive approach for modifying behaviour. The occupational therapist, particularly one with a comprehensive knowledge of SIT, is an important member of any multi-disciplinary team involved with people with fragile X. Understanding the relationship between the characteristic features of people with fragile X is crucial, and will guide professionals to work together in providing the appropriate remedial services.

References

Ayres, A.J. (1964). 'Tactile functions: their relation to hyperactive and perceptual motor behaviour'. *American Journal of Occupational Therapy* 16: 6–11.

Ayres, A.J. (1979). *Sensory Integration and the Child*. Los Angeles: Western Psychological Services.

Baranek, G.R., Greiss Hess, L.M., Yankee, J.G., Hatton, D.D. and Hooper, S.R. (2002) 'Sensory processing correlates of occupational performance in children with fragile X Syndrome: Preliminary findings'. *American Journal of Occupational Therapy* 56: 538–546.

Cheng, W. (in preparation) 'Tactile processing in children with fragile X Syndrome'. University of Surrey, Unpublished Masters thesis.

Hagerman, R.J. and A. Cronister, eds. (1996) *Fragile X Syndrome, Diagnosis, Treatment and Research*, 2nd Edition, Baltimore: Johns Hopkins University Press.

Hickman, L. (2001). 'Sensory Integration and fragile X Syndrome'. In Smith-Roley, S., Blanche, E.I. and Schaaf, R.C. (eds) (2001). *Sensory Integration with Diverse Populations*, Tucson, AZ: Therapy Skill Builders, pp. 409–420.

McIntosh, D.N., Miller, L.J., Shyu, V. and Hagerman, R.J. (1999) 'Sensory-modulation disuption, electrodermal responses, and functional behaviors' *Developmental Medicine and Child Neurology* 41: 608–615.

Miller, LJ., McIntosh, D.N., McGrath, J., Shyu, V., Lampe, M., Taylor, A.K., Tassone, F., Neitzel, K., Stackhouse, T., and Hagerman, R.J. (1999) 'Electrodermal responses to sensory stimuli in individuals with fragile X syndrome: a preliminary report' *American Journal of Medical Genetics* 83: 268–279.

Sobesky, W.E. (1996) 'The treatment of emotional and behavioural problems'. Chapter 9, in Hagerman, R.J. and A. Cronister, eds. (1996) *Fragile X Syndrome, Diagnosis, Treatment and Research*, 2nd Edition, Baltimore: Johns Hopkins University Press.

Spitzer, S. & Smith-Roley, S. (2001) 'Sensory integration revisited: a philosophy of practice'. In Smith-Roley, S., Blanche, E.I. and Schaaf, R.C. (eds) (2001). *Sensory Integration with Diverse Populations*, Tucson, AZ: Therapy Skill Builders, p. 5.

Stackhouse, T. (1994) 'Sensory integration concepts and fragile X syndrome' *SISIS Newsletter* (17 March 1994): 2–6.

Turk, J. (1998) 'Fragile X syndrome and attentional deficits'. *Journal of Applied Research in Intellectual Disabilities* 11: 175–191.

Wilbarger, P. and J.L. Wilbarger (1991) *Sensory Defensiveness in Children Aged 2–12: An Intervention Guide for Parents and Other Caretakers.* Denver CO: Avanti Educational Programs.

Williams, M.S. and Shellenberger, S. (1992). *How Does Your Engine Run: The Alert Program for Self-Regulation.* Albuquerque: Therapy Works.

Additional recommended reading

Green, D. (2002). 'Children with fragile X syndrome' in Swee Hong, C. and Howard, L. (eds) (2002) *Occupational Therapy in Childhood.* London: Whurr Pubs, pp. 231–251.

Kranowitz, C.S. (1998). *The Out of Sync Child.* USA: Penguin Putnam Inc.

Royen, C., Carreton, I. and Slavic, B. (1990) *Sensory Integration: A Foundation for Development.* Dayton, OH: Southpaw Enterprises Inc.

Oetter, P., Fichter, E.W. and Frick, S. (1993) *M.O.R.E. Integrating the Mouth with Sensory and Postural Functions.* Hugo, MN: PDP Press.

Smith-Roley, S., Blanche, E.I. and Schaaf, R.C. (eds) (2001). *Sensory Integration with Diverse Populations*, Tucson, AZ: Therapy Skill Builders, pp. 409–420.

Part IV

Development, behaviour and psychology

Chapter 16

Development in the early years

Gaia Scerif and Kim Cornish

Parents and relatives of young children, toddlers and infants with fragile X syndrome raise concerns with regards to their child's development very early in infancy (on average, before the first birthday), but a full diagnosis often comes in the second year of life or later. However, the average age at diagnosis is decreasing rapidly, thanks to advances in our understanding of the genetic bases of fragile X. With early diagnosis, the need to tailor early intervention accordingly has become an increasingly pressing issue for parents and professionals alike (Hatton *et al.*, 2000). In this chapter, we introduce the importance of investigating early development in both typically and atypically developing children. We then review recent research findings on early development in infants and toddlers with fragile X and their practical implications. The purpose of the review is twofold: first, we hope that the chapter will inform the multidisciplinary efforts of all those involved in improving future prospects for young children with fragile X and their families. Furthermore, we hope that the information will be of interest to professionals working with older children and adults with the syndrome, as a way of understanding the early origins of atypical behaviours and difficulties associated with fragile X.

The importance of investigating typical and atypical development trajectories

A crucial issue for professionals working with both typically and atypically developing children is the current state of cognitive and social skills of each child they are educating. Understanding the profile of strengths and difficulties forms the basis for targeted teaching strategies. For example, comparing expressive and productive language, as well as visuo-spatial abilities in a child, is useful in order to choose between either verbally or visually based strategies. However, it is crucial to ask what the early developmental origins of later cognitive functioning are. In what way can this knowledge help design early intervention strategies aimed at improving later cognitive outcome? Both in typical and atypical development, common profiles in late childhood and adulthood do not necessarily originate from common developmental origins. For example, language is delayed in its emergence but relatively proficient in adults with fragile X and with Williams syndrome (a rare neuro-developmental disorder). Despite this common late proficiency, the development of language may be supported by fine sequential auditory processing in Williams syndrome, whereas in fragile X, sequential processing, a relative weakness, is unlikely to aid word learning. Thus, in order to understand the processes underlying cognitive strengths and difficulties in childhood and beyond we must understand the developmental trajectories that lead to these relative strengths and difficulties (Karmiloff-Smith, 1998).

Atypical development in infants, toddlers and young children with fragile X

Delays in developmental milestones are often the first causes of concern for parents of infants with fragile X and professionals involved with them. Sitting up alone (infants with fragile X achieve this at 10 months on average), walking alone (on average at 21 months) and single words (on average at 20 months) all occur later than expected and raise alarm bells for both parents and health professionals. Are these delays also matched by delays in early cognitive development? How do these map onto cognitive outcome in late childhood and adulthood?

The cognitive profile of late childhood and young adults with fragile X is characterised by uneven abilities within and across domains. Relative strengths in language, long-term memory and holistic information-processing accompany relative weaknesses in attention, short-term memory and sequential information-processing. In addition, many adults and children display hyperactive/attention deficit disorder, hyperacusis and autistic-like behaviours.

In contrast, very few studies have addressed issues of cognitive development in young toddlers and infants with fragile X and, where they have existed, they have been based mainly on parental report questionnaires and structured interviews. Such studies have generally provided good initial descriptions of the effects of the syndrome at the behavioural level. However, in-depth investigations of the cognitive underpinnings of these difficulties have not yet been undertaken. Here, we review the current literature in the domains of motor control, language, social cognition and attention, highlighting both the characteristics of young children with fragile X as a group, the issue of individual variability and the comparison with the adult profile.

Motor skill development

Parental reports and clinical observations highlight difficulties with gross motor co-ordination and planning of fine movements, as well as hypotonia in infancy (Bailey *et al.*, 1998). With age, delays increased compared to standardised norms. Furthermore, the rate of development of infants and toddlers followed longitudinally is on average half of what is found in typically developing children and, in contrast with other skills, such as communications skills, the rate of motor development seems related to FMR1 protein expression (Bailey *et al.* 2001). Intriguingly, overall group delay in motor skills is also accompanied by larger individual differences amongst pre-school children with fragile X than in matched typically developing children.

Language

Adults with fragile X develop to have relatively stronger verbal than performance skills. However, knowledge of syntax lags behind semantics, and pragmatic conversational skills are characterised by atypical repetitive speech as well as tangential language. What are the early origins of these difficulties? Receptive language proceeded at approximately half the expected rate in a large group of children aged between 20 and 89 months, while their expressive language proceeded at approximately a third of the standard rate (Roberts *et al.*, 2001). This indicates a steady improvement in linguistic abilities, particularly understanding, although at a slower rate than in typically developing children, and this results in an increasing discrepancy between communication skills and chronological age. Furthermore, young children's language development seems to slow from approximately 48 months onwards (Fisch *et al.*, 1999), although the latter findings should be viewed with caution, because they derive from pooling children and adolescents across age groups. Studies following language development longitudinally in individual children and adolescents have also suggested a slowing in the improvement of linguistic skills, although the timing of this plateau varies (Bailey *et al.*, 1998).

As for the development of motor skills, overall delay is accompanied by large individual differences in both expressive and receptive language (Roberts et al., 2001). While the level of FMR1 protein seems correlated to the level of communication skills, it is not related to the rate of development (Bailey, Hatton, et al., 2001), suggesting that other factors impact on the speed at which language improves over time in young children with the syndrome.

Social cognition

A number of social difficulties have been well documented in adults and children with fragile X. These include social anxiety, shyness, hyper-arousal, avoidance behaviour to unfamiliar people, and gaze aversion linked to extreme social anxiety. However, social development has not been studied in young children and toddlers with the syndrome. Studies comparing gaze aversion in younger and older children found a higher incidence of this behaviour in older than in younger children. In general, young boys with fragile X but no concurrent diagnosis of autism have higher social adaptive skills than matched children with autism and children with both autism and fragile X syndrome. A concurrent diagnosis of autism seems related not only to social adaptive skills, but also to the severity of cognitive delays in boys with the syndrome (Bailey *et al.*, 2000).

Attention

Perhaps the most striking and consistent primary behavioural problem identified in *young* fragile X children is attention and hyperactivity problems, which include a behavioural triad of severe and persistent inattention, overactivity and impulsiveness. The triad of symptoms leads to many fragile X children, especially boys, being clinically diagnosed with attention deficit/hyperactivity disorder (AD/HD). Unfortunately, the majority of research has tended to focus upon children from North American schools. It is only within the past few years that the range of attention problems has been documented in UK children with fragile X. Using a teacher questionnaire to measure the scale of inattentiveness and hyperactivity in boys with fragile X, we found that teachers reported hyperactivity as a greater problem than inattentiveness. In terms of looking at the attention deficit at a cognitive level, recent research indicates core problems with the fragile X child's ability to switch visual attention and to inhibit repetitious behaviour (Wilding *et al.*, 2002). Undoubtedly the combined impact of hyperactivity (predominantly boys), poor cognitive skills, notably inhibition, and learning disability will cause tremendous difficulty in their work productivity and achievement in the classroom.

One key question is the extent to which these difficulties, which are so prominent in late childhood and early adolescence, are already present during infancy and toddlerhood in fragile X. If so, are they the result of an atypical developmental trajectory? It is very important to establish what underlies later attentional difficulties in order to focus intervention as early as possible. Indeed, while many early therapeutic tools and strategies are available for domains such as language, we know very little about early difficulties in attention and about how to intervene early and most effectively. We investigated selective attention in toddlers with fragile X, adapting a visual search task that had been previously used with older children with the syndrome (Scerif *et al.*, 2002, in preparation). Toddlers with the syndrome were as fast in finding targets as typically developing children in a control group, but they had more difficulties in dealing with increases in attentional load and committed many more repetitive errors than matched control children. These preliminary results suggest that, like adults with the syndrome, infants and toddlers with fragile X have difficulties in executive control. Furthermore, they also seem to display atypical responses to sudden changes in their external environment. Both executive control and responsiveness to external environmental changes should therefore receive special targeted focus together with more traditional domains of intervention.

Conclusions and recommendations

The study of early motor, social and cognitive development in fragile X is still in its infancy. The current research provides initial descriptions of early cognition in infants and young children with fragile X capitalising on clinical observations, semi-structured interviews and parental reports. However, early educators need to know not only about general delay, but also what the cognitive mechanisms are that result in delay. Indeed, when intervening on a particular cognitive skill, for example language, one needs to be aware of the developmental trajectory leading to performance, whether this is delayed or within the normal limits. This in turn can suggest the mechanisms that naturally aid the development of that skill in toddlers with fragile X and therefore ways in which these natural compensatory strategies can be enhanced (if they are effective and have benefits) or corrected (if they can result in later difficulties). Future experimental research should focus on these detailed aspects of early cognition to provide clearer recommendations for professionals handling intervention.

References

Bailey, D. B., Hatton, D. D. and Skinner, M. (1998). Early developmental trajectories of males with fragile X syndrome. *American Journal on Mental Retardation* 103: 29–39.

Bailey, D. B., Hatton, D. D., Mesibov, G., Ament, N. and Skinner, M. (2000). Early development, temperament, and functional impairment in autism and fragile X syndrome. *Journal of Autism and Developmental Disorders* 30(1): 49–59.

Bailey, D.B., Hatton, D.D., Tassone, F., Skinner, M. and Taylor, A.K. (2001). Variability in FMRP and early development in males with fragile X syndrome. *American Journal on Mental Retardation* 106: 16–27.

Fisch, G.S., Holden, J.A., Carpenter, N.J., Howard-Peebles, P.N., Maddalena, A., Pandya, A. and Nance, W. (1999). Age-related language characteristics of children and adolescents with fragile X syndrome. *American Journal of Medical Genetics* 83: 253–256.

Hatton, D. D., Bailey, D. B., Roberts, J. P., Skinner, M., Mayhew, L., Clark, R. D., Waring, E. and Roberts, J. E. (2000). Early intervention services for young boys with fragile X syndrome. *Journal of Early Intervention* 23: 23–37.

Karmiloff-Smith, A. (1998). Development itself is the key to understanding developmental disorders. *Trends in Cognitive Sciences* 2: 389–398.

Munir, F., Cornish K.M. and Wilding J. (2000). A neuropsychological profile of attention deficits in young males with fragile X syndrome. *Neuropsychologia* 38: 1,261–1,270.

Roberts, J. E., Mirrett, P. and Burchinal, M. (2001). Receptive and expressive communication development of young males with fragile X syndrome. *American Journal on Mental Retardation* 106(3): 216–230.

Scerif, G., Cornish, K., Wilding, J., Driver, J. and Karmiloff-Smith, A. (2002, in preparation). Visual selective attention in typically developing toddlers and toddlers with fragile X and Williams syndrome.

Wilding, J., Cornish, K. and Munir, F. (2002) Further delineation of the executive deficit in males with fragile-X syndrome. *Neuropsychologia* 40: 1,343–1,349.

Chapter 17

Behaviours and management

Jeremy Turk

Children and young people who have fragile X syndrome can manifest a wide range of behavioural tendencies which may present challenges within the classroom, and educational settings more broadly. The causes of these behaviours are many and varied. It is usual for a number of causes to be operating simultaneously. Understanding where these behaviours are coming from, and what their meanings or functions are, can go a long way in helping to address them.

Certain behaviours may be consistent with the individual's developmental level. Thus, a 10-year-old functioning at approximately the level of an average 5-year-old is likely to have the social and concentration abilities of a 5-year-old – notwithstanding the fact that this person has been alive for ten years with all the experiences and learning opportunities that implies. This is not to suggest that poor concentration span or social abilities in a student with learning difficulties is unproblematic because they are consistent with the person's general level of intellectual functioning. More, that they need to be understood within this context and helped accordingly.

Some behaviours may be indicative of a 'specific developmental delay'. Even when allowance is made for the general level of intellectual functioning and developmental difficulties, certain abilities and behaviours remain areas of exceptionally special need. In fragile X syndrome these behaviours usually include social abilities, language skills and concentration/attentional functioning, including problems with high levels of impulsiveness and marked distractibility. This profile of specific developmental difficulties, over and above those expected for the level of intellectual functioning, is referred to as being part of the 'behavioural phenotype' of fragile X syndrome. It is attributable to the underlying genetic anomaly. However, it is most important to bear in mind that such behaviours and skill difficulties can be extremely responsive to educational, psychological and social interventions. Having a biological basis for one's special educational and other needs does *not* preclude effective educational and psychological managements.

Finally, it needs to be acknowledged that some behavioural tendencies will be the consequence of an individual's social experiences and living circumstances. This emphasises the importance of taking a broad 'biopsychosocial' perspective in formulating the causes of any one person's developmental difficulties and challenging behaviours, and hence how they can best be helped.

Common behaviours witnessed in individuals who have fragile X syndrome can be classified as follows:

- those relating to the general level and profile of intellectual functioning;

- social and language difficulties;
- poor concentration, attentional skills and overactivity;
- high anxiety levels;
- other challenging behaviours such as aggression and self-injury.

General level and profile of intellectual functioning

Unlike some genetic syndromes, such as Down's syndrome, where the usual level of intellectual functioning is in the severe learning difficulties range, students with fragile X syndrome usually function within the moderate learning difficulties range with an approximate average IQ of 50–70. There will be exceptions to this rule in either direction. However, a common reason for students with fragile X syndrome being taught in schools for pupils with severe learning difficulties is the associated challenging behaviours and hence the need for a very high ratio of trained staff to students, rather than the degree of intellectual disability per se. Furthermore, the characteristic profile of intellectual abilities is just as important as the average level of intellectual functioning. Individuals with fragile X syndrome are usually reasonably adept at language skills, particularly expressive ones. However they often experience special needs with numeracy and visuo-spatial skills. Many individuals with fragile X syndrome, male and female, say just how difficult number work is for them. They also often comment on their feeling of having been misunderstood at school because of somewhat greater abilities in other academic areas. This often marked discrepancy between verbal and non-verbal ('performance') skills is a common cause of anxiety, frustration and behavioural disturbance in students with fragile X syndrome. It therefore needs sympathetic and understanding approaches from educational staff, which acknowledge, praise and reward the academic strengths while empathising and assisting with areas of particularly special educational need.

Another area of intellectual ability which is a frequent cause of frustration and distress for students with fragile X syndrome is that of dealing with and processing incoming sequences of information ('sequential information processing'). Young students will tend to process incoming information simultaneously. This is relatively unproblematic for pupils with fragile X syndrome. Examples will be the naming of objects in a picture book or describing a whole scene, for example farm or town. As development progresses, increasing demands are made of the individual's ability to process information sequentially. This can produce extreme challenges for students with fragile X syndrome. Even when level of intellectual ability, language skills and memory/recall are taken into account, the difficulties may still be pronounced. An example would be the problems experienced by a student with fragile X syndrome when faced with the sequence of instructions: 'Right class, first put the paints away, then wash your hands, then help me lay the table and then sit down ready for your elevenses'. In this sort of situation it is clearly preferable to break the sequence of commands into individual instructions which can be worked on one at a time.

A further cause of classroom difficulties, more common in the more able students with fragile X syndrome, is that of difficulties in organising one's thoughts, planning ahead, switching from one topic to another, and applying problem-solving approaches generally. These skills are known collectively as 'executive function abilities'. Difficulties in this area will manifest as high levels of disorganised thinking and behaviour, persistence on one theme even when the individual is aware of the need to shift mentally to another topic, and problems in sorting out solutions when faced with a number of possibilities of varying degrees of suitability. Particular attention to tutoring and help with problem-solving skills, and assistance with organisational aids such as check lists and diaries are helpful in this instance. Breaking down the problem-solving process into its constituents and focussing on each step one at a time is useful as illustrated by the following guide:

- Identify specific problems to be worked on.
- Decide in which order to tackle problems.
- Negotiate realistic goals.
- Clarify steps needed to achieve goal(s).
- Generate as many solutions as possible.
- Weigh up advantages and disadvantages of each solution.
- Decide on task required to tackle first step of chosen solution.
- Undertake exercise.
- Review with evaluation of success and if necessary reappraisal of how it could have gone better.
- Decide on next step and proceed.

Speech and language abilities

In fragile X syndrome all aspects of language need to be considered in relation to behaviour. These include not only verbal aspects ('speech') but the many non-verbal components such as facial expression, gesture, eye contact and physical proximity. These aspects of *expressive* language need to be distinguished from the individuals' comprehensions of what other people are trying to communicate to them – *receptive* language. In addition, the extent to which one can use language in a socially productive fashion is critical. Proficient social use of language requires good understanding of the meaning of language ('semantics') and its efficient practical use in two-way communications and interactions with others ('pragmatics'). Difficulties with social use of language and semantic/pragmatic aspects can be extreme, even with impressive expressive language skills and a large vocabulary. Such problems can be helped substantially by carefully constructed and run social use of language groups and social skill groups. Challenging behaviours can arise out of confusion with associated anxiety in a student with fragile X syndrome where unrealistic assumptions regarding receptive language skills and comprehension have been made on the basis of expressive language abilities.

Social difficulties

Not surprisingly, language problems frequently coexist with social difficulties. When extreme, and associated with ritualistic or obsessional behaviours, they may be indicative of an autistic spectrum disorder. However, in fragile X syndrome it is usually the paradoxical juxtaposition of a friendly and sociable (albeit shy and anxious) personality with certain autistic-like features which characterises individuals with the condition. A substantial minority of people with fragile X syndrome do have autism. But many more have a well-recognised profile of autistic-like tendencies. These include shyness and social anxiety, an aversion to direct eye contact, self-injury in response to anxiety or excitement (usually biting the hand at the base of the thumb), delays in imitative and symbolic ('make-believe') play, and certain repetitive behaviours, in particular hand-flapping. Conversely there is usually good understanding of facial expressions and their emotional meanings and implications. Individuals with fragile X syndrome will frequently repeat words or phrases they have heard a while ago ('delayed echolalia') or otherwise show markedly repetitive speech. Language often sounds as if there is a humorous quality to it with up-and-down swings of pitch ('jocular, litanic'). Speech may also be 'cluttered'. This refers to a combination of rapid utterances with disorganised rhythm ('disrhythmia'). It often feels as if the individual's ability to form language overtakes the ability to speak it. Words and phrases tumble over each other, impairing comprehension for the listener, and producing increasing anxiety and exacerbation of the language difficulties for the initiator. Careful guided calming and elocution strategies are helpful here in order to diminish associated anxiety and facilitate more understandable communications.

The sense of discomfort produced by direct eye-to-eye contact can be extreme. The tendency for people with fragile X syndrome to avert their gaze is not an indicator of rudeness or lack of social awareness. It requires respect and suitable adaptation of the teaching situation, for example tutoring from behind or to the side of the student rather than face to face. Averting one's own gaze when interacting with a student who has fragile X syndrome can be productive as well as appreciated.

To summarise this complicated area, a fair number of students with fragile X syndrome will have autism. Their educational needs will therefore be those of a student who has learning difficulties *and* an autistic spectrum disorder. Both these areas of developmental difficulty are important and both need to be responded to in any educational package. Many more students with fragile X syndrome can be classified as having atypical autism because of the coexistence of a friendly and sociable personality with a number of autistic-like features. They might be better described as having 'social and communicatory difficulties of a neuro-developmental nature similar to those witnessed in the autistic spectrum disorders'. Educationally, their needs will still often be similar to those students who are more clearly and obviously on the autistic spectrum. However, their sociability and good understanding of other people's thoughts and feelings need to be acknowledged and responded to.

Overactivity and attentional deficits

Boys with fragile X syndrome appear to have poorer concentration spans and poorer 'staying power' in terms of maintaining their focus on a particular topic than other students with similar degrees of intellectual disability. In addition they are also more restless, fidgety, impulsive and distractible. They may also be more overactive – but it is quite possible to have an overactive mind without an overactive body. This may manifest as blurting out answers before the question has been completed, or chattering away rapidly with frequent changes of topic. Alternatively it may show as daydreaming and being in a world of one's own. This latter presentation seems more common in girls than boys. Nonetheless it has just the same educational and therapeutic implications. Also, these attentional deficits and associated problems do not automatically improve with age, thereby emphasising just how critical early evaluation and early institution of remedial educational and psychological interventions are. Minimising distractions goes a long way to helping these difficulties. A structured, predictable and clear routine and time-table to the school day is important. So too are clear boundaries to allowable behaviour, clear and tangible rewards if these are adhered to, and equally clear sanctions if they are transgressed. Brief bursts of focussed mental activity should be interspersed with cooling-off times. Concentrating hard on a classroom topic can be exhausting for somebody with an attention deficit disorder. Regular rest and recuperation is required. Impulsive tendencies can often be helped by techniques that improve self-awareness or the need to stop and think before acting. These approaches can make use of day-to-day experiences, such as waiting for traffic lights to change, which will make sense and have meaning to the student. A high degree of one-to-one and small group tuition is also of obvious benefit for such difficulties.

Anxiety, aggression and self-injury

High levels of anxiety are very common in people who have fragile X syndrome. They frequently present as shyness or bashfulness with anxiousness in social settings. Many people with fragile X syndrome do themselves a disservice educationally, being too shy to answer a question, or being too anxious of failure to hazard a calculated guess. Patience, gentle coaxing and a demonstration of understanding can help in revealing true ability and knowledge. For example, a 21-year-old man with fragile X syndrome seemed unable to explain how an apple, a pear and a banana were the same. However, he identified correctly that the written chemical formula H_2O represented water!

Increasing anxiety may be evident through general posture and demeanour, facial expression, intensity of expressed language and even flushing of face and ears. If not recognised and responded to, there is a risk of an outburst either towards others (aggression) or towards oneself (self-injury). Thus, much aggression and self-injury will be preventable provided the underlying causes and mediating effect of anxiety are addressed in advance. An outburst of challenging behaviour, if it occurs is best managed by calming the surrounding environment as much as possible, maximising the safety of the individual and all others, and recognising the need to defuse the situation rather than standing on principle and insisting on dealing with whatever may have triggered the outburst.

Modifying behaviour – reducing the undesirable and enhancing the desirable

A person's behaviour may need to be changed in order to:

- Increase desired behaviours;
- Decrease undesirable behaviours;
- Treat distressing or unhelpful symptoms such as phobias (fears) or obsessions.

A problem with many efforts to manage challenging behaviour is that they are undertaken in a 'knee-jerk' fashion, in response to overwhelming stress experienced by teachers, parents or carers. It is tempting to go for the most problematic behaviour (which is also often one of the most resistant to change) rather than initially choosing one that is likely to modify. Choose a behaviour which is likely to respond – *not* necessarily the most problematic. Efforts to change behaviour should be based on at least the following:

- They should be made as early as possible in the development of the undesirable behaviour before it becomes entrenched or overwhelming.
- They should follow a full assessment of what the behaviour is, and why the person does it. Often people with fragile X syndrome show difficult behaviour if a task is too hard or demanding. Appearing naughty can be seen as preferable to appearing incompetent.

Conversely insufficient academic challenges will leave the student bored, frustrated and free to misbehave.

• Consider what more desirable behaviour is wanted. Make active efforts to develop it. The more time spent on desirable behaviour, the less there is left for undesirable ones. Trying to 'take away' a behaviour is rarely successful unless it is replaced with something more appropriate – usually a new skill or means of communication.

It is easy to fall into the trap of creating elaborate explanations for why somebody is doing what they do. It is better to observe, and collect data on:

• what *predisposes* someone to behave in such a way (e.g. high degrees of social anxiety caused by having fragile X syndrome);
• what triggers or *precipitates* the behaviour (e.g. television being turned off in the middle of a favourite video);
• what *perpetuates* it (e.g. repeated gaining of attention in response to challenging behaviour).

The collecting of data in this systematic and planned fashion is known as a *functional analysis* of behaviour. It leads to the development of a tailor-made behaviour modification programme.

How do people learn to behave in various ways?

The answers to this question are many and varied. At its simplest, there are three main ways that people learn:

By association ('classical conditioning')

The student learns to respond to a situation or happening by associating it with something that already triggers the behaviour.
Examples:

• Experiencing pain produces tantrum. Experience of going to dentist becomes associated with experience of pain. Going to dentist produces tantrum even without physical pain occurring.
• Feeling calm and relaxed produces diminished anxiety and overactivity. A schoolteacher is good at calming and relaxing the individual. The presence of the schoolteacher leads to the individual becoming calm, relaxed, and less overactive even without the teacher and individual interacting directly.

By learning that a particular behaviour produces a particular consequence ('operant conditioning')

The child learns that doing something results in a particular response from others.
Examples include:

• Every time the pupil finishes a meal without throwing food on the floor, he receives a sticker. Increasingly meals are finished without mess because of the incentive.

- Every time the child screams and bawls at the supermarket checkout the parent gives her a tube of Smarties. Increasingly supermarket checkouts become noisy, disruptive and uncontrollable with ever increasing Smartie tubes being bought.
- The child's constant clamouring for another toy from the Argos catalogue is diminished by studiously ignoring him.

By learning from observing other people's behaviour and the consequences ('social learning or modelling')

Examples include:

- The child repeatedly witnesses a playground bully gaining adult attention through repeated impulsive physical assaults on other children. The child starts to mimic this thereby receiving precious adult attention in a modestly staffed setting.
- At a new school the child sees that all the other pupils have to say please before getting a biscuit at elevenses time. Polite behaviour is more likely to occur from early on.

When helping children and young people who have learning disabilities to change their behaviour, a number of principles are paramount:

- Individuals do not exist in isolation from each other. Consider their friends, family and other important people such as teachers and youth club workers. What are their influences on individuals' behaviour and how are they affected by it?
- Consider the person's level of ability and understanding. A frequent cause of challenging behaviour and personal emotional distress is over- or under-estimation of abilities. This can lead, on the one hand, to frustration and feelings of being overwhelmed and misunderstood; on the other, it can produce resentment and boredom with development of less savoury time-filling activities.
- Consider language and communication skills. A large vocabulary, which can be recited, for example in response to pictures of the object being presented, may be mistaken for evidence of good communication skills. Equally, good ability to speak words ('expressive language') may be mistaken for evidence of good ability to understand what is said by others ('receptive language'). Subsequent failure to comply with instructions or to heed explanations may then be seen inappropriately as evidence of defiance and naughtiness. Teaching an effective means of communication can in itself remedy challenging behaviour.
- Be consistent. The same approach should be applied by everybody, wherever the individual is, whatever the time, and whoever is present.
- Give frequent and readily attainable rewards and incentives. It is no use constructing a programme where a pound can be earned for a day's good behaviour if the individual is unable to behave well for an hour.
- Rewards and incentives must be feasible, and easily withdrawable. Even if you know that buying a new £30 Playstation game will produce a day's good behaviour, there are few families who could afford the long-term application of such a programme.
- Personalise the programme. What are the individual's likes and dislikes? What will help them keep going with the challenge?
- The person must get more out of behaving appropriately than inappropriately. 'Do

nothing' behaviour (such as, sitting quietly and still without any further rewarding component) is unlikely to succeed.

Ways of increasing and decreasing the frequency and intensity of behaviour

There are four basic ways of increasing or decreasing the frequency and intensity of behaviour – by adding or subtracting a positive or negative consequence to the behaviour. This is illustrated in Table 17.1.

Adding a positive consequence is known as 'rewarding' or 'positive reinforcement'. Giving praise, a sticker, or the opportunity to watch a bit of a favourite video every time the child behaves throughout a lesson without screaming, makes school time behaviour better. Giving the child attention every time she cries out is likely to increase the problem. I carry on going in to work because my employers reward me with a monthly salary every four weeks or so!

Subtracting (taking away) a positive consequence is known as 'extinction'. Ignoring pupil's crying out (if tolerable) will diminish that behaviour. If I were to stop receiving payment by my employers, the chances are that my 'going to work behaviour' will pretty rapidly extinguish. Forgetting to congratulate a child for even small gains in use of language may decelerate progress. Extinction, when it works, is an extremely elegant, swift and enduring behavioural treatment. Like any treatment it may be inappropriate for a number of reasons:

- It may be impossible to prevent reinforcement of inappropriate behaviour (no amount of exhortation stops parents from rushing to their crying children the minute they start up after lights out).
- It may be undesirable to withhold reinforcement for practical reasons (parents are willing to ignore the crying but the neighbours complain bitterly).
- There is often a transient initial increase in the rate of undesirable behaviour – the so-called 'extinction burst'. This may make the programme inappropriate or dangerous (for example, it is considered unsafe to risk a head-banging child increasing the behaviour however temporarily).
- It may take too long (parents give up ignoring their children's crying after three and a half hours and go and comfort them thereby conveying the message that longer periods of crying are worthwhile to get parental attention even if the response is not immediate!).
- There may be other practical concerns such as risk of aggravating seizures in a child prone to epilepsy when emotionally aroused.

Table 17.1 Models of behaviour modification

	Positive consequence	Negative consequence
Add	Reward ('positive reinforcement')	Punishment ('aversion')
Subtract (take away)	Extinction	'Negative reinforcement'

Adding a negative consequence is known as 'punishment' or 'aversion'. This may work in the short term but can only be justified for extreme and totally unacceptable behaviours, for example the child who knowingly and deliberately runs into the road. However, its systematic use builds resentment, insecurity and unhappiness. Also, increasingly severe punishments are required over time to produce the same behaviour change, as in the caricature of the bad teacher who has to punish increasingly severely and frequently in order to maintain good behaviour – rather than providing incentives. There should be no need for aversion programmes or punishment in the management of challenging behaviour.

Subtracting (taking away) a negative consequence is known as 'negative reinforcement'. The baby who receives Smarties at the supermarket checkout from mother in order to quieten is negatively reinforcing mother's Smartie-giving behaviour by removing the aversive stimulus of screaming in public in response to receiving sweets. The baby is more likely to scream next time. Pupils who encourage the teacher to use a favourite classroom activity by only behaving in response to this are using the same behavioural technique. This makes the point that when applying a behavioural programme it is important to eat humble pie and consider what programme the individual has you on.

Fading out behavioural programmes

Your aim should be the development of desired behaviour without the need for an associated modification programme. This is helped by trying to move from rewards the person receives from others (external rewards) to internal ones, for example self-satisfaction with achieving the task. Some individuals will have such entrenched challenging behaviours or other vulnerabilities that they require an indefinite programme to maintain gains, with all the associated resource implications. Most will be able to gain at least a degree of self-control.

- The first stage is the establishment of a system of regular reinforcement. Reward the person every time the desired behaviour occurs. This is the easiest way to develop positive behaviours but is also the most prone to extinction.
- The second stage is to 'stretch the contingency' by only rewarding every second, third, fourth and so on, time ('fixed interval'). I don't need to receive money every day to continue coming in to work. I get payment at fixed intervals. This requires greater effort at establishing the behaviour, but is more resistant to extinction.
- The third stage is to develop a 'random interval' reinforcement programme. Reward desired behaviour *on average* every second, third, fourth or whatever time – but vary the number of waits before rewarding unpredictably. This is the most difficult to establish but highly resistant to extinction. Witness people's behaviour in amusement arcades on slot machines: a little reward, not very often, but it happens intermittently and unpredictably so you keep on going . . .
- The ideal final stage is for behaviour to occur for intrinsic rewards, for example liking the job or enjoying shopping, or even finding education intrinsically rewarding, fulfilling and worthwhile. External rewards can then be faded out altogether.

Progress on a behaviour programme

There is a series of characteristic phases through which individuals pass when placed on a behavioural programme.

Baseline

This is the essential observation and data-gathering phase, which is often neglected and omitted. The very act of focussing on the problem behaviour, attending to it and trying to understand it can often produce gratifying improvements. Feeling that your student never behaves may be based on the individual misbehaving regularly three times daily for twenty minutes each time. Aim to clarify what the behaviour's 'steady state' is prior to any intervention.

Period of change (either 'honeymoon' or 'extinction burst')

Honeymoon

This follows commencement of the intervention. Welcome improvement often occurs partly in response to the intervention but partly simply because things have changed in a novel way and people are paying more attention to the individual and what they do. Sometimes the honeymoon is so short you may not even notice it!

Extinction burst (or 'try harder' phase)

Behaviour worsens despite continuing the programme. The novelty has worn off. The individual may become resentful or want to return to how things were. Severity of problem behaviour may be even worse than baseline. A common mistake is to terminate the programme in response to worse behaviour associated with the extinction burst. This only causes further worsening of behaviour – the individual has been negatively reinforced for behaviour having become more challenging.

Improvement

Providing the programme is maintained, behaviour starts to improve slowly. Rate of improvement may be less than during the honeymoon but is usually more sustained.

Gathering information

Identify the behaviour you want to change. Construct a chart with three columns. Place a heading on each as follows:

- *Antecedent*: what was happening when the behaviour occurred. Where, when, with whom?
- *Behaviour*: what the individual actually did – what did you see? Be detailed.
- *Consequence*: what happened as a result? Was the individual told off, punished, removed from the setting, given an incentive to calm down, etc?

Before a programme can be drawn up, a behavioural assessment must be made of the target *behaviour*, what leads to it (*antecedents*), and what follows it (*consequences*). Details should include factors which precipitate the behaviour, in what circumstances it occurs, how people react to it, and what happens afterwards. This is best recorded in the form of a diary as follows (an ABC chart):

Date, time, place	Antecedents	Behaviour	Consequences
School assembly, the hall, Monday morning	Being bored; seeing the catering staff beginning to prepare lunch	Screaming, shouting, kicking	I was embarrassed – everyone was watching. I had to give in and offer him a Mars bar. Then the screaming stopped.

Keeping such a diary of your student's behaviour will often help you think of different ways to deal with it. If not, it can help you think of ways of modifying the antecedents or consequences so that the behaviour is changed. By collecting information from a number of occasions a picture often emerges of what it is that is triggering and maintaining the challenging behaviour. Common causes are:

- attention seeking;
- boredom;
- being overwhelmed by things going on around one;
- under-stimulation;
- being thwarted ('no you can't have a fourth Mars Bar');
- demand avoidance (for example, classroom tasks are too difficult – it is easier to misbehave and be sent out of the room);
- solitude seeking. Not all of us wish to be with others all the time. If you have autistic tendencies or a degree of shyness and social anxiety you may develop behaviours which increase the likelihood of your being alone;
- anxiety reduction for other reasons: for example, to avoid loud noise or changes in routine or the environment;
- sensory stimulation, such as licking, smelling, hand flapping, rocking.

The following outlines the above and provides a framework for devising and applying a behaviour modification programme.

Step-by-step to a behavioural programme

1 Define objectively which behaviours are problematic: (a) to the individual; (b) to the family, teachers, etc.
2 Prioritise these behaviours – which are the most important?
3 Start with a behaviour likely to respond – *not* necessarily the most problematic.
4 Do a functional analysis with comprehensive description of behaviour (when, where, what, how, with whom), antecedents and consequences
5 Try to involve the person in your assessment and intervention. Gain their co-operation whenever possible. It helps to make rewards appropriate to the behaviour – for example, getting a colouring pad or doing some painting, making a cake together or eating vegetables.
6 Evolve a plan on the basis of above findings for reducing undesirable behaviour and enhancing appropriate behaviours. Consider available methods for increasing and decreasing behaviours.

7 Relate the above plan to each stage of the behavioural sequence in question.

8 Ensure the plan is crystal clear to all involved. Ensure dissent can be voiced. Consider practicality of plan.

9 Rate response of behaviour to intervention.

10 React on basis of trends over time – not individual events.

11 Persist a reasonable time, considering possible reasons for success or failure.

You will often need to relate the behavioural programme to each stage of the desired behaviour. Sometimes behaviour is an instantaneous event, for example a spontaneous tantrum. More often it consists of a chain of linked behaviours each of which needs to be developed, for example coming in from play time, settling at the table and starting to focus on the lesson, or mealtime routines. In these instances you should work on the final behaviour in the chain until it is well developed and then move back in stages ending with the earliest behaviour required ('reverse chaining').

Finally, consider the following as well:

- It is easier to encourage desirable behaviours than to discourage undesirable ones.
- Longstanding patterns of behaviour are harder to change.
- Is the individual unwell or in pain and is this aggravating behaviour?
- All people behave badly sometimes. Does the behaviour really need to be changed? Is it really that permanent or might it be just a passing phase?
- Most behaviours won't disappear altogether no matter how hard you try. Those that do will reappear at times of change or anxiety.
- Choose the right time to tackle behaviour; for example, not when you are at a low ebb emotionally, or during the first week back at school after a break.
- There is always a reason for an outburst.
- Be calm and consistent and don't be afraid to ask for help and advice.

Chapter 18

Related conditions

Autism and attention deficit/hyperactivity disorders (AD/HD)

Kim Cornish and Julie Taylor

Children with fragile X syndrome can sometimes present with behaviours that might be considered as unusual or troublesome. For example, some children become overly impulsive, hyperactive, display atypical language patterns and aggressive behaviours on occasions. The pattern of these unusual behaviours has led many professionals and parents to wonder whether fragile X is linked with other conditions, most notably autism and/or attention deficit/ hyperactivity disorder (AD/HD). The aim of this chapter is to provide information on these two well-documented conditions and to show their relationship to (and differences from) fragile X. Current research into autism shows that it is one of the most strongly genetic of the childhood-onset psychiatric disorders. Perhaps any possible connections between autism and or AD/HD and fragile X will be confirmed or denied when the chromosome(s) responsible for autism are identified.

Autism

Given the range of social and communication impairments reported in children with fragile X, it is not surprising that this syndrome is often compared with autism. One of the most controversial and yet unresolved issues in recent years has been the extent to which there is an association between fragile X and autism (Turk, 1992). It is estimated that between 2 and 4 per cent of cases of autism are caused by fragile X and around 15 to 25 per cent of children with fragile X meet the diagnostic criteria for autism (Turk and Graham, 1997). Several studies have aimed to address the extent to which fragile X and autism overlap. The conclusions are mixed, with some researchers viewing fragile X as a pervasive developmental disorder that is best characterised as part of the autistic spectrum. On the other hand it could be possible that fragile X and autism are two separate disorders with an increased likelihood of co-occurrence if an individual has fragile X. Indeed, recent studies by Bailey and colleagues (Bailey *et al.*, 2001) suggests that co-occurrence of autism and fragile X can result in significant developmental impairments over and above those evident in fragile X alone. Furthermore, it has also been argued that the pattern of social and communicative behaviours displayed in children with fragile X and children with autism, whilst similar in some respects, differ qualitatively in many ways.

Looking first at classical autism, the most striking clinical feature is the childs pervasive lack of interest in other people including their families. Instead the child may be particularly attached to a highly unusual object (for example, a piece of cloth or a toy brick). The condition sometimes appears within the second or third year of life, but rarely after the age of three. Other atypical behaviours include stereotypes (for example, rocking, flapping hands) and a preference for these activities over and above social interactions, but it is the lack of social and communicative development that defines the syndrome. Unlike typically developing children and infants, children with autism display a lack of reciprocity in social situations, unusual eye gaze, lack of empathy and a paucity of joint play and communication skills. Furthermore, these deficits are often confounded by their poor use of social language (pragmatics), semantic problems and immediate and delayed echolalia (repetitions of words and phrases).

In fragile X, a number of autistic-like features can be exhibited and these include:

- poor eye contact
- sensitivity to touch
- hand-flapping and/or biting
- hyper-arousal
- perseveration in speech (repetition of words).

It is the *absence* of the core social impairment in children with fragile X, however, that differentiates them from children with autism. Whilst children with fragile X can often appear shy and socially anxious they are usually interested in socially interacting with others and in developing friendships but can sometimes have difficulty with accepting new faces or situations. Indeed, their lack of eye contact, which is so often misconstrued as resembling autistic behaviour, may result from their being overwhelmed or over-aroused by the sensory input involved in new social interactions rather than from a lack of social reciprocity. A further difference between autism and fragile X has been identified in a recent study by Turk and Cornish (1998), which found that children with fragile X were much better at recognising facial and emotional expressions and intonations in others compared to children with autism. Recent research indicates that when individuals with autism watch a conversation taking place, they look only at the mouth that is talking and rarely at the eyes. Hence they miss the gestures and emotions shown in the eyes, as well as other facial expressions. These clues are used by others to make social sense of what they see and hear. Children with fragile X, who resist eye contact and thus avoid watching eyes or moving mouths in conversations, may miss the same social clues albeit for a different reason.

At a cognitive level, numerous research studies have argued that a deficit in 'theory of mind' might underlie the social and communicative impairments that are characteristic of autism. By 'theory of mind' we refer to the ability to infer mental states (beliefs and intentions) in others and oneself. Children with autism typically perform poorly on these tasks compared to other syndrome groups. In a recent study we examined a range of theory-of-mind skills in children with fragile X alongside children with autism and children with Down's Syndrome. The results of the study indicate that although children with fragile X do have impairments in theory of mind, the intensity of this deficit is not as severe as that reported in autism but is comparable to the deficit reported in other learning disabled groups (Down's syndrome). What is especially interesting is that when errors occur, the type of error appears to be syndrome specific, reflecting the differing cognitive strengths and difficulties within fragile X. For example, the children with fragile X had impairment in the ability to transfer the real knowledge about an object's function to other representations of that object. In contrast, the errors made by the children with autism seem to reflect an inability to comprehend that different perceptual information about an object does not override an object's real function (Cornish, Grant and Munir, under review). There are other social difficulties experienced in autism that cannot be explained by poor intuitive mentalising. Impairments in emotion control, imitation, identifying with others and poor attention to social cues are all found in autism but not in fragile X. Children with autism also have weak central coherence where they process details well at the expense of global meaning.

Attention deficit/hyperactivity disorder (AD/HD)

AD/HD refers to a triad of symptoms, a so-called 'holy trinity' of chronic inattentiveness, and /or impulsivity and hyperactivity. These features tend to present early in development and across a wide range of situations. A child with AD/HD will often fail to pay close attention to details or make careless mistakes in schoolwork, he/she may find it difficult to follow through on instructions in class and have difficulty in waiting their turn. If hyperactivity is present, the child will often fidget with hands or feet and may constantly get up and down from their seat in a classroom. AD/HD is one of the most frequent disorders associated with behaviour problems in children. It makes up as much as 50 per cent of the child psychiatry clinic population and approximately 3 to 5 per cent of school-age children in the general population. Boys with AD/HD tend to outnumber girls by 3 to 1, although AD/HD in girls continues to be diagnosed – possibly because girls are more likely to show inattentive-only symptoms without hyperactivity and are thus less destructive in a classroom. The disorder persists into adolescence in 50 to 80 per cent and into adulthood in 30 to 50 per cent of cases clinically diagnosed in childhood. In terms of associated problems, children with AD/HD are at greater risk from social or adaptive problems, which can include aggression and anti-social behaviours.

In children with fragile X, there is now accumulating evidence to indicate that attention problems and hyperactivity are highly prevalent in boys and that many would meet the clinical criteria for AD/HD. For example, in 1984, Fryns and co-workers reported that hyperactivity and concentration difficulties were the most striking behavioural difficulties encountered in their sample of 21 boys; and in 1988 Bregman, and co-workers found 93 per cent of their 41 boys with fragile X met the DSM-III criteria for AD/HD. In 1987, Hagerman also found 73 per cent of 37 fragile X boys exhibited higher scores on attention and hyperactivity items on the Conner's teacher rating scale. Even when the level of learning disability is taken into account, boys with fragile X exhibit more symptoms of AD/HD than matched control children. In a UK study in 1998 by Turk, boys with fragile X were compared to boys with Down's syndrome and boys with learning disabilities of unknown aetiology. Turk reported that fragile X boys demonstrated significantly higher scores on items relating to hyperactivity and restlessness on the Child Behaviour Checklist (CBCL – teacher version) and on the Parental Account of Childhood Symptoms (PACS) questionnaire, than the two comparison groups of children. Furthermore, he reported these attributes were not diminished in the boys who had higher developmental ages.

The problem, however, of using only behaviour rating scales in assessing attention problems is that only a behavioural profile can be established. Such studies have not examined the different cognitive aspects of attention. They therefore tell us nothing about the difficulties encountered by children with fragile X on tasks requiring them to attend to stimuli while ignoring distracting stimuli (selective attention) or their ability to inhibit responses or to sustain attention over time on task. Studies on children with AD/HD as their primary diagnosis have documented not only behavioural profiles but have also identified core cognitive deficits including a primary deficit in the ability to inhibit automatic responding, that is difficulty in inhibiting automatic forms of behaviour when new rules come into operation. Similarly, recent research on children with fragile X has attempted to bridge the gap between what is known about the behavioural characteristics of the syndrome and what is known about the cognitive deficits of attention. In our own research we have found that the level and persistence of impulsive and repetitive behaviour displayed by young boys on cognitive assessments may be the consequence of a deficit in their inhibitory system (Wilding, Cornish and Munir 2002). To this end, the cognitive profile is almost identical to those children with AD/HD but without significant learning disability.

Using the information we know about AD/HD it might be useful to extrapolate this knowledge and apply it to dealing with the behaviour problems encountered in the classrooms of children with fragile X. We know, for example, that the AD/HD child will respond better if instructions are repeated a number of times, and, if novel or difficult tasks are performed during the morning session with recreational or less attention-based activities placed in the afternoon. However, an awareness of the cognitive strengths and difficulties of children with fragile X is also crucial. In particular, given that tedious, abstract or novel information is difficult for the fragile X child to absorb, it might be more useful to organise this type of activity into bite-size units, with greater clarity. In doing this, it is possible to draw on the child's strength in verbal skills and in their ability to remember information that is presented in a salient, meaningful context.

One area that remains unaddressed is the extent of the attention problems in girls with fragile X. No published study has yet addressed whether affected girls will present with AD/HD symptoms to the same extent as affected boys. Research in children with AD/HD as their primary disorder, reports that boys are three times more likely to have AD/HD than girls and six to nine times more likely than girls to be seen with AD/HD in a clinical setting. Indeed, there is an emerging consensus that in girls the core deficits may be related to their chronic inattentiveness rather than hyperactive-impulsive behaviours that combine with inattention in boys. If this is the case, then it may be more appropriate to target and develop interventions differently according to gender in fragile X.

Stimulant medication for symptoms of AD/HD

One area of continued controversy in the UK is whether children with a learning disability (such as fragile X) but who have additional symptoms that mirror those of classical AD/HD, would benefit from stimulant medication such as methylphenidate (Ritalin) (see Chapter 19). Undoubtedly, the prevalence of Ritalin-prescribing for AD/HD in children with learning disability is increasing in the UK. However, there is a current paucity of published findings on how Ritalin may impact upon a child with fragile X, although a flurry of recent studies suggests that children with a learning disability with IQs above 45 may have a more positive clinical response to stimulant medication than those children with severe levels of learning disability. However, other findings have reported a higher rate of unacceptable side effects due to Ritalin in children with learning disability compared to the range typically experienced in children of normal IQ. There is currently no published study of a British cohort of fragile X children that would inform clinicians and teachers about the effects of stimulant treatment in terms of cognitive functioning and behaviour management.

Conclusion and recommendations

This chapter has outlined some of the important findings that relate to two conditions often associated with fragile X: autism and AD/HD. A review of the current literature suggests that AD/HD is especially prevalent in boys with fragile X and appears to mirror the cognitive and behavioural profile of classical AD/HD. However, the profile of AD/HD in girls with fragile X is less well established but it is highly likely that the main deficits will focus around inattentiveness and impulsive behaviour rather than include hyperactivity. In some respects, the lack of hyperactive behaviour (combined with chronic shyness and social anxiety) places many girls at risk from not benefiting or gaining access to educational programmes that could target their specific attention deficits. Teachers and other professionals need to be aware that girls with fragile X will more often display a subtype of AD/HD referred to as inattention-only (IO) which will not include hyperactive behaviour. This aspect of their behavioural profile needs to be recognised as a core difficulty alongside the more classical AD/HD profile displayed in boys with fragile X.

In contrast to the prevalence of AD/HD, the prevalence of autism in fragile X is still controversial and we have sought to outline some of 'autistic-like' features that children with fragile X can display alongside the core differences between the fragile X profile and the profile of classical autism. In spite of the differences between these three complex conditions, there are similarities in the type of approach best used. All three require high levels of support both at home and at school. A predictable, consistent environment with clear boundaries and appropriate motivators suits them all. Systems and strategies that aim to reduce anxiety and raise self-esteem should be established to ameliorate all three conditions.

Selected reading

Bailey, D.B., Hatton, D.D., Skinner, M. and Mesibov, G. (2001). Autistic behaviour, FMR1 protein, and developmental trajectories in young males with fragile X syndrome. *Journal of Autism and Developmental Disorders* 31: 165–174.

Cohen, I.L., Sudhalter, V., Pfadt, A., Jenkins, E.C., Brown, W.T. and Vietze, P.M. (1991) Why are autism and the fragile-X syndrome associated? Conceptual and methodological issues. *American Journal of Human Genetics* 48: 195–202.

Turk, J. (1992). The fragile X syndrome: on the way to a behavioural phenotype. *British Journal of Psychiatry* 160: 24–35.

Turk, J. and Graham, P. (1997). Fragile X syndrome, autism and autistic features. *Autism* 1: 105–27.

Turk, J. and Cornish, K. (1998). Face recognition and emotion perception in boys with fragile X syndrome. *Journal of Intellectual Disability Research* 42(6): 490–499.

Wilding, J., Cornish, K.M. and Munir, F. (2002) Further delineation of the executive deficit in males with fragile X syndrome. *Neuropsychologia* 40(8): 1343–9.

Chapter 19

Medication matters

Jeremy Turk

The use of medication for problematic behaviours in individuals with learning disabilities has a chequered history. An era of overuse with little regard for potential short- and long-term side effects, sometimes irreversible, was followed by a period of time when medication of any form seemed to be frowned upon. This phase had the extremely positive effect of focussing our attention on the psychological and social determinants of behaviour and what could be done to improve quality of life by these means alone. However, recent years have witnessed acknowledgement that however sophisticated our understanding of psychological and social determinants of behaviour, there is still the occasional place for the judicious use of certain medications for particular indications.

It is important to remember that intervention and support for children and young people with fragile X syndrome who show challenging behaviours has many dimensions. Psychological, educational and social approaches should always be considered – the use of medication being viewed as a temporary addition to these rather than a substitute for them. There are a number of crucial issues that must be born in mind when considering the use of medication for behavioural reasons.

1 Medication should never be the initial intervention

Consider psychological, educational, family and social approaches before considering medication. It is a common misconception that because the roots of a behavioural problem are partly biological, then the treatment must be medical. There is in fact much good evidence that behaviour problems of an undeniably biological cause (such as those following head injury) can be helped substantially by psychological means. Conversely problems of a very 'psychological' nature (such as sudden severe depression following bereavement) may, if serious, require a brief course of medication to facilitate psychological treatment. Furthermore, severity of the problem is a poor indicator of whether medication is needed – extreme behaviours may be helped very readily by straightforward behavioural advice while mild and relatively trivial problems may require medication if they are felt to be troublesome enough to be treated (for example, nervous tics).

2 A thorough multi-disciplinary assessment must be undertaken

The only way to know what combination of multi-disciplinary interventions is required is to have a comprehensive multi-disciplinary assessment. For example, tantrums in an individual who has learning disabilities may often result from a combination of factors: frustration over poor communication skills, a high degree of impulsiveness and inability to wait, combined with distress over unrealistic schooling expectations, physically and emotionally over-burdened carers and a predisposition to high levels of anxiety. Such a combination of contributors to the problem behaviour indicates the need to attend to a wide range of social, family, educational and psychological issues. To prescribe medication without these issues being addressed would be unethical and inappropriate. However, the problems may have become so entrenched as to seem self-perpetuating. In such circumstances the use of medication *in addition to the above* may be justified.

3   Other interventions should have been tried

There is no such thing as a medication without side effects. The decision whether or not to prescribe is therefore a balance between severity of problem, potential benefits, possible adverse effects, and whether other forms of treatment are available and have been tried. Medication may work as well as psychological approaches for some problems and may seem attractively simple. However, used as a first line of intervention, medication will not allow the individual to develop their own ways of coping better with their problems. It will also leave the person prone to unnecessary side effects.

4   If problems still persist, consider medication in addition to other approaches as a means to an end – not an end in itself

The decision as to whether one should try psychological or medical treatments is not an 'either-or' one. Necessary psychological, educational, familial and other social supports should be in place and must continue. If required, medication can then be added as a means of facilitating these other treatments, for the shortest possible time, with careful monitoring by an experienced and appropriately trained medical practitioner.

5   Treat the symptoms (for example, self-injury, aggression) not the syndrome

There is no medication for specific causes of learning disability such as fragile X syndrome. However, certain medications may be indicated for some challenging behaviours and other problems experienced commonly by individuals with the condition. Most individuals with fragile X syndrome will never require medication. Of the remainder, most will need a specific agent for a short duration as an addition to the inputs described above. The decision to treat medically is based on whether a certain emotional or behavioural problem (for example, self-injury, depression, hyperactivity) has been present severely enough for a persisting amount of time to cause concern – and whether it has responded to other approaches or not.

6   Undertake a clinical trial of medication. Does it work or not? Are there side effects?

Medications for emotional and behavioural difficulties are notoriously unpredictable in their effects – particularly in individuals with learning disabilities or autistic features. There is often no way of knowing in advance how a person will react to a particular medication. Assessment and initial prescription is therefore but the start of the process. Careful monitoring by the individual, carers and professionals is required, if possible using rating scales to get as clear an idea as possible as to whether there are changes coincident with the medication having been started, and whether these changes are beneficial or not. For example, only about two-thirds of children prescribed stimulants such as methylphenidate (Ritalin, Equasym) or dexamphetamine (Dexedrine) for severe hyperactivity benefit with increased attention span and reduced restlessness and impulsivity. Some of the remainder will respond with worsened hyperactivity! This thankfully resolves as soon as the medication is stopped. Medications also take a very variable time to start working. Stimulants for hyperactivity act very quickly; often within half an hour, and the effects can be vivid. Antidepressants may take six or so weeks to create a noticeable and enduring change in mood. Each medication has its own profile of side effects. Families and school staff should always be made aware of these so they can be on the lookout for them and also so that they can include this information in making an informed decision as to whether a certain medication is worth trying or not.

7   Consider the 'cost-benefit' ratio. What is the likelihood of improvement? How important is this? What are the likelihoods of side effects? How serious might they be?

There is always the need to weigh up the 'pros' and 'cons' of medication. Is the problem really that bad? Have other non-medical approaches really been tried properly? Am I worried that medication is being suggested because of a lack of other more appropriate services and interventions locally? Does the person really have a condition or symptom that is recognised as being likely to respond to a particular class of medications? Or do people seem to want to just 'dampen down' his or her behaviour or render the person more 'manageable' in an overstretched setting?

8   Beware of the increased risk of adverse effects in people with learning disability and other developmental disabilities

The effects of medication are difficult to predict at the best of times. It is even more problematic in people with learning and other developmental disabilities. Even more caution and thought is required for this group before a decision to prescribe is reached.

9   If medication does not work, stop it!

Obvious advice but sadly often ignored. Resolution of the problem that triggered commencement of medication does not mean automatically that the medication was responsible for the improvement. It certainly doesn't imply that long-term prescribing is therefore indicated. So many other things in the individual's life may have changed simultaneously. Even the decision to prescribe and the taking of tablets will have had a profound psychological effect on all concerned without a hint of drug having entered the body. Some medications, if beneficial, should be continued for a reasonable time to minimise risk of relapse when stopped. For example, antidepressants should usually be given for four to six months even if mood has lifted quickly. Conversely, stimulants for hyperactivity have a very short duration of action, no more than four or so hours. These medications can therefore be stopped intermittently (under medical supervision) to monitor whether they are still required or whether the individual has grown out of the need for them.

10 If medication does work, give it for the minimum time possible with frequent monitoring and reviews regarding continuing need and possible adverse effects

There is no room for medication on a 'repeat prescription' basis where there is a lack of regular careful monitoring to ensure continued need and benefit and absence of serious adverse effects. Properly monitored drug treatments can be as time-consuming for professionals as other approaches. If the time, expertise and willingness are unavailable then medication really should not be commenced.

11 Don't ask whether medication works for children with fragile X who have emotional and behavioural problems. Ask whether a specific medication works for a specific child who has a specific behavioural difficulty

We are all individuals. We all have our own complicated reasons for being who we are and for doing what we do. There can therefore be no recipe book listing the 'right' medication for any particular behaviour. The reasons for the behaviour and its functions must be elucidated for each individual. On this basis there may sometimes be a useful role for medication in addition to other approaches as a means to an end – not an end in itself.

There are a number of relatively common reasons for considering medication in children and young people with fragile X syndrome:

Epilepsy and associated emotional and behavioural problems

Epilepsy occurs in 10–30 per cent of individuals who have fragile X. It usually takes the form of generalised 'tonic-clonic' or 'grand mal' convulsions. Anticonvulsants such as carbamazepine (Tegretol), sodium valproate (Epilim) and lamotrigine (Lamictal) are often sufficient to control even severe and frequent convulsions with relatively few side effects. Newer anticonvulsants such as topiramate (Topamax) may be used in addition. There is some evidence that these medications may be of benefit for predictable and regular swings of mood and behaviour even in the absence of obvious epilepsy. Blood levels of these medications usually require monitoring because of the great variation in the amount absorbed from the gut, and the levels needed to produce benefit without side effects. Epilepsy can also take the form of generalised absences ('petit mal'). These absence states consist of the individual appearing to enter into a state of suspended animation for a few seconds before continuing whatever they had been doing, oblivious to the fact that they have experienced a seizure. Such episodes can be very difficult to identify in a busy classroom, especially if they are particularly transient and if the individual is suspected of having concentration problems as well. Absence seizures do not include loss of muscle control. The individual does not collapse or show muscle twitching or jerking. Diagnosis is by means of analysing the person's brainwaves using an electroencephalogram (EEG). Medication may be similar to those mentioned above, for example sodium valproate. It may differ, an example being ethosuximide (Zarontin). Occasionally epilepsy shows as altered mood states. This may be a direct effect if the seizure is affecting the part of the brain which is concerned with emotions. At other times it may be because of abnormal experiences the seizure is producing such as strange, puzzling and disturbing smells, sounds, sights, tastes or even physical sensations. These episodes where the state of consciousness is affected are known as 'complex partial seizures'. They can be particularly difficult to diagnose because of their unusual nature, their confusion with psychologically or socially induced outbursts, and the fact that the EEG abnormality is only present during an actual seizure.

Hyperactivity and attention deficits

Psychostimulants such as methylphenidate (Ritalin) and dexamphetamine (Dexedrine) boost concentration skills and the individual's ability to resist impulsive tendencies and distractions. They are very highly researched medications which when used for the right individuals can dramatically improve their behaviour and attentiveness. They appear to work by stimulating the brain's 'inhibitory circuitry' – those parts which act as a brake and balance the other main 'excitatory' system. Benefits can be dramatic and rapid in terms of reduced activity levels, increased concentration span, less restlessness and fidgetiness, better control of impulsive tendencies and enhanced freedom from distractibility. They do have a number of possible side effects that require that they be treated with respect. These include worsening of hyperactivity, poor sleep, poor appetite, weight loss, stunting of growth, tummy aches, headaches, dizziness, mood changes, palpitations and nervous tics. If these problems occur stopping the medication can reverse them. Unfortunately only two-thirds of individuals benefit from the stimulant medications and it is difficult to predict who the responders are likely to be. Those with epilepsy may be at risk of the condition being worsened by these medications. There is now a sustained release long-acting version of methylphenidate, known as Concerta. This has the benefit of only one daily dosage as opposed to the morning and lunchtime doses that are usually needed with the more traditional stimulant medications. These medicines can be equally useful where the concentration problems exist without overactivity, so-called AD/HD, predominantly inattentive type.

Clonidine (Catapres, Dixarit) is also beneficial for disorders of attention and overactivity. It has the benefit of not affecting appetite or aggravating epilepsy. It also has a mildly calming effect which is of use if the behaviour problems coexist with sleep disturbance or tic disorders. Clonidine can be combined with a stimulant medication if necessary, for example methylphenidate being taken in the morning and at lunchtime, with a small dose of clonidine in the evening to help prepare the individual for sleep.

Aggression and violence

These extreme challenging behaviours often prove very difficult to treat by any means. It is particularly important to have considered and tried non-medical approaches including psychological, educational and social approaches. The *reasons* for the extreme behaviours must be searched for and addressed. It is important to avoid the understandable temptation to reach for sedatives, which often paradoxically make things worse. Nonetheless, sometimes the challenges are so great that some form of behavioural control is really essential to ensure the individual's safety and welfare. The more modern major tranquillisers (so-called 'atypical antipsychotics') such as risperidone (Risperdal), amisulpiride (Solian), olanzepine (Zyprexa) and quetiapine (Seroquel) can have a beneficially calming and mind-focussing effect. Their main complication is often dramatic appetite stimulation with equally dramatic consequent weight gain. Dizziness and faintness can also occur as well as occasional tremor, slowness and muscle stiffness similar to that seen in Parkinson's disease. Very low doses may be all that is needed. Indeed, excessive doses may produce side effects without allowing for benefit.

The main indication for these medications is to stabilise individuals and hopefully render them more receptive to psychological and social therapeutic approaches. They should be discontinued after the need for medication has resolved.

Self-injurious behaviour

Again, other approaches and the underlying reasons for the behaviour must be considered (such as attention-seeking, solitude-seeking, demand avoidance). Sadly there are no magic medications for such problems but the following may be of use:

- newer antidepressants such as fluoxetine (Prozac), paroxetine (Seroxat), sertraline (Lustral) and citalopram (Cipramil) where the self-injury seems to have an obsessive-compulsive quality. These medications are of obvious use where depression is part of the clinical picture.
- 'anti-tic' agents such as pimozide (Orap) or sulpiride (Dolmatil) if self-injury takes a repetitive tic-like form.
- 'opioid antagonists' such as naltrexone. These are thought to work by blocking the body's release of substances similar to chemicals called opiates. These chemicals are released in increased amounts in response to injury and can produce a calming and mildly euphoric effect. It is thought that this pleasant sensation may be a reinforcer for seemingly purposeless and self-destructive activities. By blocking the release of these chemicals, the pleasant reinforcing consequence of self-injury is removed, the behaviour becomes unrewarding or even somewhat aversive, and it should diminish.

Each of these medication groups will benefit a small number of individuals with serious self-injury, when combined with an individualised behaviour modification programme which addresses the self-injury's function in that person.

Mood disorder

Depression is one of the most common of all medical conditions. It is even more common in people with learning disabilities for a number of predictable psychological and social reasons as well as a probable heightened vulnerability. Psychological treatments are usually highly effective and the treatment of first choice. Antidepressants, as described above, may be needed temporarily or intermittently in addition. The newer antidepressants are also recognised as being of use for obsessive-compulsive behaviours, anxiety states including social anxiety, and even the consequences of post-traumatic stress disorder.

Where swings of mood between euphoria and depression occur, a mood stabiliser may be indicated. Traditionally lithium (Priadil, Camcolit) has been used. However, lithium has a number of quite serious side effects. For this reason, cyclical mood and behaviour disorders are being increasingly treated with medications traditionally used for epilepsy, such as carbamazepine and sodium valproate, often with highly beneficial outcomes.

Sleep disorder

Disturbances of sleep are another very frequent cause for concern. A good bedtime routine and attention to other factors contributing to poor settling and sleep are essential. Sleep difficulties may comprise:

- difficulties in settling and falling asleep;
- problems in remaining asleep with repeated awakenings throughout the night;
- early morning waking.

Sleep problems have been shown to be some of the most responsive to behaviour modification programmes. These should always be tried first. The following medications may be of benefit in extremis:

- Hypnotics such as trimeprazine (Vallergan). This medication is in fact an antihistamine which has been found to have the useful side effect of intense drowsiness. It may however make some children less sleepy and more irritable as well as producing headache and dry mouth. The irritability and drowsiness can persist well in to the school day, interfering with classroom learning and behaviour. For similar reasons the older sedatives such as diazepam (Valium) chlordiazepoxide (Librium) and nitrazepam (Mogadon) should be avoided. They too can produce increased irritability, daytime drowsiness and blunted concentration as well as having addictive potential.
- There is increasing interest in melatonin, which is produced by a gland at the base of the brain and released in response to falling light levels as picked up by the eyes. It can facilitate sleep onset and reduce night-time waking in children with developmental disabilities who have failed to respond to psychological interventions. In the short term it appears to be a remarkably safe medication. Long-term safety has not as yet been researched. Benefits can also dwindle over time.
- Some preliminary data suggests that clonidine (see above) may be useful in helping sleep when repeated night-time waking is a problem.

Summary and conclusions

From the above it should be clear that although there are a number of medications of potential benefit for some of the problems experienced by children and young people who have fragile X syndrome, they all need to be treated with substantial respect. They must be prescribed and monitored by a specialist trained and experienced in this complicated field, and should follow attempts at non-medical approaches. These should include psychological, educational, family and social interventions. Medication is not a magic cure. It can however be of some further benefit when combined with the above treatments following a thorough assessment. No one treatment is suitable for all people who have a particular problem. The decision to medicate is therefore a very individual one. Long-term as well as short-term side effects can occur and the risks of these must always be weighed up against the possible benefits.

Part V

Family and social matters

Chapter 20

The genetics of fragile **X** syndrome

Angela Barnicoat and Barbara Carmichael

An understanding of the genetics of Fragile X Syndrome is of value to those involved in the teaching or training of affected individuals. An insight into the genetic patterns of inheritance aids understanding of the practical and emotional difficulties some families may have.

Practical importance of genetics to education

There are two particularly important issues. Firstly the condition may affect other family members. Mothers and siblings are the most likely close relatives to be affected. Females are frequently less severely affected than males because of the pattern of inheritance. This milder degree of difficulty may delay or prevent diagnosis. It can be especially useful to understand that the mother of an affected child may be struggling with her own cognitive and psychological difficulties as well as trying to help and support a child with learning and behavioural problems. Awareness of the risk to sisters may allow early diagnosis and intervention for biologically based difficulties, which might otherwise be attributed to social factors or lack of application.

Secondly because of the genetic nature of the condition a young person who has fragile X is at risk of passing on the gene to any children they may have. There may be other pressing issues related to the possibility of raising a family for affected individuals, but the risk of transmission to the next generation is an additional burden. This is generally a greater concern for young women with fragile X than men not only because their genetic risk is higher (see below), but also because the milder problems they usually experience makes reproduction more likely for them.

Genes and chromosomes

Humans have 46 chromosomes, which contain the genetic instructions handed down from parent to child. Each chromosome contains a large number of genes. A gene is a length of chemical code, containing the information for cells to make specific protein molecules. The different proteins are important to allow the cells to develop a full range of functions. In total humans are estimated to have around 80 thousand genes.

Genes are made from molecules of DNA (deoxyribonucleic acid). Chromosomes are made from coiled up genes and other DNA molecules, which separate and control the genes, as well as proteins packing the chromosomes together.

Chromosomes are inherited in matching pairs. The pairs are numbered from 1 to 22 based on their relative size. Each individual receives one copy of each chromosome from their mother and one from their father. This is the mechanism by which genes are mixed up as they are passed from parent to child and means that each child inherits half of each parent's genes. It also means that for each gene a child inherits two copies; one from the mother and one from the father. In most cases only one gene is needed so the second copy is rather like an insurance policy in case of a gene failing to work normally.

The exception to this is one pair of chromosomes, the X and Y, which make up the twenty-third pair. Females have two X chromosomes and males an X and a Y. The Y chromosome contains genes leading to the development of male characteristics; when it is absent female features will develop.

Fragile X syndrome was originally named because of an unusual appearance of the X chromosome in those with the condition. It looked as if one end of the chromosome was breaking off. In fact this appearance is caused by the uncoiling of the strands of genetic material in the chromosome at a particular site. The gene FMR-1 (fragile site mental retardation-1) that functions abnormally in fragile X is located at the position of the apparent fragility of the X chromosome.

FMR-1 or fragile X gene

The molecules of DNA that make up the FMR-1 gene are altered in fragile X in a way that prevents the gene performing its usual function.

The DNA molecules of all genes are made of a coding pattern of chemical bases. There are four bases, adenine, guanine, thiamine and cytosine, known by their initial letters A, G, T and C to make up the code. These bases are arranged in groups of three, specific groups of three coding for particular amino acids to be part of a protein.

The change in the FMR-1 gene in people with fragile X is twofold. Firstly there is an increase in the size of a CGG repeat section within the gene. Secondly when this CGG repeat number becomes quite large (roughly over 200) a second chemical change occurs whereby a controlling part of the DNA has a chemical added to it in a process called methylation. It is the second change of methylation that effectively turns the gene off, and stops the FMR-1 protein being made. People who lack the FMR-1 protein have fragile X.

Pre and full mutations in FMR-1

The change in the gene has two stages. There may be a small increase in the size of the CGG repeat (from about 50–200 repeats) – this is termed a premutation. People with pre-mutations do not seem to have fragile X but whether they may have subtle problems with cognitive and psychological processes is much debated. However, when a premutation is handed down from a mother to a child it may increase in size leading to a full mutation with more than 200 repeats and methylation of the gene. Those males who have the full mutation are expected to have fragile X.

For girls who have a full mutation around half are expected to have the condition. The lower chance of girls being affected is because they have two X chromosomes. In each cell of the body a girl only uses one X chromosome the other is inactivated or turned off. It is a random process determining which X chromosome is inactivated (either the one she inherited from her father or the one she inherited from her mother). A girl with the full mutation is likely to escape the effects of fragile X syndrome if her brain cells have randomly turned off a high proportion of the X chromosomes that carry the altered gene. Conversely, if a high proportion of the unaffected X chromosomes are turned off, she will show more features of fragile X syndrome.

Pattern of inheritance of fragile X

The pattern of inheritance of fragile X can now be understood. Boys who have the condition have an unusual X chromosome that they have inherited from their mother. (They must inherit their Y from their father.) Mothers of affected boys may be carriers of pre or full mutations (if the latter they may themselves be affected). In each pregnancy a woman is equally likely to hand on either of her X chromosomes. For a carrier mother on average half her children will inherit the X chromosome with the change in the FMR-1 gene and half will inherit the normal X chromosome.

If a woman carries a full mutation it is likely to be handed on without much change to her children, so that half of her sons would be expected to be affected and around a quarter of her daughters (half will inherit the full mutation and half of these will be affected). If a woman carries a premutation there is a risk that this will change to a full mutation as it is handed on. The level of this risk depends on several factors, not all of which are yet fully understood. The risk is high if there is relatively large increase in the CGG repeat and if there are close family members affected with fragile X. Boys who have a premutation will always pass this on. The premutation does not seem to increase when a man transmits the gene. Since a man passes his X chromosome to his daughters but his Y to his sons, such a man will have daughters who all carry the premutation and sons who are free of the disorder. Males who have the full mutation are expected to pass this to daughters too. However, there is a small amount of evidence that the daughters of full mutation males are premutation carriers rather than full mutation carriers.

Rarely, a different change in the FMR-1 gene prevents its usual function. Most commonly this is a section missing from the gene (a deletion).

Genetic diagnosis and counselling

The diagnosis of fragile X is undertaken in genetics laboratories usually by checking for the expansion in the CGG repeat and methylation of the gene in DNA extracted from a sample of blood. Examination of the chromosomes for the fragile site has largely been abandoned as the newer technology usually gives more information to families.

When a paediatrician assesses a developmentally delayed child, a test for fragile X is frequently suggested. If the diagnosis is confirmed, discussion with a genetics specialist should be offered to the family. Clinical geneticists who see such families construct a family tree and explain the pattern of inheritance. This is important in explaining the risks that further children may be affected, and in deciding who else in the family could be carrying the unusual gene. Testing is offered for other family members as appropriate. It is not usual to test children about whom there are no developmental concerns within a family until they are teenagers. In the UK clinical geneticists may be the first professionals a family come into contact with who have seen other children with fragile X and so can be a valuable resource for general information.

Where a couple already have a child with fragile X there is always a substantial risk that further children will be affected. Testing during pregnancy can be offered to women at risk of an affected child. It is technically complex and needs to be discussed in detail with a geneticist. When it is predicted that a pregnancy will result in an affected baby the parents may be offered an abortion. There is no treatment to ameliorate the syndrome before birth.

New reproductive techniques are becoming available. The most promising at present is called preimplantation genetic diagnosis. This involves fertilisation in a laboratory using eggs and sperm taken from the parents. When the human embryo reaches a critical size a single cell is removed and checked for fragile X. Only embryos free of the abnormal gene are returned to the mother's womb to grow. Techniques like this may help families avoid the birth of affected children in the future.

Summary

Understanding the genetic nature of fragile X is important for teachers of those who are affected. This is because teachers can be alert to the possibility of other family members, particularly mothers, themselves having problems from the condition. In addition, it can aid teachers as they help affected adolescents think about themselves and their possible future as parents, aware of the risk that the condition may be transmitted to another generation.

Chapter 21

Adults with fragile X syndrome

Greg O'Brien

Introduction

'But what are the prospects for the future, doctor?' This question is frequently on the minds of the parents whose children have learning difficulties or the more serious learning disabilities, and certainly so in respect of fragile X syndrome. We still have much to learn about this issue, but there are some pointers we can give.

In this chapter, we will consider the long-term outlook for people affected by fragile X. There is a great deal to consider. The question arises whether gazing into the future is really helpful. However, it is vital to remember that, while we can make generalisations about outcomes being more or less likely in fragile X, we cannot say for sure what will happen in the case of any individual. But we can advise that certain problems are more or less likely to occur, to get worse, or even to improve. Clinicians try to give pointers to what parents and others should watch out for, and what they might do about it.

I will also describe two of my studies: one compares children and adults with fragile X; the other looks at adult 'low expressors' of the condition. Both studies provide information about being an adult living with fragile X, how families can be aware of the complexities of affected adults and help people attain their maximal potential.

Crystal ball gazing or prediction? The adult outcome of fragile X syndrome

There are fundamental questions to be asked when considering the adult outcome of childhood learning disabilities. These concern:

- life expectancy
- general health and quality of life
- skills for daily living in adulthood
- adjustment to adult life.

Life expectancy

There is a long tradition of research into the life expectancy of people with learning disabilities. These studies help us to put the life expectancy of people with fragile X into perspective. They have shown that people with learning disabilities, including those living in the community, have a shorter life expectancy than other people. But can just having learning disabilities really reduce life expectancy? In fact, people with severe learning disabilities, most notably IQ levels below 40, do not live so long. Other high-risk factors, which predict or are associated with earlier death in people with learning disabilities, include additional physical disabilities or medical problems, particularly cerebral palsy and poorly controlled epilepsy. Non-mobile people and those incapable of self-feeding are especially at risk of short life expectancy. This doesn't fit the pattern of fragile X. Adults with fragile X may well live to a ripe old age, because they have few of the high-risk factors. But any additional health problems, especially poorly controlled epilepsy, does not hold out promise for greater longevity.

General health and quality of life

Closely related to the study of life expectancy, there has been long-standing interest in the general health of adults with learning disabilities. Fragile X syndrome has no specific health problems associated with it which are particularly likely to impact on adult life.

Parents do ask whether problems with the heart valves of children with fragile X can cause problems in later life. These valves are a bit floppy, a bit like the finger joints of people with fragile X. They tend to leak a bit; or in medical language, they are 'incompetent'. But to our knowledge, this does not cause problems in adult life. I would recommend that this be kept under review for each person with valve incompetence, as would happen in other causes of valve incompetence. In fragile X, this is something we do not yet know enough about.

Just like the rest of us, the health of affected individuals is mostly determined by their diet and lifestyle. Making responsible personal choices, and being in control of their own circumstances, is central to enhancing the quality of life of people with fragile X. A variety of important interactional effects are apparent when considering general health outcomes. For example, the individual's own perception of any physical illness, such as epilepsy, can play a crucial role in outcome, as can family and parental adjustment to the whole business of the stress of disability. All in all, general health in adulthood for most people with fragile X is determined by the same influences as the rest of us. Smoking, poor diet and an inactive lifestyle are the worst possible combination. Attention to health problems, a balanced diet and an active lifestyle promote better adjustment. But it is not likely to work if it is forced on the person concerned. They need to make choices, and those around them need to point out the advantages of a healthy lifestyle, rather than just leaving it up to the individual.

Skills for daily living in adulthood

The fundamental question is 'How much will this person be able to do for themselves in adulthood?' To explore this question in respect of fragile X, we need to identify the most powerful factors influencing the capacity for independent living in any person with learning disabilities. This issue can be broken down into several parts. Firstly, is there evidence that severe learning disabilities in childhood (in terms of lower IQ) predict adult daily living skills? Clarke and Clarke (1988) concluded that early severe learning disabilities predict very powerfully long-term dependency and disability, much more than mild disability. The studies they reviewed indicated the importance of other childhood factors to predict subsequent adult living skills. Notably, conduct disorder in childhood was found to be an important adverse factor. A more recent review (King *et al.*, 1992) agreed that child variables are an important determinant of subsequent adult functioning, but emphasised that environmental variables are also crucially important. The consensus is that the severity of childhood learning disabilities may be *of itself* a most powerful predictor of later subsequent adaptive functioning, in all people with learning disabilities. Faced with such a prospect, some researchers have concentrated on how best to maximise social adaptive functioning of children with learning disabilities. One long-standing debate concerns patterns of parenting. Marfo (1990) noted that, while it had been widely believed that certain patterns of parenting such as 'maternal directiveness' were likely to have an adverse effect upon development, this was not based on empirical evidence. Another possibility was that 'maternal directiveness' is better seen as an indicator of the severity of early intellectual and behavioural challenges. A directive style of parenting may be a response to behavioural problems in the child, rather than the cause of the child's difficulties.

This evidence is very helpful to parents who have found that a 'directive' parenting style is most appropriate in helping the growing person with fragile X develop skills for adult daily living.

Adjustment to adult life

Parents' most fervent hope is that their child will enjoy a satisfying, fulfilling and, in every possible way, a successful life. Once again, follow-up studies on these themes reveal both good news and bad. Many people will enjoy futures that live up to these expectations, but the bad news is inescapable. Follow-up studies of key indicators of adult adjustment, such as employment, relationships, criminality and adult mental health, are not optimistic. It is known that the more severely disabled child is at greater risk, in respect of most outcome indices of general integration into adult life. The outcomes for children with mild learning disability have improved in more recent years. Findings of early studies have been substantially corroborated by more recent work

This latter observation has been pivotal. Traditionally, many of us have derived much optimism from studies of the situation of people with learning disabilities over the closing decades of the twentieth century. By the mid 1970s, it was widely believed that the outcome and situation of people with mild learning disabilities had improved so much that it must only be a matter of time before the same improvements applied to the situation of people with more severe learning disabilities. Sadly, there are no signs of the emergence of such a change. On the contrary, all available evidence emphasises that the more severe the child's learning disabilities, the less promising the prospects for adulthood.

Summary

While it would be folly to try to predict definitive adult outcomes for an individual child with learning disabilities, whether or not these were caused by fragile X, certain key issues are helpful. First of all, the severity of childhood learning disabilities in terms of IQ exerts a major influence on subsequent development and adjustment. Secondly, the presence of a major physical disability has a substantial bearing on outcome. Furthermore, self-perception, parental and family factors, and wider societal influences are important mediators of these key variables. In clinical practice, the task is to identify opportunities for intervention in these various domains, in order to promote the maximal outcomes for any people with learning disabilities. It is here that the person with fragile X merits the most careful attention.

Study one: child to adult comparisons in fragile X syndrome

This study was carried out with the kind co-operation of a large number of family members of the UK Fragile X Society. It explored whether, and to what extent, problems in children with fragile X continue into adulthood.

Sample

Two groups, each of 35 affected people identified as having FraX-A, were studied in childhood and adulthood. The child group comprised boys aged 6–9 years, while the adults were men aged 20–40 years.

Questionnaire

The study employed the parent and child versions of the SSBP (Society for the Study of Behavioural Phenotypes) questionnaire (O'Brien and Yule 1995; O'Brien, 2002). This widely used measure was designed to assess behavioural phenotypes. It is intended for use in postal surveys, for completion by parents or principal carers. The questionnaire explores behaviours in: feeding; sleep; social behaviour; language; motor functioning; unusual interest; self-injuring and aggression; anxiety and mood.

Results: continuities and differences from childhood to adulthood in fragile X syndrome

Developmental differences: developmental continuities

In terms of basic self-care and self-organisation skills, the adults showed significant improvements on the children (see Figure 21.1). For abilities such as washing and dressing, bowel and bladder control, and capacity to use a pencil appropriately, there is evidence of considerable improvement with age. However, there is far less evidence of improvements in language function. In verbal language use to express basic needs ('needs communication'), and communication for reasons other than basic needs ('social communication') there is only marginally improved functioning in the older group. These findings demonstrate that, in common with all children with developmental disability, substantial improvements in basic self-care and organisation are observed with increasing age and development in fragile X, but specific developmental disabilities in language are more persistent into adulthood.

This matters when we plan intervention and management strategies to address these patterns of development. The implications are that:

- Conventional strategies geared towards the acquisition of basic social, self-care and organisational skills are appropriate. Maturation over the course of development will facilitate such work. Some of the basic self-care development strategies used for all people with learning disabilities are therefore appropriate throughout their life
- In designing and implementing such programmes, it is important to bear in mind the persisting problems in language. In fragile X, language will be delayed over the course of development, more so than the acquisition of basic self-care and organisation skills.

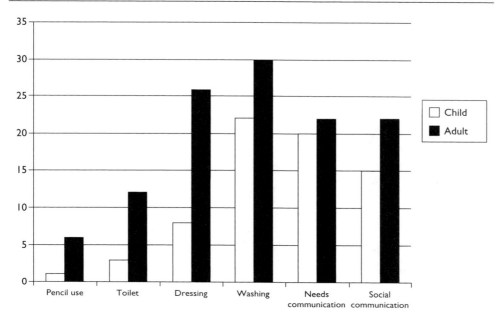

Figure 21.1 Developmental differences and continuities

• The persistence of the marked language deficit over the course of development highlights the need for speech and language therapy, not just in early life but into adulthood.

Behavioural differences

In some respects, behaviours that were prominent problems in the children were less apparent in the adults. Figure 21.2 summarises the key changes in behaviour between the children and adults with fragile X. 'Settling to task', which is a marker of the person's observed capacity to attend and complete an activity, was markedly deficient in the children but substantially improved in the adults. In keeping with this maturational change, the adults were far less likely than the children to 'create chaos' in their immediate environment, by being unsettled, noisy, and interfering with the activities of others. These findings are in keeping with reports of a high prevalence of attention deficit/hyperactivity disorder (AD/HD) in children with fragile X (Turk, 1992). 7 of the 35 boys had persistent pica, the eating of non-nutrient material, while none of the 35 adults showed this difficult behaviour.

Behavioural continuities

The most striking findings were of similarities between the boys and the men with fragile X in their social behaviour (Figure 21.3) and in observations of what may be considered 'peripheral autistic' behaviours. These are behaviours that are more common among autistic individuals, while not being diagnostic of autism (Figure 21.4). In terms of social behaviour, the boys and men with fragile X were both characterised by: a lack of social interest in others; over-familiarity towards strangers; a pattern of unusual eye contact. This latter is gaze avoidance; it is most marked in affected people at the onset of any social encounter or

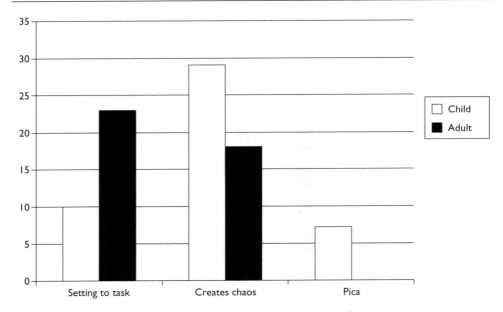

Figure 21.2 Behavioural differences: general disturbance, attention and pica

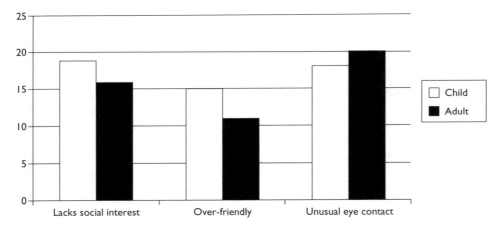

Figure 21.3 Behavioural continuities: social behaviour

interaction, as previously described in fragile X by Turk (1992). The 'peripheral autistic' behaviours common among both the boys and men with fragile X which showed little or no evidence of any reduction in intensity among the older group were: hand-flapping; obsessional behaviour; self-injury.

In designing management strategies to address these behavioural findings, the implications are:

• In fragile X, AD/HD becomes less common with increasing age through childhood into adulthood. Orthodox approaches such as prescribing stimulant medication

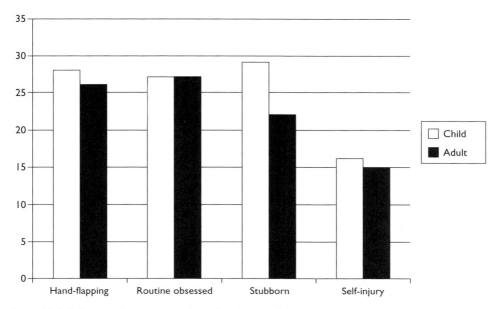

Figure 21.4 Behavioural continuities: 'peripheral autistic' features

coupled with behavioural management are often helpful, but are not typically required in adulthood.

- Behavioural problems that persist from childhood into adulthood need ongoing attention. Exactly how this will be best done for individual people depends as much on what support structures and services are available, as on types of specific treatment. Behavioural approaches such as limit setting and slowly implemented graded extinction of problem behaviours are helpful, while more challenging interventions are less successful and may well provoke further behaviour problems.

Study two: low-expressing males with fragile X syndrome

Some men within families affected by fragile X syndrome are recognised as 'premutation' males. The question arises whether the 'premutation' represents a dilute or lesser form of the syndrome. One way to investigate this is to examine these men, and compare them with men in their families who are similar in other respects. This is important when investigating what may be potentially mild problems. Any differences found in the premutation men could thus be considered a result of the premutation, and not due to other environmental influences.

Method

The subjects of this study were men with a fragile X expansion of 50–200 repeats. All of them had been detected during screening of families with a fragile X member. Men were selected who were aged over 18 years, who had a first-degree male relative, and who did not have such an expansion. 6 premutation men and 7 unaffected brothers were studied. Both subjects, those with the premutation and those without, were twice interviewed in their homes by clinicians who were 'blind' to the diagnosis.

During the first interview, the subjects were observed for their patterns of social interaction, and systematically examined for their physical appearance. Clinicians looked specifically for physical symptoms of anxiety, and the subjects' eye contact patterns were timed. At the end of the first interview, another clinician (also 'blind to diagnosis) completed two psychiatric rating scales, the Clinical Anxiety Scale and the General Health Questionnaire. At the end of the first interview, the first clinician judged which were the premutation men, and which the unaffected relatives.

The second interview was audiotaped. A medical history was taken, plus a detailed account of the subjects' social, employment and everyday living situation. The aim was to produce a 20-minute conversation for analysis of language and speech style, all of which are of interest in fragile X syndrome.

Results

Some of the results were negative; the premutation men did not prove to be different from their unaffected relatives:

- The employment for subjects with the fragile X expansion included long-distance lorry driver, apprentice mechanic, chef, senior lecturer at technical college, legal executive, desk-top publisher and electrician. Employment for the control males included fitness consultant, vending machine repair-man, electrician, hospital maintenance supervisor, self-employed accountant and factory shift manager.
- There were no apparent differences with employment or social occupation activities.
- On review of the audiotapes no patterns of speech typical to fragile X were found in either groups of men.

In two other respects, however, the premutation cases proved to be different from their relatives:

- The clinician who examined them was 'blind' to diagnosis, and decided, on the basis of their appearance and behaviour, which were the premutation cases. The clinician was correct in almost all cases. All 6 of the unaffected controls were correctly identified, as were 5 of the 7 premutation men. In appearance and general behaviour, the premutation men were distinct from the unaffected controls, in a way usually noticeable to the trained eye.
- The premutation men scored highly on social anxiety, of the type found in fragile X.

Concluding comment

These two studies make some key statements about adults with fragile X syndrome, which have been corroborated elsewhere. Firstly, some of the behavioural problems causing major problems in childhood, notably AD/HD, general restlessness and over-activity, are not typical of adults with fragile X. Secondly, problems with language and social anxiety do persist and need careful attention in adulthood. In this respect, it is equally important to arrange for intervention in early life, and to maintain longer-term support for adults with fragile X. In addition, we now know from a variety of studies that adults with the pre-expansion should no longer be regarded as unaffected carriers. They are in fact a less extreme variant of the syndrome. Finally, when we consider the broader impact within the family of living with this condition, it is not accurate to talk of any 'unaffected relative'. The social, language and emotional problems of people with fragile X inevitably impact on the whole family.

References

Clarke, A. and Clarke, A. (1988) 'The adult outcome of early behavioural anomalies', *International Journal of Behavioural Development* 11: 3–19.

King, E.H., Logsdon, D.A. and Shroeder, S.R. (1992) 'Risk factors for developmental delay among infants and toddlers', *Children's Health Care* 21: 39–52.

Marfo, K. (1990) 'Maternal directiveness in interactions with mentally handicapped children: an analytical commentary', *Journal of Child Psychology and Psychiatry* 31: 531–549.

O'Brien, G. (ed) (2002) 'Behavioural phenotypes in clinical practice', *Clinics in Developmental Medicine*, No 157, Mac Keith Press, London UK.

O'Brien, G. and Yule, W. (eds) (1995) 'Behavioural phenotypes', *Clinics in Developmental Medicine* No. 138, London: Mac Keith Press.

Turk, J. (1992) 'The fragile X Syndrome. On the way to a behavioural phenotype', *British Journal of Psychiatry* 160: 24–35.

Chapter 22

Behaviour and cognitive profiles in adults

Kim Cornish

Although this past decade has seen unparallelled advances in our understanding of the child with fragile X syndrome, both at the cognitive and at the behavioural level, relatively few studies have documented the pattern of strengths and difficulties in late adolescence and young adulthood. This chapter will attempt to redress that balance by presenting recent findings that highlight the profile from 18 years onwards in both men and women. The main question to be addressed is to what extent the childhood profile of behaviour and cognition changes with increasing age. Specifically, do certain skills or behaviour problems intensify or decline in adulthood? What, if any, skills and problems remain constant from childhood into adulthood?

Only by understanding the course of any changes can important issues regarding post-secondary education and career pathways be appropriately developed and encouraged.

The behavioural profile

As described in previous chapters, boys with fragile X can display a wide range of behavioural problems including:

- attention deficit disorder with or without hyperactivity (AD/HD) symptoms
- aggressive outbursts
- stereotypes (such as hand-flapping and biting)
- social anxiety
- excessive shyness
- some autistic-like features, such as perseveration of speech, tactile defensiveness and hyper-arousal.

It is of major concern whether the intensity and frequency of these behaviours continue into adulthood. Of the few UK studies that have examined the adult male profile there is some indication that certain behaviours *reduce* post-puberty (Cornish, 1996). This is shown in Table 22.1. These are:

- faddy eating
- sleep problems
- stereotypies (such as hand-flapping)
- hyperactivity self-injurious behaviour
- mood swings
- aggressiveness.

Table 22.1 Summary of the behavioural characteristics of children and adults with fragile X as measured by the Society for the Study of Behavioural Phenotype Questionnaire

Items	FX child (<16 yrs)		FX adult (>16yrs)	
	male %	female %	male %	female %
Feeding				
Eating less than normal	0.0	7.1	6.7	7.1
Normal intake of food	67.7	71.4	33.3	57.1
Eating more than normal	33.3	21.4	59.9	35.7
Faddy eating	35.7	14.3	14.3	21.4
Eating inappropriate substances	6.7	0.0	13.3	0.0
Sleep				
Difficulty getting to sleep	35.7	7.1	20.0	21.4
Regular sleep pattern	80.0	78.6	75.3	78.6
Frequently wakes in night	28.6	21.4	20.0	21.4
Disturbed behaviour during sleep	40.0	28.6	20.0	7.1
Social behaviour				
Isolated	33.3	30.8	71.4	57.1
Too friendly with strangers	26.7	21.4	13.3	28.6
Unusual eye contact	71.4	72.9	60.0	57.1
Facial grimacing	50.0	28.6	40.0	14.3
Difficulty showing emotion	46.2	50.0	53.3	57.1
Communication				
Repetitive language	86.7	50.0	60.0	50.0
Conversation meaningless	61.5	28.6	20.0	38.5
Shouts and screams unexpectedly	42.9	14.3	20.0	21.4
Unusual interests and movements				
Unusual movements	86.7	50.0	40.0	42.9
Peculiar object attachment	20.0	7.1	6.7	14.3
Liking routine/obsessive behaviour	86.7	42.9	42.9	57.9
Unusual reaction to light/smell/sound	71.4	42.9	40.0	7.1
Aggression/self-injury				
Deliberately destroys things	33.3	7.1	6.7	7.1
Self-harming behaviour	73.3	21.4	40.0	28.6
Physically attacks family	46.7	14.2	13.3	7.1
Frequently very stubborn	26.7	35.7	26.7	35.7
Not a problem	53.3	50.0	53.3	50.0
Minor problem	20.0	14.3	20.0	14.3
Major problem	40.0	14.3	7.1	7.1
Anxiety/mood				
Mood changeable	78.6	35.7	26.7	50.0
Excessively happy	60.0	42.9	26.7	28.6
Excessively unhappy	42.9	35.7	21.4	35.7
Often fearful	46.7	42.9	40.0	7.1
Serious temper tantrums	46.7	14.3	28.6	35.7
Mood out of place	35.7	42.9	26.7	7.1

Some behaviours however, remain *stable* from childhood to early adulthood:

- unusual eye contact
- difficulty in showing emotion and unusual or inappropriate moods
- stubbornness
- inattentiveness
- impulsivity.

Unfortunately, a few behaviours appear to *increase* with age:

- overeating
- preferring to be alone
- panic attacks (Hagerman, 1996)
- violent outbursts (Hagerman, 1996).

There still remain too few published studies outlining the trajectory of behaviours in males with fragile X, although the above findings provide positive encouragement that a number of debilitating problems in childhood (most notably hyperactive behaviour) do decline with age whilst others remain constant. In contrast, few behaviours increase in intensity with age.

In females with fragile X we know surprisingly more about the course of their behaviour problems from childhood to adulthood. These changes are going to be much less dramatic because problems reported in childhood are not to the same degree of impairment as that reported for boys with fragile X. The main problems displayed by girls with fragile X relate to their chronic levels of shyness, anxiety and social avoidance (Keysor and Mazzocco, 2002), and some parents have noted that these problems are present in their children as early as pre-school. A number of recent studies now highlight how this profile changes from childhood to adulthood (see Table 22.1, Cornish 1996).

Cornish (1996) has shown that the behaviours that *reduce* post-puberty include:

- sleep problems
- hyperacusis (hypersensitivity to sensory stimuli)
- inappropriate moods.

Behaviours that remain *stable* from childhood to early adulthood:

- unusual eye contact
- difficulty in showing emotion and unusual or inappropriate moods
- repetitive language
- depression (approximately a third)
- social withdrawal.

Behaviours that *increase* with age:

- preferring to be alone
- mood swings
- temper tantrums.

Similar findings have been reported in North America (and also in Australia, see Chapter 23) where studies have emphasised that the woman with fragile X is characterised by problems associated with social isolation, poor eye contact and a persisting difficulty in establishing a good rapport with people, especially in social situations. One suggestion for the consistency of this profile over time is that many women may find it difficult to integrate past information when making judgments about themselves in the present, and end up presenting themselves in an unrealistic light (Sobesky *et al.* 1994).

The cognitive profile

The cognitive profile of the fragile X child, which has been presented and discussed in previous chapters, includes weaknesses in short-and long-term memory for abstract, sequential information, visuo-spatial performance, concentration, inhibition, and in the planning and organising of information. However, given the important gender differences, this section will explore the adult profile separately for men and women.

In adult men with fragile X the profile appears to strongly reflect similar patterns of features associated with cognitive functioning in childhood. Poor inhibitory and switching skills and reduced concentration skills still characterise the profile into adulthood (Cornish *et al.*, 2001), although some aspects of attention, namely selective attention (the ability to select relevant information while ignoring distraction) appear to be much better developed. What is also encouraging is that the study reported relatively unimpaired short-term memory for faces and pictures. This finding reflects an important strength in childhood that continues to develop into adulthood.

In women with fragile X, again the profile seems to mirror that seen in childhood with a primary deficit in executive functioning (such as planning and generating successful strategies, abstract concept formation, perseverative thinking) alongside difficulties in mental arithmetic, visuo-spatial skills and visual memory (Bennetto *et al.*, 2001).

Post-18 years – what next?

There is currently very little information available on vocational training opportunities for young adults with fragile X. However, given the pattern of strengths and difficulties in the behavioural and cognitive profile of young adults with fragile X, it would appear crucial that vocational training and direction should come sooner rather than later in the school experience. Importantly, educators need to take into account the unique cognitive and behavioural features of fragile X when encouraging specific types of job placements or training schemes. For example, placing a fragile X adult in a work environment or college course that requires sustained attention and concentration over long periods of time during a given day would not be appropriate and may well increase levels of maladaptive behaviour (such as ritualistic behaviour and aggression).

In young women with fragile X, academic emphasis should be on providing training opportunities that focus upon increasing their strengths (verbal abilities) and reducing their difficulties (social avoidance, anxiety). Life courses that help women to develop their self-esteem and social skills would be of tremendous benefit, especially as they relate to job applications, interviews, working with colleagues and adjusting to new environments. Indeed, for all individuals with fragile X, training should incorporate a more *functional* approach that seeks to develop independent living skills (for example, learning to budget, making deposits into a bank account, handling the correct change before and after a purchase). The importance of developing and consolidating these skills early within an academic environment cannot be emphasised enough if the transition from school to workplace is to be a successful experience for all concerned, including the individual themselves as well as future employers.

Conclusions and recommendations

This chapter has outlined the emerging profile of the behavioural and cognitive features that characterise the fragile X adult. The pattern of findings is very encouraging and suggests that many problem behaviours that dominate in childhood either reduce in intensity or remain at a plateau during early adulthood. Few behaviours increase with age. It is also important to remember that some problem behaviours are non-existent or marginal in fragile X children and adults compared to the profiles in other genetic conditions. For example, the incidence of malnourishment, pica, deliberate aggressiveness or destructiveness, and overly friendliness to strangers are all reported to have minimal impact in fragile X. However, in conditions such as Down's syndrome or cri-du-chat syndrome and others, many of these behaviours represent significant problems for families and teachers. Likewise, some of the problems associated with fragile X do not apply to individuals with other conditions, thus highlighting the importance of recognising the distinct behavioural and cognitive profiles ('phenotype') of different genetic conditions.

Clearly, research also needs to address how the phenotype develops beyond early adulthood into mid life and old age. We currently have no knowledge of the pattern of strengths and difficulties of older adults with fragile X. The findings of such a study would enable us to give better information to families and professionals who work with young adults about what to expect and how to intervene so that any help received is better targeted.

Equally, there is a pressing need for investment in longitudinal assessments of males and females with fragile X that begin in childhood and continue through adolescence and beyond so that we can better understand the developmental trajectory of the behavioural and cognitive profile. By doing this we will ensure that strategies are in place that will allow the young fragile X adult to develop to their academic potential and to find fulfilment in a work or college environment that caters for their individual needs and where their unique contribution may be appreciated.

References

Bennetto, L., Pennington B.F., Porter D., Taylor A.K. and Hagerman R.J. (2001) 'Profile of cognitive functioning in women with the fragile X mutation.' *Neuropsychology* 15: 290–299.

Cornish, K.M. (1996) 'Identifying the cognitive and behavioural profiles of children and young adults with fragile X syndrome.' *Fragile X Society Newsletter no.* 13 (April).

Cornish, K.M., Munir, F. and Cross, G. (2001) 'Differential impact of the FMR-1 full mutation on memory and attention functioning: A neuropsychological perspective.' *Journal of Cognitive Neuroscience* 13: 1–7.

Hagerman, R.J. (1996) 'The physical and behavioural phenotype.' In R. Hagerman and A Cronister (Eds) *Fragile X Syndrome: Diagnosis, Treatment, and Research.* Baltimore: Johns Hopkins University Press.

Keysor, C.S. and Mazzocco, M.M.M. (2002) 'A developmental approach to understanding fragile X syndrome in females.' *Microscopy Research and Technique* 57: 179–186.

Sobesky, W.E., Pennington, B.F., Porter, D., Hull, C.E. and Hagerman, R.J. (1994) 'Emotional and neurocognitive deficits in fragile X.' *American Journal of Medical Genetics* 51: 378–385.

Chapter 23

Emotional and social difficulties of women with fragile X syndrome

Lesley Powell

The special concerns and difficulties of women with fragile X syndrome fall within a range of professional interests, including clinicians, gynaecologists and obstetricians, psychiatrists, psychologists, geneticists and counsellors. They are also important for teachers, because the behaviour and success of the adult individual is the prime outcome of education. The genetics of fragile X syndrome which give rise to these concerns and difficulties have been discussed in earlier chapters, but it is important for professionals to understand the emotional and social problems often experienced by women with fragile X.

Although women can be classified as having either a full mutation or a premutation, women with a full mutation can also be subdivided into those who have learning disabilities and those who do not. To indicate that they are not affected intellectually, women may use the terms 'carrier' or 'carrier only', and this is often because they were tested in the 1980s using cytogenetic procedures and their diagnosis was unclear. Unfortunately, these women can exhibit emotional and social difficulties, as well as inappropriate social behaviour if their intellectual functioning falls within the borderline area (IQ between 70 and 80). The emotional and social difficulties for each of these three groups, premutation, full mutation and, full mutation with learning difficulties, will be discussed separately.

Premutation

Women who carry a premutation exhibit no intellectual, educational or social difficulties, but there is evidence of some clinical manifestations associated with a premutation classification. Research indicates that women with more than 100 CGG repeats within the gene suffer significantly higher levels of depression than women who have an allele size below 100 repeats. Also, 28 per cent experience premature ovarian failure (menopause) before the age of 40, with the median age of menopause being six to eight years earlier than for women in the general population.

Full mutation

Most women who carry the full mutation, but do not exhibit learning difficulties, are capable women with a wide range of careers and interests, who raise families. However, since the early 1990s, it has been recognised that they can present with a wide range of academic, social and emotional difficulties. It must be emphasised that the following difficulties are not present in all women with a full mutation, but many women do experience at least some of these debilitating conditions.

Academic difficulties:

- poor reading comprehension
- mathematics difficulties
- poor sequencing skills
- poor planning and organisational skills.

Emotional difficulties:

- depression
- difficulty initiating and maintaining friendships
- low self-esteem
- general anxiety.

Social difficulties:

- inappropriate social behaviour
- social anxiety
- shyness
- poor conversation skills.

The combined effects of the above difficulties often make it difficult for affected women to cope with organising employment, the running of a household, planning their day's activities, budgeting, shopping and, in many cases, raising one or more affected children. Also, many of these women suffer abnormal levels of guilt if their child or children have inherited the faulty gene. This can exacerbate their emotional and social difficulties, especially anxiety, low self-esteem, shyness and depression.

Professionals should be aware that women with poor conversation skills, shyness, low self-esteem and social anxiety find it difficult to formulate appropriate questions, describe symptoms, or express their concerns to doctors and counsellors. People with fragile X learn better visually so if it is necessary to explain complicated medical procedures, a diagram may help them to understand the explanation.

A previous chapter discussed the options regarding pre-natal testing and the inability to predict how affected, if at all, a female child with a full mutation will be. If a mother decides to terminate her pregnancy because of the presence of the full mutation, regardless of whether the child is a boy or a girl, she will suffer the emotional difficulties listed above and may need extensive counselling. It should be noted that these are women just like other women, who wish to have a child and, in terminating their pregnancy, are losing a much wanted and much loved child. Also, if they choose to terminate a female child they do so not knowing to what extent the child would have been affected. This can also lead to feeling of doubt, guilt, depression and anxiety.

As previously stated, not all women who carry the full mutation are affected. If, however, they suffer from any of the above-listed difficulties then professionals need to watch for signs of anxiety and depression, social isolation, guilt and an inability to cope with the organisation of their daily life. These women should then be referred to the appropriate agencies, counsellors or clinicians.

Full mutation with learning difficulties

Research has revealed that approximately 60 per cent of women with a full mutation have some degree of intellectual impairment (defined as an 1Q below 70). Because of their learning disabilities, these women are more likely to be identified than women with no intellectual impairment. In general, these women are less affected than males with a full mutation; most women will be classified as having a mild, or mild to moderate impairment.

The possible social and emotional difficulties listed for women with a full mutation also apply to this group of women, but they usually exhibit most of the difficulties rather than some or none. Also, while the poor social skills of women with a full mutation include difficulties with conversation and making and maintaining friendships, this group of women will often present with inappropriate social behaviours and an inability to use appropriate language or topics of conversation in different social settings.

During my research over the past decade I have interviewed many women in their own homes. This has led to our being brought together in an informal encounter, set within a social context. Although these were inevitably short-term relationships, limited to the research purpose, nevertheless they took place in the social setting of a home, often with shared eating and drinking. The social rules of these simple encounters are so familiar that we perform the routines automatically. It is not so for many of these women. I have lost count of the number of interviewees who, during a meal, have eaten from my plate, drunk from my teacup, or drunk the dregs from my water glass before washing up. During an enjoyable afternoon tea with one very articulate woman, she proceeded to remove her false teeth and lick them clean before replacing them.

On another occasion, I drove over 400 kilometres in 42-degree heat to a family I was meeting for the first time. On my arrival, the woman opened the front door and said that she was thrilled to meet me, and informed me that she was having an affair. This is a perfect example of 'inappropriate topics of conversation' and her indiscretion could have had a devastating effect on her life. What was even sadder was her distorted view of what constitutes a good working relationship within the limited personal boundaries of research. She explained that she was entitled to have an affair because her husband was too tired to be a good husband, and she was well aware of what makes a good marriage because she watched the soap opera *The Days of Our Lives* on television every day.

Another sweet woman, who has a mild intellectual disability and is raising three daughters of similar ability, has no friends, no social life and rarely leaves her house. She cried at the end of my initial visit and as we all hugged and kissed goodbye she stated that I was her friend. She beamed as she told me that she knew what friends did – they drank cappuccino! We have since had cappuccinos together and while the simplicity of her friendship is precious to me, her inability to enter into a deep and meaningful relationship with another woman is heartbreaking.

Social training at school, practising the rules of social behaviour and types or degrees of relationships, could have avoided the worst effects of these social difficulties. They would have been spared the embarrassment of committing these social faux pas, of choosing infidelity as a result of a distorted concept of marriage, and the loneliness of a friendless existence.

Women with a mild to moderate impairment often marry and raise their family while having limited skills in literacy, numeracy, social behaviour, child-raising, and conflict resolution. They need the support of family and professionals, social skills training, functional life skills training and strategies to cope with emergencies. In fact, they may well need to stay in formal education as long as possible, and continue with some learning assistance, and practical assistance throughout their lives.

Many women are capable of working within the paid employment system. There are many courses at college for girls to complete both in Britain and TAFE (Technical and Further Education Colleges) in Australia. These girls are better suited to employment that delivers services to the community. Many are happily employed in the hospital system, the beauty industry, catering firms, plant nurseries, or as carers or nursery school assistants.

Many of the difficulties experienced by this group of women are also present to some degree in the women who do not have learning disabilities. Their social and emotional difficulties, therefore, should not be assumed to be the result of an intellectual impairment but rather as conditions associated with the full mutation and treated accordingly.

Further reading

Johnson, C., Eliez, S., Dyer-Friedman, J., Hessl, D., Glasser, B., Blasey, C., Taylor, A. and Reiss, A. (1991) 'Neurobehavioral phenotype in carriers of the fragile X premutation.' *American Journal of Medical Genetics* 103(4): 314–19.

Mazzocco, M., Hagerman, R. and Cronister-Silverman, A. (1992) 'Specific frontal lobe deficits among women with the fragile X gene.' *Journal of the American Academy of Child and Adolescent Psychiatry* 31(6): 1,141–1,148.

Partington, M.W., Moore, D.Y. and Turner, G.M. (1996) Confirmation of early menopause in fragile X carriers.' *American Journal of Medical Genetics* 64(2): 370–2.

Chapter 24

Support for individuals with fragile X syndrome and their families

Jeremy Turk

Introduction

This final chapter focuses on the more personal aspects affecting individuals who have fragile X syndrome and their families. The content goes beyond the specifically educational and explores what it is like and how it feels to have fragile X syndrome, what families with an affected member go through emotionally as well as practically, and how services should be configured in order to address these needs to the greatest effect.

There is currently no cure for the fragile X syndrome. However, there are many treatments – biological, psychological, educational and social – which are of established benefit in helping to maximise individuals' potentials, minimise their handicaps and enhance quality of life for them and their families. Despite the great variety of treatments available, there are some important principles common to all of them that should be adhered to if maximum benefit is to be obtained.

Assessment and intervention work should always be within a multidisciplinary framework with contributions from a range of professionals. Fragile X syndrome is a complex condition producing special needs in many different areas. Hence, no one individual can hope to have all the necessary talents or expertise. Work must be undertaken within a biopsychosocial context, recognising that many biological, psychological and social factors contribute to the developmental, emotional and behavioural needs of people who have fragile X syndrome. All assessment and intervention work, wherever it takes place, must reflect this. The aim of such work should be the generation of practical solutions to practical problems. Sympathy and understanding is necessary but not sufficient. Essential therapist attributes must be accompanied by the ability to provide practical directive advice and suggestions where appropriate. Work between clinicians and families must therefore be problem-focused with initial clarification of what are the challenges, which need to be tackled, in what order and by what means. Active and planned monitoring of interventions is essential to ensure they are of continuing benefit. Finally all work must be individualised. What is important to the person with fragile X syndrome? What do they see as an incentive for more appropriate behaviour? What will be their likely response to social attention, solitude, pressure to conform, or frustration?

In such work we must remember that developmental or behavioural challenges may occur for a variety of different reasons:

- as a normal component of an individual's developmental stage;
- as an understandable response to experiences;

- as a result of vulnerabilities produced by having learning disabilities;
- as the result of having fragile X syndrome.

One problem may occur for one or more of the above reasons. This will influence what interventions are considered to be appropriate.

We must always be mindful of the need to enquire whether there has been comprehensive and up-to-date genetic counselling and advice. The process of genetic counselling is a good example of a situation where people mean many different things by the term. This will affect the nature and level of support received by families. Counselling is a broad concept with both educational and psychotherapeutic components. Educational aspects should include information-sharing about the genetic nature of fragile X and its mode of inheritance. Less often, families are informed of the large and increasing body of knowledge about developmental and behavioural aspects, only finding out about these areas slowly through their own reading of the literature and talking to other families and support groups. However, families usually know as much information as possible earlier rather than later. Old ideas that too much knowledge may produce negative and fatalistic views of the child have thank-fully been replaced by awareness of the importance of forewarning families of challenges to be faced and hence allowing them to prepare for these. Psychotherapeutic components of counselling should include both non-directive and directive aspects. Non-directive psychotherapy relies on established therapist attributes known to be important in facilitating client acceptance and change: emotional warmth, genuineness, empathy and unconditional positive regard. These attributes are important in helping families reflect on their predicament and hence gain greater understanding of the situation they now find themselves in and what personal adjustments may be required. In conjunction with these necessary prerequisites, the therapist must also be adept at directive problem-solving approaches. These are required to tackle the many practical challenges faced by families, such as how to encourage early development, how to help organise appropriate educational provision and how to change inappropriate behaviour such as social difficulties, hyperactivity, aggression and self-injury. Thus counselling is a complex and multifaceted process requiring contributions from a number of professionals, and extending over a long time.

Educational aspects

Wherever education occurs, teachers must be aware of the wide range of possible intellectual functioning and the common significant discrepancy between verbal and performance skills. It must be remembered that individuals may be extremely articulate with a good vocabulary and good conversational skills yet may have exceptional needs in mathematics, numeracy and visuo-spatial abilities. It is important that difficulties in these areas are recognised and that the individual's poor performance or aversion to such tasks is not attributed to stubbornness, laziness or being difficult. There must also be awareness of the characteristic developmental trajectory whereby the rate of increase in intellectual functioning of individuals with fragile X syndrome tends to plateau towards puberty thereby increasing the discrepancy between their levels of intellectual functioning and those of their learning disabled peers. This is because of particular problems with sequential processing of information – a skill increasingly required as development proceeds. Teaching must therefore be modified to reduce the need for sequential information-processing strategies and to rely more on simultaneous information-processing skills. There is also increasing evidence that female carriers show the above tendencies even if their average intellectual functioning level is within the normal range. Many such carriers report having developed a number of strategies to compensate for these difficulties including the use of diaries and lists, alarm clocks to prompt action at certain times and sticking to strong routines to maximise familiarity. We need to learn from these many and varied coping strategies and to incorporate them into our own repertoire of teachable skills.

Early interventions

Early pre-school interventions for children with fragile X syndrome should address medical and intellectual needs evident during this time. A thorough medical and developmental assessment by a multidisciplinary child development team is mandatory. So too is the early and vigorous treatment of any identified medical problems which may complicate the developmental difficulties, for example glue ear or visual disturbances. Practical home-based interventions, such as Portage, help structure parental input to aid development and facilitate monitoring of progress. As well as the possible direct benefits of the procedures involved, there is much to be gained from the developing relationship between parent and professional in partnership. These approaches complement subsequent special nursery provision and ensuing assessment of special educational needs culminating in recommendations regarding school placement and educational provision.

Educational requirements

Many of the educational requirements of children with fragile X syndrome are similar to those of children with other causes for their learning disabilities. Small class size with access to small group and individual tuition is essential to ensure a high proportion of time spent by the teacher with each pupil. There must be attention to noise level and lighting in order to help minimise distractions and enhance concentration. This is helped further by a highly structured and predictable environment and class routine. Graduated increasing involvement in group (as opposed to individual) teaching will help encourage independence and self-motivated learning as will interaction with more able pupils. Respect for specific special needs must be maintained at all times. Awareness of sequential processing difficulties and the need for reliance on simultaneous techniques with concrete information must be accompanied by sympathy regarding the common gaze aversion. The school day should contain a minimum of surprises and the staff group should remain as consistent and predictable as possible with everybody using the same teaching and discipline approaches. Communications between staff and pupils should be simple, concrete, and outcome and rule-based. The same phrases should be used to convey the same messages at all times and should be linked to the same predictable expectations and outcomes. Staff must be aware of the broader context of communication including not only speech but also eye contact, facial expression, body posture and gesture.

Helping autistic features

The indifference to social interaction often witnessed in typical autism is rarely seen in fragile X. Instead there is often a tendency towards anxiety in social situations in the presence of a friendly and sociable personality. This usually coexists with awareness of the need for, and importance of, social interaction. This social anxiety is potentially treatable with social skills groups and behavioural desensitisation techniques. Other useful techniques include tutoring on perspective and turn-taking, anger management and emotion-recognition classes. The eye contact aversion so characteristic of fragile X syndrome contrasts with the commoner eye contact indifference in typical autism. Poor imitative and symbolic play is a feature of young children with fragile X but many seem to develop these skills later unlike many children with typical autism. Hand-flapping when excited or anxious is a very common behaviour. Fragile X syndrome and autism can occur together. The two conditions are far from being mutually exclusive. Also, there is much behavioural variability within both groups.

Helping the attentional deficits

Parents, teachers and clinicians frequently report that attentional deficits and impulsive and overactive behaviours are the most common and challenging of the behavioural difficulties experienced by students who have fragile X syndrome. Boys with fragile X are indeed more inattentive, restless and fidgety than other boys with similar degrees of intellectual disability. These features are often accompanied by markedly impulsive and distractible tendencies. Overactivity is common but not universal, and is less often witnessed in girls with fragile X. Short bursts of focussed tuition, interspersed with frequent times out from learning and equally frequent readily attainable rewards for even brief durations of concentration are helpful.

Medical interventions

Any associated physical problems should be identified as early as possible and treated vigorously. There should be comprehensive hearing and vision checks with remedial action where necessary. Medication has a small but important role to play in the treatment of epilepsy, hyperactivity and attentional deficits, and sometimes aggression, self-injury, obsessive-compulsive tendencies, mood disorders and sleep disturbance (see Chapter 19).

Psychological interventions

Psychological approaches are pivotal in the management of unresolved familial and personal grief reactions relating to diagnosis, family adjustment, management of challenging behaviour and enhancement of normal developmental processes. Non-directive counselling is often necessary to help familial reflection on their predicament, how it has arisen and what steps should be taken to optimise further family and individual development and sense of fulfilment. Family therapy may be required to aid bereavement feelings and adaptation and to attend to the needs of parents and siblings. Sometimes a child with disabilities can become a scapegoat for the family's problems and may be excluded from family processes. More often they can become the focus of attention and family activities to the extent that the needs of other family members may be at risk of being ignored with consequent detrimental effects for not only those individuals but also the child with disabilities.

Cognitive psychotherapy deals with people's thoughts – what they think and why and whether such beliefs and expectations are useful or not. Inappropriate or 'maladaptive' cognitions can underlie emotional disturbance and may affect the efforts of the individual and the family to achieve the best for themselves. They are amenable to being challenged and tested within a therapeutic relationship. Work also includes problem-solving approaches and the development of useful coping strategies.

Behavioural psychotherapy and modification advances have revolutionised management of some of the most distressing and destructive tendencies such as self-injury and aggression. A comprehensive behavioural approach should commence with a thorough functional analysis of behaviour whereby diary and chart keeping of antecedents and consequences of the target behaviour are documented methodically in order to try to identify common patterns which may indicate important triggers or reinforcers. This allows for the development of appropriate practical intervention strategies, which may be based on:

- rewarding appropriate behaviour (positive reinforcement);
- ignoring inappropriate behaviour (extinction);
- punishing inappropriate behaviour (aversive techniques);
- removing aversive or unpleasant stimuli in response to appropriate behaviour (negative reinforcement).

In practice aversive techniques should not be necessary. In all behavioural approaches there is a need to consider all people and networks with whom the child comes in contact. These include in particular family, friends and school. The child's developmental level must be considered in terms of his or her level of understanding and the age-appropriateness of the programme. Too sophisticated an approach may confuse leading to worsening of behaviour. Too simplistic an approach may be seen as patronising. It is necessary to maintain the child's dignity and sense of self-control. Rewards must be appropriate for the individuals, meaningful for them, frequently and readily obtainable and capable of being easily withdrawn. The programme must be personalised to reflect the child's needs, wishes, likes and dislikes – not those of the therapist or teacher. At all times one must consider the antecedents and consequences of the child's behaviour in order to discern what factors have predisposed the child to develop such behaviour, which have precipitated the behaviour ('triggers') and which may be perpetuating such tendencies ('reinforcers').

Other therapeutic interventions

Speech and language therapy is required for individual assessment of speech and language skills and needs, and should occur in collaboration with family and school input. Some language tendencies may be maladaptive but there is evidence that others serve important functions in compensating for information processing and other difficulties, for example echolalia and repetitive speech. Speech and language therapists also give advice on augmentative communication techniques such as sign languages (e.g. Makaton), picture communication boards (e.g. Bliss symbolics) and schemes for enhancing social interactions as a way of getting needs met (e.g. PECS – Picture Exchange Communication System). Occupational therapy individual assessment can provide invaluable information on fine motor functioning and visuo-motor co-ordination. Sensory integration approaches are gaining popularity in the management of the frequently present generalised sensory defensiveness and intolerance of frustration. Physiotherapy may assist motor delay difficulties, joint hypermobility problems and clumsiness.

Social interventions

Attention to social aspects is an essential component of comprehensive multi-disciplinary intervention packages. Welfare benefits provide invaluable family support and can, if appropriate, be saved in a trust for future use by the disabled individual later in life. Respite care arrangements provide important breaks for the family from caring for their disabled member. They also provide opportunities for individuals to experience different living environments – an important part of socialisation. Similar benefits arise from special holiday organisations. Clubs, societies and organisations frequently exist within the private and voluntary sector to help link families who have members with similar difficulties and to assist in developing mutual support arrangements.

Family support groups provide excellent mutual support networks as well as systems of disseminating information and arguing for improved facilities. There is also the need for long-term planning regarding accommodation, occupation, continuing education and financial security.

The views of the consumers

Finally, we reflect on what individuals with fragile X syndrome and their families frequently state as their needs and what they expect of us as supportive professionals. This is a list of some of the more common expressions voiced by families regarding the help they have received and how it could be improved.

- Educational, social service and health professionals are generally good at expressing sympathy. However, they frequently lack practical knowledge and the ability to provide practical guidance which relates specifically to those aspects reflecting the underlying cause of the student's problems, such as fragile X syndrome.
- These professionals usually have adequate general knowledge but lack specialist knowledge of fragile X syndrome, its consequences and useful interventions and services.
- There can be resistance to the idea of challenging behaviours having a genetic basis, even if they can be influenced dramatically by psychological and social factors. We don't like the implication that such behaviours are 'our fault'.
- Even when there is acknowledgement that behaviour may have a genetic origin, this is often framed as a 'vulnerability' – implying the need for strong social influences to disclose the behaviour. This is not usually the case.
- Professionals can get stuck on their own background and philosophy, whether it is educational, social or medical. They can end up 'overholding' a student and family rather than sharing and working together with other agencies at an early stage in the problem's development.
- There can be a lack of multi-agency joined-up thinking and working. What we want is an integrated, seamless service.

Responsibilities of professionals

How then can we as caring professionals respond best to the above? Here, in ending, are a few personal suggestions as starting points. We need:

- To be aware of not only the psychological and social, but also biological contributions to development, personality, temperament, emotions and behaviour.
- To ensure that we have sufficient specialist knowledge to advise and counsel about the important interactions between these biological, psychological and social factors, and their practical implications.
- To have the knowledge and ability to develop appropriate therapeutic and educational packages in conjunction with other relevant resources and agencies.
- To ensure that all necessary genetic investigations and genetic counselling have been undertaken.
- To maintain a broad and balanced view of all the biological, psychological and social issues pertaining to our clients and their families, in terms of evaluation, intervention and ongoing support.

Conclusion

Denise Dew-Hughes

The primary aim of this book is to enhance the teaching and learning of people with fragile X syndrome. It also aims to develop general and transferable teaching skills, capable of being applied to a wide range of pupil difficulties and strengths, and to improve classroom practice by developing deeper understandings of pupil needs. These aims are served by a series of objectives, such as easing access to multi-professional expertise, providing factual information without exclusive terminology, and encouraging educational practitioners to consider wider issues contributing to the uniqueness of individual learners.

Educating any child with complex learning difficulties challenges the professional knowledge and practice of teachers. Conditions such as fragile X syndrome present a wide range of learning difficulties, many of which are familiar to general teaching practice. Because of this, the special expertise and understanding required from teachers in meeting the needs of pupils with fragile X are capable of crossing all boundaries of school placement. Learning how to meet the needs of these very special children can endow teachers with valuable and non-specific skills, which not only help individual pupils, but also result in deeper understandings of the nature and processes of teaching and learning.

The contribution of information to the development of teachers' practice has been discussed earlier in this book. It is a fundamental constituent of their professional knowledge, and is necessary at all stages of professional development. Teachers are very aware of their ongoing need for accurate information about specific pupils' learning needs, and how these relate to wider physical, social and environmental contexts. This is particularly so for conditions such as fragile X syndrome, which may predispose a pupil to specific difficulties and require specialist approaches, while at the same time constituting only a part of the pupil as an individual.

Teachers in a nation-wide survey[1] identified many ways in which information about a pupil's specific condition could enhance their response to a pupil's learning needs. They considered that being better informed brought advantages to all aspects of their practice, and that their teaching was improved at the most fundamental level in three key areas. Better information brought:

- professional advantages, which caused a general improvement in the teacher's standards of practice;
- practical advantages, which improved or informed specific aspects of teaching and pupil support;
- personal advantages, which enhanced the teacher's values and attitudes towards people with learning difficulties.

Teachers are well aware of the reasons why they need information about a condition such as fragile X syndrome. Most commonly identified in the survey were the safety, support and treatment regime of the pupil, the psychological implications of a specific condition, and the risks and responsibilities in maintaining a safe classroom environment. Teachers also wanted to know how learning might be affected by the pupil's specific condition, and how to develop appropriate teaching strategies and approaches to meet learning needs. A better-informed teacher was seen as a more successful practitioner, who was more likely to understand and value the whole pupil. In addition, such teachers would be more aware of their own personal values, likely to avoid pre-judgements and to develop empathy and positive attitudes towards pupils with difficulties.

Classroom teachers in the survey accessed a wide range of different sources to acquire information about a specific condition that might cause learning difficulties. They chose information at hand (records, medical personnel, colleagues, special educational needs coordinators) and a wider research base, including publications and support agencies. Most sought information about specific conditions and individual pupils from several different sources. In short, they were willing to commit time and effort to undertake research because they considered being better informed was equivalent to being better teachers.

Societies offering support and information were rated highly by teachers as a prime source of information about pupils' learning, and physical and emotional difficulties. These support agencies were regarded as an ongoing pedagogical resource; they were easily accessible and provided relevant and accurate information and advice. Teachers believed that support agencies promoted more effective teaching by determining expectations for a pupil, identifying appropriate tasks and setting a realistic range for outcomes. Above all, they encouraged teachers to value the individuality of each learner. Because support agencies draw on wide areas of expertise and experience, information from this source encouraged teachers to view their own role and practice as multi-faceted and closely linked with other professions.

Fragile X Society

A specific condition such as fragile X syndrome, which has a worldwide support agency, can offer all the teaching benefits identified above. The UK Fragile X Society was founded in 1990 as a national charity to provide support and information to families and professionals caring for children and adults affected by fragile X syndrome. Through its support and information services, publications, newsletters, and conferences, the Society gives help, information and guidance to parents and professionals. In addition to depth and breadth of expertise from its specialist advisors and its ongoing promotion of research, it also offers the practical experience of those who care daily for children and adults with the syndrome. Because of the range of ability of its members, and the successful learning featured in newsletter articles, teachers are encouraged not to underestimate the potential of learners with fragile X syndrome.

The Society actively encourages research into all aspects of fragile X syndrome and its members commonly participate in studies. It has supported 26 major studies into fragile X during its first twelve years, providing a wealth of practical data and first-hand experience from almost 1,500 families in the United Kingdom, and provides links with international fragile X foundations. Many of the current leading fragile X researchers have contributed chapters to this book. The most vital outcome of this research has been the dissemination of new knowledge derived from academic study to practitioners at the front line in teaching, medicine, psychology and ancillary therapies. Knowledge and understanding gained from research can stimulate and inform their practice, and ultimately help people with fragile X to enjoy more rewarding and fulfilled lives. In this way, the Society provides a conduit, feeding research directly into practice to benefit those whom the research is intended to help.

The Society maintains a database of research into fragile X syndrome and encourages practitioners to access its findings. Teachers, genetic counsellors and other health-care providers in the UK are encouraged to refer concerned professionals and families affected by fragile X syndrome to the Society. Membership is free to fragile X families and carers; those with a professional interest in fragile X syndrome are welcomed as associate members. Links are maintained through overseas groups with the fragile X community worldwide.

Note

1   A general sample of teachers, primary, secondary, special, subject-specialists and SENCOs, in 74 schools, units and colleges in England and Wales. Described in 'Professional knowledge and the response of teachers to pupils with special educational needs'. Ed.D thesis. Oxford Brookes University. Dew-Hughes, D.M. (1999).

Addresses

The following organisations provide information about themselves and about fragile X societies in other countries.
The UK Fragile X Society
Rood End House
6 Stortford Road
Great Dunmow
Essex
CM6 1DA
Tel: (+44) 01371 875100
Family contact: (+44) 01424 813147
Fax: (+44) 01371 859915
Email: info@fragilex.org.uk
Internet: www.fragilex.org.uk
Registered Charity No. 1003981

National Fragile X Foundation (USA)
PO Box 190488
San Francisco
CA 94119–0488
USA
Tel: 800–688–8765
Fax: 925–938–9315
Email: NATLFX@FragileX.org
Internet: www.FragileX.org

FRAXA Research Foundation (USA)
45 Pleasant Street
Newburyport
MA 01950
USA
Tel: 978 462 1866
Fax: 978 463 9985
Email: kclapp@fraxa.org
Internet: www.fraxa.org

Index